In Bondage to Evil

In Bondage to Evil

A Psycho-Spiritual Understanding of Possession

T. Craig Isaacs

PICKWICK *Publications* · Eugene, Oregon

IN BONDAGE TO EVIL
A Psycho-Spiritual Understanding of Possession

Pickwick Publications
An Imprint of Wipf and Stock Publishers
199 W. 8th Ave., Suite 3
Eugene, OR 97401

www.wipfandstock.com

PAPERBACK ISBN: 978-1-5326-3141-2
HARDCOVER ISBN: 978-1-5326-3143-6
EBOOK ISBN: 978-1-5326-3142-9

Cataloguing-in-Publication data:

Names: Isaacs, T. Craig.

Title: In bondage to evil : a psycho-spiritual understanding of possession / T. Craig Isaacs.

Description: Eugene, OR: Pickwick Publications, 2018 | Includes bibliographical references.

Identifiers: ISBN 978-1-5326-3141-2 (paperback) | ISBN 978-1-5326-3143-6 (hardcover) | ISBN 978-1-5326-3142-9 (ebook)

Subjects: LCSH: Spirit possession | Exorcism | Demoniac possession—Psychological aspects | Mental disorders—History | Psychology, Religious

Classification: BX2340 I83 2018 (print) | BX2340 (ebook)

Manufactured in the U.S.A.   01/18/18

Contents

1   Introduction | 1

2   A Brief History of Possession | 7

3   Mysticism and Possession | 21

4   A Christian View: Possession by Evil | 34

5   A Christian View: Possession by the Holy Spirit | 49

6   Possession States in Voodoo | 63

7   Possession States and Shamanism | 74

8   Spiritualism and Possession | 84

9   Witchcraft, Satanism, and Possession | 93

10 The Compatibility of Possession States | 105

11 The Cultural Explanations | 108

12 The Neuropsychological Explanations of Possession | 116

13 Possession and the Hypnosis Theory | 126

14 Possession and the Dissociative Disorders | 129

15 Other Disorders to Which Possession is Commonly Attributed | 134

16 Possession and Hysteria: A Psychoanalytic View of Possession | 137

17 Possession and the Human Spirit: An Existentialist Perspective | 142

18 Jungian Psychology and Possession | 148

19 Three Cases of Possession | 173

20 The Diagnosis of Possession | 186

21 The Fall of Satan: The Intrapsychic Dynamics
of the Possession State | 213

Bibliography | 233

1

Introduction

Either you believe in possession or you do not. It is that simple, or at least that is how it often seems. However, the existence of the possession state in the human condition is not a matter of faith, it is a phenomenon that demands exploration.

A man walks into the psychotherapist's office. He is visibly nervous, fidgeting with a button on his shirt, gazing absently at the floor as he begins to describe what brings him in for consultation. It is embarrassing for him to talk about, but he has nowhere else to turn. He already went to his priest, but the priest said he needed to see a therapist. He went to a psychiatrist, but the medications only helped him sleep, they did not stop the thoughts or the fears. He begins to tell how his son committed suicide just over a year ago. How a few days after this he began to have disturbing intrusive thoughts, thoughts about killing his wife and his grandchild. He describes how these thoughts have been extremely difficult not to act upon, and the terror he has been in, a terror multiplied by what he learned only a few weeks ago. As he felt he could no longer contain his secret thoughts and impulses and hide them from his family, he shared his fears in a tearful session with his youngest son. It was then that he learned from his son the distressing fact that the boy who had recently committed suicide had had the same thoughts, the *exact* same thoughts. It was even because of this that he had killed himself, because he too could not restrain himself from action any longer. A dread came over the man, and the fear that this was no ordinary obsession. He began to question, "Am I possessed?"

Three men and a cat are sharing an apartment. It becomes obvious to two of the men that the third is into some very weird interests. He is burning candles in odd places, and bringing some very questionable people home. The two decide that they will ask him to move out. He agrees, but only after cursing the others and the apartment. The two scoff at this and use it as a topic of joking for weeks. One day, a few weeks later, the house cat dies. The veterinarian says that the internal organs had "seized up" for some inexplicable reason. They are saddened but think no more of it. A week later they find themselves in the local emergency room. One of the roommates is in extreme abdominal pain. He dies. The emergency room physician tells the remaining man that his friend has died, that his internal organs seemed to have "seized up" for some as yet unknown reason. In understandable terror the remaining man tells the physician the story of the curse; the physician says, "Sir, you don't need a doctor, you need a minister!" Are they suffering the effects of a curse?

Whatever the reasons may be, whatever belief system one uses to interpret these events, a phenomenon has occurred that warrants investigation; an investigation that will take us to that liminal place between psychology and religion.

During the last century the concept of spirit-possession fell into increasing disrepute. As psychological knowledge increased, and the scientific study of psychological phenomena became more prevalent, the thought that the supernatural might be involved in individual pathology became discredited. Consequently, we moved from a belief that demons or spirits were causing the ills of humanity to the thought that people were suffering solely from mental illnesses.

With this shift in thinking many improvements were instituted in the treatment of the mentally ill. No longer were the insane placed into prisons and treated like animals. No longer were they seen as evil and as in league with the Devil. Rather, they were given treatment, much as a victim of any physical disease was treated. This advent of what is now called "Moral Treatment" was one of the launching points for today's work in psychology. However, with the resurgence of belief in demonic possession, and the increase in the practice of both formal and informal exorcism, the question arises whether or not we have really done away with the phenomenon of possession. It appears that even though we may have witnessed the removal of the *belief* in demonic possession from our diagnostic categories, the phenomenon that was once described with attributes of the demonic still remains with us.

Much of what was once seen to be demonic possession can today be fit into one of the many psychodiagnostic categories available to us. We are able to view the schizophrenic aspects of the possession. We can see the hysterical attitudes of the possessed. The paranoid characteristics of those individuals, as well as the dissociative qualities involved, are clearly visible. Our problem arises when attempting to narrow the diagnostic criteria down to a point of truly classifying the possessed, and then attempting to treat the possessed as if he or she were schizophrenic, hysterical, paranoid, or suffering from dissociative identity disorder. It is at this point that we find ourselves at a loss, trying to accurately *fit* the possessed into any current classification. This may be because none of the current diagnostic categories can adequately describe as a whole the various phenomenon encountered in a possession. Possession may be a category of its own.

When we threw out the supernatural explanations of the universe, did we also then force ourselves to ignore certain of the stranger phenomena associated with possession, so that we could avoid the connotations which the concept of demon possession carried? If we did, and if a phenomenon of possession does exist—distinct from any other disorder that we now acknowledge—then we are being negligent in our service to those who are suffering from this malady. If such a phenomenon is present as a distinct manner of functioning, then it is time that we once again begin to recognize it and to learn how to treat it on its own merits, rather than attempting to treat this manner of functioning "as if" it were schizophrenia or any other diagnostic possibility.

The present work is an attempt to distinguish the possession state as an independent diagnostic category, and to begin to form a picture of the phenomenology and dynamics of possession so that it might be more easily distinguishable from the other forms of functioning that are similar in appearance.

The concept of spirit-possession is one that elicits a variety of responses in the modern person, from fear and respect to ridicule and disbelief. Yet in almost all known societies and cultures there have been the phenomena of persons entering into those altered states of consciousness commonly attributed to possession; states such as seeing visions, hearing voices, and acting as if a new and different personality has taken over.

Erika Bourguignon[1] once grouped and classified these behaviors and beliefs under the rubric of what she called "trance behaviors and associated beliefs." This classification assists us to better understand and differentiate among the various phenomena that have historically been seen as forms of possession.

Different cultures tend to understand trance behaviors by either a naturalistic or a supernaturalistic form of explanation. The Western technological societies tend to view the world in a more rationalistic and scientific manner and so have more frequently preferred the naturalistic form of explanation. Within this frame of reference, altered states of consciousness can be seen as the result of some form of inducement such as hypnosis,

---

1. Bourguignon, *World Distribution and Patterns of Possession States.*

extreme fear, and drugs. They might be seen as the consequence of an illness, whether somatic or psychological in origin. The most common somatic explanation that Bourguignon has encountered for the cause of an altered state of consciousness is fever. She has found the primary psychological explanations to have been either multiple personality (today's dissociative identity disorder), hysteria, some form of psychosis, or even epilepsy. We shall look more closely at how these psychological explanations have been elucidated later in our discussion.

The naturalistic explanation of these behaviors is relatively new in comparison to its counterpart. Explaining the altered states of consciousness by means of the supernatural has historically been the prominent method, and still is in many cultures today. Even in our highly technological society there remains a large sub-culture that explains the world in a supernatural manner. The supernatural way of thinking is evident even in people who would prefer to believe themselves to be "modern" and "rational," as is obvious from the simple fact that almost every large newspaper still carries the daily horoscope.

As with the naturalistic system—which has a variety of ways for explaining the possession phenomena—so too, the supernaturalistic system is complex and varied. A belief in involuntary possession is not common to all cultures, but the similar phenomena, of persons entering altered states of consciousness, is common. The explanations of these similar phenomena are what differ more than do the phenomena themselves. Bourguignon divided these explanations into non-possession beliefs and possession beliefs, which is similar to Oesterreich's[2] description of voluntary and spontaneous (or involuntary) forms of possession.

Under the rubric of non-possession beliefs we find the practices of witchcraft, mysticism, mediumship (communication with spirits), and shamanism. Though Bourguignon refers to these as non-possession beliefs, Oesterreich sees these as forms of voluntary possession. The person has intentionally become possessed for some specific purpose, for a short period of time. The witch may become possessed with mana—or power—or with a certain spirit in order to curse, bless, or create medicines. The shaman may go on the spirit-journey to gain power, knowledge, or to find a lost soul and return it to its owner: all for a price. The medium may be possessed by the dead or other spirits to bring information to those still living or "confined to the earthly plane." The mystic may enter an altered state of consciousness in order to find God, or to lose his or her ego into a form of "cosmic

2. Oesterreich, *Possession, Demoniacal and Other, among Primitive Races, in Antiquity, the Middle Ages, and Modern Times.*

consciousness." Even though in almost all of these practices the person may have felt a call to enter the altered state—whether it was the witch seeing Satan ask her to join him, or the Native American shaman hearing the call of the wolf as a call to spiritually join Brother Wolf—still it was the person's choice to become possessed by either the new personality or the new-found ability or power.

This is illustrated in an event related by Pattison.[3] He tells the story of a teenage Native American girl who one day saw ghosts in the forest and thereafter became haunted by a ghost, and seemingly possessed. Later she found out from her mother that this was the ghost of her dead grandfather who had been a powerful shaman. Before his death, the grandfather had chosen to pass his powers on to the girl when she was ready. The possession was believed by both the girl and her mother to be the grandfather attempting to pass on his powers to the girl at this point in her life. But she had the ability—with the help of her mother and the community—to either accept these powers or to reject them. She had the choice of whether to be possessed by her grandfather's power, and so then to possess them as a shaman in her own right, or to reject the power. The incident concluded with the girl deciding to reject the power, and upon doing so the haunting and possession ceased.

This is the difference between the two forms of possession. With the voluntary—or non-possession—form, the person is able to reject the possession. But this is not case with what Bourguignon has called the possession belief—the involuntary possession.

Possession, as most people think of it, is best described by Bourguignon's description of possession belief, or Oesterreich's spontaneous possession. It is within this category that such stories as *Dracula* and *The Exorcist* are to be found. It is here that we encounter the belief in, and fear of, demons and devils. It is this phenomenon—the phenomenon of involuntary possession—that we will be focusing upon in this work. In the following pages we will be examining the various explanations of involuntary possession, from antiquity to the present.

As mentioned before, for many today, demonic possession (which is a form of involuntary possession) is merely the historical explanation for certain diseases and mental illnesses. Freud saw it as such when he said that "the neuroses of . . . early times emerge in demonological trappings."[4] Thus we are led to believe that in antiquity all forms of mental illness were seen as possessions by either demons, the gods, or ghosts and so conversely that in

---

3. Pattison, *Psychosocial Interpretations of Exorcism.*
4. Freud, *A Seventeenth Century Demonological Neurosis,* 72.

our day all expression of what was classically seen as possession is in actuality mental illness. We will explore the validity of this belief by examining the place of involuntary possession in the beliefs and medical practices of societies from antiquity into classical and medieval times.

We will also look at the role of spirit-possession in various religious and cultural practices: in mysticism, Voodoo, shamanism, spiritualism, witchcraft, and Satanism. We shall also take a look into the concept of illness, and possession, in the Christian community today, as well as the concept of possession by the Holy Spirit. We will be doing all this in order to gain an understanding of the history and phenomenology of spirit-possession.

We will then move on to discuss the various explanations utilized for the phenomenon of involuntary possession, both sociological and psychological. Possessions still occur in many societies and cultures today. From these cultures, anthropologists have derived many explanations—other than the demonic—for the phenomena they have observed. We will examine these explanations to get a better understanding of the societal impact upon the possessed individual.

Then we will more closely investigate Freud's contention that the demonic possessions of yesteryear are actually neuroses, or psychoses, masquerading in demonic garb. We will be looking at the question, "Is there a certain area of psychopathology into which involuntary possession usually falls?"

Finally, we will illustrate a clinical differentiation between the currently recognized categories of psychopathology and involuntary possession. Many writers, thinkers, and researchers at the interface of religion and psychology have attempted to provide a distinction between what they see as two separate phenomena. What this differentiation has usually come to is very similar to what the Roman Catholic Church for centuries has used as the criteria for a true possession: the possession usually is accompanied by certain parapsychological happenings, while these are noticeably absent in the presently described psychological disorders. Therefore, we will not only be studying the symptomology and personality characteristics of the possessed persons, but also the presence or absence of those phenomena commonly attributed to the occurrence of an involuntary possession.

This work looks at the results of fourteen cases of exorcism that worked to heal the possessed person. From these we are able to identify the phenomena that surround possession and differentiate it from other psychopathological disorders, producing an objective manner of distinguishing possession from recognized psychopathologies. We will assemble a set of diagnostic criteria that will in the future enable us to distinguish possession, or what might then be called the *possessive states disorder*, from schizophrenia, paranoia, hysteria, and other psychological syndromes.

2

A Brief History of Possession

The history of possession by evil is inextricably tied to the history and development of the concept of the Devil, as well as to the demonologies of the various cultures in which possession is encountered. Jeffery Burton Russell has written what is possibly the best analysis to date on this topic in his books, *The Devil, Satan,* and *Lucifer*; works in which Russell traced the development of the concept of a devil from antiquity up to the Middle Ages.

The Devil has not always been viewed as a singular entity that embodied a culture's, or a religion's, concept of evil. Rather, Russell sees three progressive stages in the human understanding of the Devil.

> Stage one, represented by most monist religions and early Hebrew thought, was characterized by a lack of distinction between good and evil analogous to the early stage of human psychological development when good and evil are not fully differentiated. Stage two, represented by Iranian, Gnostic, and Manichean dualism, postulated that good and evil are totally different, opposed, and unconnected; this stage is analogous to individual development in youth, when things are seen in terms of black and white. The third stage, hinted at by Nicholas of Cusa and expressly stated by C. G. Jung is the notion of a unity transcending good and evil; this suggests that evil can be overcome not by denying it but by transcending it.[1]

Connected with each stage of human understanding of good and evil is a stage of understanding in regard to possession.

> Stage one is exemplified by most of the religions and cultures found in antiquity. The outlook in the Mesopotamia region of

1. Russell, *Lucifer*, 310.

the Sumero-Akkadian religion, the Assyro-Babylonians, the
Hittities and the Canaanites, as well as the early Hebrews and
Egyptians, can all be described as monist in nature. That is, there
is one absolute principle—or God—that rules the universe, of
which there may be many aspects reflected in a pantheon of
gods and goddesses. This form of thinking can also be observed
in the Far East in much of Hinduism and Mahayana Buddhism,
and in the West in the Greco-Roman conceptions of the gods.[2]

The fight between good and evil is not as clear in these monist religions
as it will be in the later forms of dualist philosophies. Each of the gods and
goddesses maintained certain aspects of good and evil within themselves.
Yet there were gods and goddesses who were considerably more good than
evil, as well as some who were more evil than good. It is this latter category
that comprises the closest approximation to a devil in these cultures. For
example, in Assyro-Babylonian thought there is the hero Marduk—a young
god—battling the older gods, including his parents—in order to bring order
(cosmos) out of chaos. Thus, Marduk battles Tiamat, goddess of the prime-
val waters and chaos, as well as the eldest of the old ones, Kingu, and a horde
of demons that Tiamat conceives in order to assist Kingu. Examining this
we can see that this is not a battle between the forces of good and evil but
between those of consciousness and unconsciousness; between order and
chaos; between the new and the old order.[3]

The battle between the newer, or younger gods, and the older gods is a
common motif throughout most of these monist religions. The Greeks had
their older generation of gods, as well as the even more ancient Titans, all of
whom were fought by the younger generation who usurped these older ones
and then inhabited Mt. Olympus. The Hebrews had the *bene ha-elohim*, the
sons of God, who created a race of giants because they had intercourse with
the women of the earth. These sons of God have at times been seen as the
precursors to the later Hebraic and Christian concept of demons. Thus it is
not so much that a moral sense of good and evil were at war in these cultures, but that there was the continuing sense of struggle to maintain order
in a world which was quite chaotic and dangerous.[4] The closest approximation to a devil concept in the Assyro-Babylonian religion can be found in
their gods of the underworld. But, as Russell illustrates, even these gods are
ambivalent in nature.

2. Russell, *The Devil.*
3. Ibid.
4. Ibid.

The deities of the Babylonian underworld manifest qualities that are at best dubious. The "queen of darkness" is Ereshkigal, originally a sky goddesses carried off by force to the underworld by the dragon Kur and there enthroned as its lady. She shares her throne with Nergal, the son of Enlil and originally a sun deity. Nergal forces his way into the underworld using heat and lightening as weapons and threatens to destroy Ereshkigal, who averts ruin only by agreeing to marry him. These dark deities are gods of destruction, plague, war, and death, yet they show their ambivalence both in their functions (Nergal is also a god of healing) and in their origins as sky gods who have fallen to their present chthonic state.[5]

Such ambivalence of the gods is also common in Hinduism.

Most of the gods and goddesses of Hinduism have both their light and their dark sides. The goddess Kali is possibly one of the starkest examples of this. Kali in her lighter aspects is a goddess who brings life and nourishment to the earth, while with the other hand she deals out death and destruction. This is true also of her consort Shiva and most of the other deities of the Hindu pantheon. . . . Not always is the ambivalent nature of the gods and goddesses so starkly seen. In the Canaanite, Hittite, and Greco-Roman traditions the gods and goddesses tend more to exemplify a specific aspect of the one God. Thus in Canaanite religion we encounter the battle between Baal and Mot. Baal, the evil pagan god found in the Bible, is the good fertility god of the Canaanites. Baal is in perennial combat with Mot, the god of death and destruction. Yet, the Canaanites did not conceive of this battle as a fight of good against evil, but as a description of a yearly cycle, and so Baal and Mot are actually a doublet, a description of the opposite acts of the same monist God.[6]

In Greece, once again, we do not find a singular description of evil but encounter it in many places and forms. Yet, as in the other monist religions, these gods are not absolutely evil or good. Hermes psychopomp, the god who led the dead to the underworld, was also the messenger of the gods. Hermes's son, Pan, was the god of sexual desire, which was both creative and destructive. Hades, god of the underworld, brought death, but was also known as Plouton, the god of wealth, for "the underground not only consumes the dead, receiving their souls as well as their corpses, but it also pushes up the tender crops in the spring and therefore promises renewed

5. Ibid., 90.
6. Ibid., 94–97.

life."[7] The list could continue for most of the gods of Greece. There was Alastor the tempter and many minor spirits of a malicious nature that would also afflict the earth and humanity with illness and misfortune. Many of the qualities, and symbolic images, of these darker gods and goddesses would later be combined to form the early and later Christian images of the Devil. Yet, in Greece there was no such singular entity.

For most of these monist religions the earth—and the creatures which inhabited it, including humanity—was out of harmony with heaven and the one God. Because of this, humanity needed to appease the gods in order to maintain order, prosperity, and health. This they did through sacrifices and devotions to the gods. Misfortune and illness were therefore seen as the retribution of the gods for misdeeds in relation to the cultic practices they required. This is directly related to the ambivalent nature of the gods. If one were to maintain a correct cultic relationship with the god or goddess, then one would see the beneficial actions of that god or goddess. But if one were to even accidentally offend the deities then the dark side would show forth and the person would experience misfortune or illness. This concept was a later manifestation of the monist viewpoint, for in the earlier conceptions in Sumer it was primarily lack of caution, or fate, that caused evil spirits to possess a person.[8] One manner by which the gods could afflict persons was by sending a specific demon to them. Thus a god might send a demon of headaches, or of backaches to an individual. Whatever the illness might be, there was a specific demon associated with it. It was then the job of the priest-doctor to help the afflicted person by either appeasing the god, or by driving out the demon. Both methods of healing prevailed; pungent, evil-smelling remedies were seen to revolt the demon and so it would leave, while the good-smelling or tasting remedies might appease the god who would then leave of his or her own accord. Thus medicines, though also seen to have true physical effects, were primarily viewed as means of dealing with demons, the physical cure merely being a side-effect.

> Incantations, magic rites, symbolical ceremonies had precisely the same object in view as medicine proper—to drive or coax the demon out of the body, or, vice versa, medical treatment was supposed to act on the demon, while the cure of the patient was merely an incidental though obvious consequence that followed upon the exorcism of the demon. Such we find to be actually the theory on which medicine rested among the Babylonians and Assyrians down to the latest days; it formed an integral part

7. Ibid., 126–27.
8. Sigerist, *A History of Medicine*, v.1.

of the incantation division of the religious literature, and while prescriptions of a purely medical character are to be traced back to quite an early period, they are invariably accompanied by certain magic rites of precisely the same character as are found in incantations proper. . . . If a certain treatment was good for a patient, it was so because it was bad for the demon. If certain herbs and certain concoctions acted favorably on a sick man, it was because the demons did not like the smell or taste of the herbs, or because the ingredients of which the concoction was made were unpleasant to the demons and caused them to leave their victim, rather than be subjected to the annoyance of unpleasant ordeals.[9]

Not all of the monist cultures maintained this rather limited view of disease and healing. The Greeks, for example, had a culture that maintained three forms of medicine: the Orphic, the Hippocratic, and the Pythagorean. Thus, some Greeks would turn to the cult of Aesculapius for healing, while others might look to a form of the rational medicine which was also on the rise. Thus, the Greek could conceive of a natural cause for certain illnesses while at the same time understanding a supernatural cause for another. This began to indicate an independent concept of possession that was valid alongside of an organic concept of disease.[10]

This was also true for the Egyptians. The Egyptians maintained a monist form of religion, with no singular concept of evil. Rather evil, or the instigation of misfortune and disease, could be seen in many of the gods, especially in Horus, Seth, and Sekhemet.[11] There were many incantations and magical rites found in Egypt in order to exorcise those gods and demons who might afflict a person with illness. But alongside these magical rites is an empirico-rational medicine.[12] The Egyptians seem to have conceived of at least two origins for illness: the gods (or demons) and nature.

Speculative as these theories [of Egyptian medicine] are I find them nevertheless very impressive, as they represent the beginning of medical science, a science which was different from our sober natural science but still one which endeavored to explain the phenomena of life and death, of health and disease, rationally without having recourse to the gods. It was a way of thinking in terms of a philosophy of nature, and in doing it the Egyptians

9. Jastrow, *The Civilization of Babylonia and Assyria*, 250.
10. Cf. Russell, *The Devil* and Sigerist, *A History of Medicine, vol. 1.*
11. Russell, *The Devil.*
12. Sigerist, *A History of Medicine., vol. 1.*

anticipated views and methods of the pre-Socratic philosophers of Greece.[13]

As would be true later in Greece, the Egyptians were conceiving of illness as both a natural occurrence and as a form of possession. The question arises of whether they actually held to these different forms of etiology simultaneously, or whether—like in many areas today—there was a confusion among the healers as to whether the illness was to be viewed exclusively as the fault of the gods or as the fault of nature. But this is clear in the Egyptian culture.

> I still believe in the common origin of all Egyptian medicine, one in which magic, religious, and empirical elements were interwoven inextricably as they are in primitive medicine. But the Papyrus Edwin Smith makes it evident that the empirico-rational element was stronger than we had assumed and that the split between magic, religion, and medicine proper occurred rather early. This may justify the discussion of these various aspects, . . . although I should like to repeat that there are not sharp borderlines. The magician did not hesitate to prescribe drugs at times as part of his ritual, just as the most rational physician in certain cases took recourse to prayer and magic then as he sometimes does today.[14]

The first true embodiment of a principle of evil arises not with the monist religions but with the rise of dualism in ancient Persia. In the sixth century B.C., a man named Zoroaster developed a religion that would later usurp the religion of the Magi and their devas. He replaced these with the two spirits, Ahura Mazda and Ahriman. Ahura Mazda embodied the principle of good and light, and was seen to have created all that was good in the world. Ahriman was the embodiment of all that as dark and evil, and it was to Ahriman that all disease and misfortune was attributed.[15]

Even though Ahriman was the author of "9 and 90 and 900 and 9000 and 9 times 10,000 diseases" this did not mean that *all* disease was attributed to demonic possession. Ahriman and his demons were seen to be spirits possessing no material bodies of their own, thus they inhabited other bodies, causing uncleanness in certain animals, as well as disease, insanity, and death in human beings. But disease could also be a general evil with which Ahriman or a demon afflicted the person. Thus there were three kinds of

13. Sigerist, *A History of Medicine, vol. 1,* 355.
14. Ibid., 298.
15. Russell, *The Devil.*

healers in Persia: the surgeons, the herbalists, and the incantation priests. Each had his specialty in types of diseases or afflictions to be healed. Yet most mental or nervous diseases were seen to be the result of an indwelling spirit which required exorcism.

This same outlook is held in some form by the other major schools of dualism that arose in the ancient world. The later forms of Christian heresies such as Gnosticism and Manicheism posited a worldview with an absolute principle of good and an absolute principle of evil with like effects on the individual as those of the Zoroastrian deities. Much of this gnostic thought was of utmost importance in the development of the Christian concepts of the Devil and of demonic possession. But much of it was also rejected. The later Christian conceptions—though influenced by dualism—actually take us into the third stage of human conception in regard to the principles of good and evil: the stage where God is viewed as being transcendent to either of these principles. It is to this stage that we now turn.

The Christian tradition is incomprehensible apart from the Hebrew tradition from which it sprung. The Hebrews began with a monist form of religion. During this period the Hebrews conceived of the universe as ruled by a singular principle that was seen to contain aspects of both good and evil. Thus, Israel's first king, Saul, could be afflicted with the evil spirit of God,[16] but elsewhere in 1 Samuel[17] the author also can speak of the spirit of Yahweh in a positive manner.

The monist form of the religion soon gave way to a true monotheistic form. Here Yahweh became the one God in whom all these principles rested. Thus Yahweh could be a God of mercy, while at the same time instructing the Israelites to spare none of their enemies in Canaan, killing all down to the children.

At this point in the development of the Hebrew religion possession was attributed not to demons or a devil, but to Yahweh. But, by the time of the prophets the monotheistic God would begin to transform into the transcendental God: the God who no longer was in part evil, but who transcended evil. In such a conception, God was still ultimately responsible for everything that happened in the universe—being its creator—but the principle of evil specifically was being transferred to one member of the creation: the Devil.

A problem of theodicy then arose for the Hebrew people. How could a good God allow evil? The answer to this allowed dualism to creep into the monotheism of their religion. The Hebrews posited the existence of an evil

16. 1 Samuel 16:16.
17. 1 Samuel 10:6.

creature, called by various names: Satan, Sammael, and Semyaza being a few. This seemed to parallel the Zoroastrian concept of a good god and an evil god engaged in universal combat. Yet the Hebrews could not accept this dualistic position and still maintain the uniqueness of their God Yahweh. Thus Satan never became an absolutely evil principle within Judaism. Satan, and his demons, have generally been seen to be a part of the creation of Yahweh, and so ontologically subservient to Yahweh. Satan and the demons have been described in various ways. At times they were viewed as the sons of God— the *bene ha Elohim*—who lusted after women and so left the heavenly court and descended to earth; but because of their lust, Yahweh sent the archangels to punish them and so cast them into the pit and deep valleys.[18]

Another view of Satan and the demons is that these were angels of God—*malak Yahweh*—who rebelled against God and attempted to usurp God's position. The leader of this rebellion was the then supreme angel in the choir of the cherubim: Lucifer, who became Satan. Because of his presumption and pride he was cast out of heaven by the faithful angels of God, and with him were cast down a third of the angels in heaven who had followed Satan in his rebellion. When cast down to earth these fallen angels saw that they could still overcome God if they were able to alienate Him in heaven while they controlled the earth. How would they gain control of the creation? By gaining control over the stewards of creation; by controlling God's image in the creation: humanity. Thus, these fallen angels, led by Satan, became the demons that would tempt and possess human beings to rebel against Yahweh and against His laws.[19]

Evil entered the world through the rebellion in heaven, but evil is propagated in the world because human beings sin. If human beings were not to follow the temptations or promptings of these demons then the creation would still be in God's will and evil would exist only in the persons of these demons and not in the actions of any other part of creation. But this was not the case. Human beings did follow the rebellious ways of these fallen angels, and so the creation became cursed by God; death and destruction entered the natural order.

This is a later Hebrew explanation of evil. Ultimately evil comes about because a part of God's creation is in rebellion to the will of God, and he allows this because he has given angels and human beings the capacity to will. By so doing, by allowing these creatures volition, God has set up the universe to run by love rather than by compulsion and fear. If God were to force the angels and the human beings into doing his will, he would then

18. Russell, *Satan*.
19. Bennett, *The Holy Spirit and You*.

have to break his law of love, something he appears unwilling to do. This is a partial solution to the theodicy problem brought about by a monotheism that denies the existence of evil in the Godhead. Evil may ultimately be traced to a supernatural origin, but this does not mean that the Hebrew viewed all misfortune or disease as the result of a demon's intervention. Human responsibility played a great part in Hebrew thinking. Thus, demons, or the evil spirit of Elohim, might tempt the person, but it was the person's responsibility to avoid contact with such evil and to follow the law of the Lord. Thus, a person's misfortune or illness might be the result of a personal sin, and only indirectly caused by supernatural evil.

The concept of possession did exist though. We see that Yahweh compelled Pharaoh to resist the will of God as brought by Moses. Yahweh also caused the leaders of those opposed to Israel to "harden their hearts" and so led them into destruction. We also see in the Bible that Satan is a cause of sin and misfortune. The Book of Job is probably the most clear and lengthy example of a person's misfortune brought about by a character that Christians came to identify as Satan, with no personal sin involved. But as we saw with sin, possession was not the common explanation for all diseases.

Sin, as well as possession, could cause disease and misfortune. Because of this differentiation between natural and supernatural causes, the Hebrew people were able to distinguish, to a greater degree than their neighbors, between demonic possessions and mental illnesses. There is ample evidence of this in the Bible. In 1 Samuel—the same book we looked at earlier to see Saul afflicted by the evil spirit of Elohim—we see David feigning insanity.[20] We can also see that there is a madness due to drunkenness,[21] and one due to unforgiveness and hatred.[22] Despair and misfortune can also cause insanity.[23] These are merely a few examples of the Hebrew's understanding of a mental disorder.

Thus, the Hebrew knew of various causes of disease and misfortune, only one of these being demonic in nature. They understood the presence of physical illness, of psychological illness, and illness due to demons. They comprehended the concept of a physical or objective sin, a subjective or mental sin, as well as sin caused by the action of the fallen angels, or in the early years, the action of the evil spirit of Elohim. This comprehension is well described by the Hellenistic Jew, Philo, when he differentiated four types of ecstasy.

20. 1 Samuel 11:13–14.
21. Jeremiah 25:16.
22. Hosea 9:7.
23. Deuteronomy 28:34.

1. Ecstasy is a mad fury producing mental delusion, owing to old age or melancholy or other similar cause.

2. Extreme amazement at the events that so often happen suddenly or unexpectedly.

3. A passivity of mind, if indeed the mind can ever be at rest.

4. And the best form of all is the divine possession and frenzy, to which the prophets as a class are subject[24]

We can see that, for the Hebrew, possession was not the explanation for disease in particular; much less for mental diseases. The Hebrew had a concept of mental disease alongside that of demonic action. This became more clouded in later Rabbinic Judaism, where the evil principle would be further refined into the *Yester ha-ra*, the evil principle in humans through which Satan would work. It became less well-defined in Christianity, and it is to this that we now turn.

The New Testament does not develop any coherent, or unique, diabology or demonology. Rather, it carries on the Old Testament and Intertestamental concepts. The Devil as a fallen angel is alluded to a number of times, but a precise and developed concept of the Devil is nowhere indicated. Primarily this is because the New Testament writers were not interested in setting down a precise dogmatic system nor a coherent theology. What was of interest was the gospel message that the kingdom of God had appeared.[25] Thus, the central message of the New Testament was that the kingdom of God, the kingdom of light and truth, had arrived to overthrow the kingdom of darkness and evil. The stories of healings and of exorcisms in the New Testament are, therefore, primarily illustrations of this fact and only secondarily are they indicators of what we are to believe about this cosmos. The stories of healings and exorcisms are illustrations of how the kingdom of God, present in the person of Jesus Christ, had the power to overthrow the kingdom of this world, the kingdom of the devil. Even though this is the primary message, still we may look at these stories to attempt to find indicators to what Jesus Christ and the apostles believed.

Jesus seems to have made the same differentiation among physical sickness, demon-possession, and certain "mental illnesses" such as epilepsy, as we saw in earlier Hebrew thought. Early in Matthew's Gospel we can see Jesus treating epilepsy as a mental illness.[26] However, later in this same

---

24. Pulver, *The Experience of the Pneuma in Philo.*

25. Russell, *Satan.*

26. Matthew 4:24.

Gospel, we see Jesus casting a demon out of an epileptic boy.[27] This leads to a confusion as to whether Jesus saw epilepsy as something due to natural causes or as due to demonic influence—as separate from demon-possession—or as something intermediate to both. One way in which to clear up this confusion is to take both passages as separate statements about epilepsy. If this is done, then we can see that Jesus saw some forms of epilepsy—a term which also included many other forms of "mental illness"—as due to natural causes, while other forms were due to demonic causes. This viewpoint is true in other aspects of New Testament thought in regard to illness. Any form of illness may have its natural component or cause, but it may also have its spiritual component. Thus Jesus can heal a physically sick person by forgiving sins—the spirituality of sin being the root cause of the illness.[28] Yet in another place he can say that the sick person has not sinned, but rather is only sick and so can be healed.[29] Likewise, we can see how in one place Jesus spoke about epilepsy as an illness separate from demon-possession, and in another that the epilepsy has as its root cause a demonic component. We can also see how Judas Iscariot had Satan enter into him and so cause him to betray his Lord, and then a few hours later Judas is driven not by Satan to commit suicide, but by remorse—a psychological element.[30] This ability to discern the root cause indicates to us that Jesus and the apostles had a very interconnected and fluid concept of the human being where the body could be affected by the environment, by the soul, or by the spirit.

As Christianity began to develop it had no set or coherent dogmatic doctrines to follow. Because of this the teachings of Jesus Christ began to take on many forms, later to be identified with such beliefs as Gnosticism, Manicheism, Elkesaitism, Docetism, and the like. Because of these flourishing offshoots from the teachings of the apostles, a doctrine which would stand for the true faith was perceived as necessary if the church as a whole was to survive as a unity. Therefore it was with the early fathers of the church that we first encounter a developing diabology and demonology.[31]

Gnosticism was especially important for the early church to combat. It posited a dualistic worldview that called for an implicit equality and opposition of the Devil—not necessarily Satan, who could be seen as subordinated to the true principle of evil, the Devil—and Christ. The early church fathers, though, could not reconcile this with their understanding of the teachings

27. Matthew 7:14.
28. Luke 5:17–26.
29. John 9:1.
30. Matthew 27:3–5.
31. Russell, *The Devil.*

of Jesus Christ as brought to them through the missionizing of the apostles. The common consensus of the church fathers was that the Devil was Satan, and that Satan was an angel who rebelled against God and was thus cast out of heaven with a total of one-third of all the angels, all who had taken part in the rebellion.[32] Satan, thus being an angel, was subordinate to Jesus Christ, but was still in opposition to him. However, in the cross of Christ, Satan and his rebellious angels—who were also seen as the various demons one would encounter—were defeated. Because of this the followers of Jesus Christ, in whom he still lived by means of the Holy Spirit, also had power over Satan and his demons. Therefore, even though the Devil still existed and still would attack the righteous, there was now a truly effective means to combating this Devil and his hosts: exorcism in the name and the blood of Jesus Christ.[33]

With the development of this demonology, and with the increase in the ascetic practices of the church, there also came an increasing dualism. Even though the intention of the church fathers was to combat dualism, great parts of it crept into the doctrine of the early church. Because of this, a movement toward the viewing of all evils as the result of Satan, or a demon, had begun. Misfortunes and illnesses were seen to be the direct result of Satan's actions. The persecutions and the resulting martyrdoms of many early Christians were attributed to Satan's inciting the political hierarchies to attack Christians. Thus, in their attempt to maintain a unified church in the face of the various forms with which it was struggling, the church fathers were unable to maintain a strict monotheism, but took up a modified monotheism which bordered on dualism. With this the differentiation amongst the body, the soul, and the spirit began to give way to a more dualistic aspect of either the body and the soul, or matter versus spirit. This would be exacerbated in the medieval period.[34]

The medieval period in Christianity was marked by the increasing paganism of its doctrines.[35] The increasing Christianization of Europe was to a great extent also the paganization of Christianity. The Christian missionaries did not attempt to do away with the indigenous religions as a whole; instead they attempted to Christianize the feasts, ceremonies, and folklore of these religions. Because of this many new forms of belief entered into popular Christianity; forms of belief that could hardly be maintained by

32. Cf. Russell, *Satan*; Rahner, *Earth Spirit and Divine Spirit in Patristic Theology*.

33. Bennett, *The Holy Spirit and You*.

34. Russell, *Satan*.

35. Russell, *Lucifer*.

even the most naive of theologies—for they were still more pagan than they were Christian, yet were accepted.

With these converts to Christianity came a plethora of new demons and new aspects to the Devil. The fairies and trolls, monsters and gods of the previous folk religions became demons within the newly founded Christian faith amongst these people. As these forms of belief flourished, the Greek and Roman philosophical influence begin to wane. It was still present as seen in such exemplars as Aquinas and Anselm, but for the majority of the clergy which taught the populace, it was this newer Christianity—a Christianity mixed with folk belief—that predominated.

With this the church moved into an even greater belief in a modified dualism. The world became composed of either good spirits or demonic spirits. The people saw themselves as powerless in a corrupt world and so they were afflicted by demons and the Devil with diseases, misfortunes, and death. God the Father had become very removed from the people, and Jesus Christ was seen to be a weak and essentially ineffectual person. He was commonly portrayed as beaten and dying on the cross. It was believed at this time that the Devil was in control of the world. The Devil was portrayed as the father of terrors. The Devil had become the true god of the age, with only a hope left that Christ would soon come again with His kingdom to save the people. The theology was faulty at best, yet it was maintained because it fit the needs of the people. A people who were powerless and beaten needed to identify with a God who also seemed powerless and beaten, yet who also promised to come again with power to overcome the Devil and once again save the people.

The separation of a rational and intellectual teaching among the people not only allowed the rise of folk religious beliefs, but also doomed the advancement of previous medical practices. As the Devil and his demons were seen to be the authors of all ills, if a person was sick the Devil must be behind it. To some extent the people of the Middle Ages still maintained a concept of disease. They knew to burn a hut in which the plague existed, and that draining of blood by leeches may assist in healing by removing the bad elements from the person. Yet, for many, exorcism was the prescribed cure, and exorcisms abounded.

At this time exorcism did not resemble most earlier forms, nor the forms that exist today. During this dark period, a possessed person could be confronted with an array of tortures which were designed to drive out the demon or the Devil. This could mean the rack, burning, or excessive whipping. This was especially true for one thought to be a witch.[36]

36. Cf. Kieckhefer, *European Witch Trials: Their Foundations in Popular and Learned*

The medieval period was a time of excesses, with a seeming deification of the irrational aspects of the human psyche. In response to this a backlash occurred with the advent of the age of Enlightenment. The Enlightenment brought the Western world out of its period of irrationality, but it did so by attempting to repress the irrational and in turn deify the intellect and a newer sense of positivism. This continued right into the modern period. The modern period added little to a coherent diabology, but rather tended to draw on the concepts of the past. Today we stand in what is considered to be the postmodern period of our civilization, yet in many ways we are still children of the Enlightenment. We continue to deny the irrational and so are confronted with our shadows in the form of genocide and global oppression. We deny the existence of an evil principle and we are confronted with evil's creation: nuclear holocaust and environmental destruction. Because the symptoms of evil's presence have become now so gross and so clear, it is harder for us to continue to deny it.

The new physics attempts to deal with both its understanding of evil and of God in a concept of the "mystery," that which it knows exists but which it can never touch.[37] Christianity has had to take a new look at its concept of the Devil, as well. As evils arise which its intellectual theologies cannot explain, and as cases of demonic possession seem to increase, the church as a whole has been confronted with how to deal with irrational evil once again. Because of this a new form of diabology is alive, one that takes the historical tradition and applies it to our world, which is in the grip of the rational and the irrational. It is to this present-day Christian concept of illness and possession that we turn our attention.

Culture, 1300–1500.; Russell, Lucifer.

37. Schilling, The New Consciousness in Science and Religion.

3

Mysticism and Possession

In today's world, possession is still with us in many forms and aspects. We encounter it in the highly developed religions of both East and West, as well as in the archaic practices of shamanism. Many of these forms are not commonly seen to be possessions, nor do the practitioners view them as such. Yet, as we will see in our following investigation, there is a commonality among the forms of possession that draw them all together.

The phenomenon of possession lies along a spectrum, a spectrum of motivation in approaching the transcendent aspects of our perceived reality. This spectrum is bordered on one end by what we call mysticism, and on the other end by magic. Mysticism and magic are often confused with one another, while, in actuality they are polar opposites. Evelyn Underhill, in her classic work on mysticism, has seen that these two "represent . . . the opposite poles of the same thing: the transcendental consciousness of humanity."[1] The difference between these two poles of transcendental consciousness lies with the will of the individual involved, or the goal of the religious movement as a whole: in mysticism the person desires to surrender the self to the absolute, while with magic the user attempts to manipulate this transcendent consciousness to further his or her own ends in the world of normal consciousness. "The fundamental difference between the two is this: magic wants to get, mysticism wants to give."[2]

> In mysticism the will is united with the emotions in an impassioned desire to transcend the sense-world, in order that the self may be joined by love to the one eternal and ultimate Object of love; whose existence is intuitively perceived by that which we used to call the soul, but now find it easier to refer to as the "cosmic" or "transcendental" sense. This is the poetic and religious

1. Underhill, *Mysticism*, 70.
2. Ibid.

temperament acting upon the plane of reality. In magic, the will unites with the intellect in an impassioned desire for supersensible knowledge. This is the intellectual, aggressive, and scientific temperament trying to extend its field of consciousness, until it includes the supersensual world: obviously the antithesis of mysticism, though often adopting its title and style.[3]

Mysticism is the surrender of the individual will in favor of a will transcendent of the individual. Magic, on the other hand, is the exaltation of the individual will.[4] In the following pages we explore this spectrum of transcendental consciousness as we begin to investigate representative forms of possession. We will begin with mysticism in general, but especially as it is found in Christianity and Hinduism, as representative of all the great religions of the world. We will then look at forms of possession in Christianity as representative of formal religious practices. The reason for choosing Christianity is two-fold: first, Christianity is the major religion with an active possession belief in the Western world; secondly, it is with Christians who have been possessed that we will be dealing later in this study. After this we will move further down the spectrum toward the more magical end as we study Voodoo, shamanism, Spiritualism, witchcraft, and finally Satanism. Each of these forms is complex and meriting greater independent investigation than is practical in the scope of this study. Therefore, we may barely be able to scratch the surface of the complexity of these practices. So we will only briefly review the essential features and beliefs contained in each of these and concentrate on the cognitive and objective phenomena associated with the possession state in these practices.

We begin our review with a look at mysticism. Mysticism is common to most established religions in the world today. It can still be encountered in Christianity, Hinduism, Buddhism, Islam, Judaism, Taoism, and the other great religions of humanity.[5]

In the minds of many, a mystic is perceived as either a person whose consciousness is other-worldly, or as a person who has supernatural abilities. Even though both of these may be seen with the mystics, this is not the essence of the mystic way, for the goal of this activity is not power or special ability, or even a change in consciousness in order to experience another reality—these, rather, are the goals of the magician. The goal of the mystic is

---

3. Ibid., 71.

4 Ibid.

5. cf., Almond, *Mystical Experience and Religious Doctrine*; Parrinder, *Mysticism in the World's Religions*.

to be united with transcendent reality, whether it is seen as God, the cosmic consciousness, or nirvana.[6]

> What then do we really mean by mysticism? A word which is impartially applied to the performances of mediums and the ecstasies of the saints, to "menticulture" and sorcery, dreamy poetry and medieval art, to prayer and palmistry, the doctrinal excesses of Gnosticism, and the tepid speculations of the Cambridge Platonists—even, according to William James, to the higher branches of intoxication—soon ceases to have any useful meaning. Its employment merely confuses the inexperienced student, who ends with a vague idea that every kind of supersensual theory and practice is somehow "mystical." Hence the need of fixing, if possible, its true characteristics: and restating the fact that Mysticism, in its pure form, is the science of ultimates, the science of union with the Absolute, and nothing else, and the mystic is the person who attains to this union, not the person who talks about it. Not to know about, but to Be, is the mark of the real initiate.[7]

Mysticism is thus defined by its goal: the union of an individual with the absolute. This move toward union with the absolute is a developmental process, a person does not have it magically bestowed upon them. Mysticism is a process of development in consciousness taking the seeker from the baser levels of human existence to the lofty heights of continuous consciousness of the reality transcendent to our normal state. Underhill outlines the phases of this mystic way. She sees it as a move from first becoming aware that there is a reality transcending that which is commonly experienced, to a complete union with that reality, with various intervening steps. Underhill's description of the phases is:

1. The awakening of the Self to consciousness of Divine Reality. This experience, usually abrupt and well-marked, is accompanied by intense feelings of joy and exaltation.

2. The Self, aware for the first time of Divine Beauty, realizes by contrast its own finiteness and imperfection, the manifold illusions in which it is immersed, the immense distance which separates it from the One. Its attempts to eliminate by discipline and mortification all that stands in the way of its progress towards union with God constitute Purgation: a state of pain and effort.

6. Underhill, *Mysticism*.
7. Ibid., 72.

3. When by Purgation the Self has become detached from the "ornaments of the spiritual marriage," its joyful consciousness of the Transcendent Order returns in an enhanced form. Like the prisoners in Plato's "Cave of Illusion," it has awakened to knowledge of Reality, has struggled up the harsh and difficult path to the mouth of the cave. Now it looks upon the sun. This is Illumination: a state that includes in itself many of the stages of contemplation. . . . Illumination is the "contemplative state" par excellence. . . . Illumination brings a certain apprehension of the Absolute, as sense of the Divine Presence: but not true union with it. It is a state of happiness.

4. In the development of the great and strenuous seekers after God, this is followed—or sometimes intermittently accompanied—by the most terrible of all the experiences of the Mystic Way: the final and complete purification of the Self, which is called by some contemplatives the "mystic pain" or "mystic death," by others the Purification of the Spirit or Dark Night of the Soul. The consciousness which had in Illumination, sunned itself in the sense of the Divine Presence, now suffers under an equally intense sense of the Divine Absence: learning to dissociate personal satisfaction of mystical vision from the reality of mystical life . . . the human instinct for personal happiness must be killed. This is the "spiritual crucifixion" so often described by the mystics: the great desolation in which the soul seems abandoned by the Divine. The Self now surrenders itself, its individuality, and its will, completely. It desires nothing, asks nothing, is utterly passive, and is thus prepared for

5. Union: the true goal of the mystic quest. In this state the Absolute Life is not merely perceived and enjoyed by the Self, as in Illumination: but is one with it.[8]

To this point, this description of the mystic way best describes Christian mysticism, for in Christian mysticism the self finds itself united to the Absolute, but not dissolved in the Absolute. Union, rather, propels the self to an active life with God. But in non-Christian forms of mysticism another stage is added to these, a sixth stage beyond that of Union. This is the stage of complete annihilation, or the absorption of the individual into the cosmos. This is a major distinguishing factor in the differentiation of Christian and non-Christian mysticism: the Christian self is *enhanced* in a relationship with the Absolute, the non-Christian self is *lost* into the Absolute.

8. Ibid., 169–70.

As the mystic progresses along the way, the increasing consciousness of what is transcendent of commonly experienced reality makes communication more difficult. The mystic therefore turns to symbol and metaphor to describe the vision which he or she experiences. So we encounter the art and prose of a Blake, as well as the symbolic language of a St. John of the Cross or a St. Teresa of Avila. Others do not even attempt to communicate their experiences to the uninitiated, but only to those on a common quest. When one of the early twentieth century's Hindu mystics, Paramhansa Yogananda, inquired of another mystic, Bhaduri Mahasaya, as to why he did not write a book on yoga in order to tell the world about his knowledge and experience with the transcendent reality, Mahasaya responded, "I am training disciples, they and their students will be living volumes, proof against the natural disintegration of tome and unnatural interpretations of the critics."[9] Mahasaya was well aware of the difficulty a mystic has in translating his or her experience of the transcendent to the immanent.

But communication of their experience is not of primary importance to the mystic: the Absolute is their goal. This is one of the major differences between the mystic and the shaman: the shaman may travel into the supernatural realms to perform a task and to tell others about the supernatural; the mystic desires only union with what is even beyond these other realms. This is seen in Underhill's four rules for distinguishing mysticism from other forms of religious practice.

1. True mysticism is active and practical, not passive and theoretical. It is an organic life-process, something which the whole self does; not something as to which its intellect holds an opinion.

2. Its aims are wholly transcendental and spiritual. It is in no way concerned with adding to, exploring, re-arranging, or improving anything in the visible universe. The mystic brushes aside manifestations. Though he does not, as his enemies declare, neglect his duty to the many, his heart is always set upon the changeless One.

3. This One is for the mystic, not merely the Reality of all that is, but also a living and personal Object of Love; never an object of exploration. It draws his whole being homeward, but always under the guidance of the heart.

4. Living union with this One—which is the term of his adventure—is a definite state or form of enhanced life. It is

9. Yogananda, *Autobiography of a Yogi*, 83.

obtained neither from an intellectual realization of its de-
lights, nor from the most acute emotional longings. Though
these must be present, they are not enough. It is arrived
at by an arduous psychological and spiritual process—the
so-called Mystic Way—entailing the complete remaking of
character and the liberation of a new, or rather latent, form
of consciousness; which imposes on the self the condition
which is sometimes inaccurately called "ecstasy," but is better named the Unitive State.[10]

This fourth and last rule of mysticism illustrates the reason for viewing it as a form of possession. The goal of the mystic is union with the
Absolute, which is attained only by *complete surrender of one's self* to this
transcendent reality. This surrender of the self to another reality is actually
a form of possession, for the person has attempted to give all of him- or herself to a power other than the self. This is tempered to a degree in Christian
mysticism, where the surrender does not include the annihilation of the
self—as occurs in most other forms—but rather is satisfied with the union
of the self with God. Yet, even in Christian mysticism, where a semblance
of selfhood is maintained, the complete surrender of the individual's will
to the will of God is imperative. Even if we observe the subtle differences
in the various mystic forms, and take into account the variations in self-
abnegation, the telling criteria for mysticism as a form of possession is seen
in two statements made by Evelyn Underhill. First, Underhill understood
the mystic to be "possessed by the transcendent."[11] But in her second statement, she clearly illustrated the possession qualities of giving one's body
and will over to another to control, for she observed that the mystic did
attempt to abandon independent bodily and intellectual activity, because
"the abandonment of bodily and intellectual activity is . . . undertaken in
order that they may, in the words of Plotinus, 'energize enthusiastically'
upon another plane."[12] Thus, mysticism may be considered a high form
of possession, for in it the possessor is none other than the Absolute, not
merely some nature-spirit, god, or demon.

Common to most forms of possession, and no less prominent here, is
the state of ecstasy experienced by the possessed. Underhill expresses this
commonality between mysticism and other forms of possession in her description of the physical condition of one in ecstasy.

10. Underhill, *Mysticism*, 81.

11. Ibid., 174.

12. Ibid., 173.

Such ecstasy as this, so far as its physical symptoms go, is not of course the peculiar privilege of the mystics. It is an abnormal bodily state, caused by a psychic state: and this causal psychic state may be healthy or unhealthy, the result of genius or disease. It is common in the little understood type of personality called "sensitive" or mediumistic: it is a well-known symptom of certain mental and nervous illnesses. A feeble mind concentrated on one idea—like a hypnotic subject gazing at one spot—easily becomes entranced; however trivial the idea which gained possession of his consciousness. Apart from its content, then, ecstasy carries no guarantee of spiritual value. It merely indicates the presence of certain abnormal psychophysical conditions: an alteration of the normal equilibrium, a shifting of the threshold of consciousness, which leaves the body, and the whole usual "external world" outside instead of inside the conscious field, and even affects those physical functions—such as breathing—which are almost entirely automatic. Thus ecstasy, physically considered, may occur in any person in whom (1) the threshold of consciousness is exceptionally mobile and (2) there is a tendency to dwell upon one governing idea or intuition. Its worth depends entirely on the objective value of that idea or intuition.[13]

Ecstasy is an important aspect of the mystic's life, for it is during the ecstatic state that many mystics encounter the transcendent reality to a greater degree. Ecstasy is actually a form of trance, and trances can vary in duration and in onset. Onset of the trance is what technically distinguishes ecstasy from rapture. Ecstasy is a more gradual onset of a trance due to a "period of absorption in, or contemplation of, some idea which has filled the field of consciousness."[14] Rapture, on the other hand, "instead of developing naturally from a state of intense absorption in the Divine Vision, may seize the subject abruptly and irresistibly, when in his normal state of consciousness."[15] Both ecstasy and rapture are common to the mystic. Whether rapture or ecstasy, the effects of the trance are similar: "during the trance, breathing and circulation are depressed. The body is more or less cold and rigid, remaining in the exact position which it occupied at the oncoming of the ecstasy, however difficult and unnatural this pose may be."[16] We will see, as we explore

13. Ibid., 360.
14. Ibid., 359.
15. Ibid., 375.
16. Ibid., 359.

other forms of possession, that the phenomena of both rapture and ecstasy are commonly observed in possession states.

Along with trance-like states, many other unusual phenomena surround the life of the mystic. In order to review some of these, we will look into the lives of two twentieth-century mystics: the Christian priest (now saint) Padre Pio (1887–1968), and the Hindu Swami, Paramhansa Yogananda (died 1952). In the lives of these two we find most of the phenomena commonly experienced by mystics. These two also illustrate the commonality of mystical phenomena, apart from the difference in doctrinal beliefs which each held.

Most mystics have what might be considered enhanced perceptual abilities. They are able to read the thoughts of others and to see the future to some extent. They also experience seeing visions, hearing voices, and encountering apparitions of spirits. These voices and visions are in many ways a manner of communication between the invisible and the visible.

> Visions and voices, then, may stand in the same relation to the mystic as pictures, poems, and musical compositions stand to the great painter, poet, or musician. They are the artistic expressions and creative results (a) of thought, (b) of intuition, (c) or direct perception. All would be ready to acknowledge how conventional and imperfect of necessity are those transcripts of perceived Goodness, Truth, and Beauty which we owe to artistic genius: how unequal is their relation to reality. But this is not to say that they are valueless or absurd. So too with the mystic, whose proceedings in this respect are closer to those of the artist than is generally acknowledged. In both types there is a constant and involuntary work of translation going on, by which Reality is interpreted in the terms of appearance.[17]

The vision or the voice may be perceived intellectually or concretely. Most often, the mystic will perceive the vision or voice as coming from deep within him- or herself. An equally deep maturity in the mystical life is needed in this regard to discern the difference between the voice of the mind and the voice of the Absolute. At times, though, the mystic may see concrete visions of spirits, angels, and the like, or hear an externally audible voice.[18] But both visions and voices are suspect from the mystic's point of view.

Vision, then, is recognized by the true contemplative as at best an imperfect, oblique, and untrustworthy method of apprehension: it is ungovernable, capricious, liable to deception, and the greater its accompanying hallucination

17. Ibid., 272.
18. Cf., Carty, *Padre Pio: The Stigmatist*, 5–6; Underhill, *Mysticism*, 266.

the more suspicious it becomes. All, however, distinguish different classes of visionary experience; and differentiate sharply between the value of the vision which is "felt" rather than seen, and the true optical hallucination which is perceived, exterior to the subject, by the physical sight.

> We may trace in visions, as in voices—for these, from the psychologist's point of view, are strictly parallel phenomena—a progressive externalization on the self's part of those concepts or intuitions which form the bases of all automatic states. Three main groups have been distinguished by the mystics, and illustrated again and again from their experiences. These are (1) Intellectual, (2) Imaginary, and (3) Corporeal vision: answering to (1) Substantial or inarticulate, (2) Interior and distinct, (3) Exterior words; . . . as to corporeal vision, it has few peculiarities of interest to the student of pure mysticism. Like the "exterior word" it is little else than a more or less uncontrollable externalization of inward memories, thoughts, or intuitions.[19]

Though Underhill interprets the mystic's corporeal vision and exterior word as an externalization of inward memories, there is a difference between these mystic experiences and the average hallucination of the psychotic. The difference lies in the integrity of the perception. The psychotic's hallucination is usually lacking in integrity and may be fleeting in duration; the voice may speak incoherently or in gibberish.[20] In some extreme forms of psychosis there is an integrity to these perceptions, but this is very rare. In mysticism, though, the distinct integrity of the perception is the norm. The mystic clearly understands this perception to originate not in his or her self, but in another, transcendent reality. "The self, wholly absorbed by the intimate sense of divine companionship, receives its messages in the form of 'distinct interior words'; as of an alien voice, speaking within the mind with such an accent of validity and spontaneity as to leave no room for doubt as to its character."[21]

These mystic visions also have a continuity over time, and do not fluctuate to the same extent as in psychosis. A psychotic, as he or she begins to reintegrate the fragmented self, will begin to realize that the vision or voice was actually a part of the self. The mystic, on the other hand, will continue

19. Underhill, *Mysticism*, 281.

20. Pao, *Schizophrenic Disorders: Theory and Treatment from a Psychodynamic Point of View.*

21. Underhill, *Mysticism*, 278.

to regard the vision or voice as a separate entity, even when out of the crisis period of the trance-state.[22]

Not only does the mystic tend to hear, see, and otherwise experience spirits—poltergeist-type phenomena are commonly experienced by mystics—but he or she has a degree of control over them. Padre Pio illustrates this in his capacity as an exorcist. Using the power and authority of his Lord—Jesus Christ—Padre Pio was able to dispel spirits from others.[23] He was also able to bring healing to the sick by means of prayer.[24]

Most mystics astonish the normal person with his or her outstanding ability to control the physical body. The ability to levitate seems to be a common occurrence for mystics. Padre Pio was said to be able to walk over the heads of others when in a pressing crowd, while many other saints of the past were known to levitate while in meditation.[25] Yogananda relates to us his experience with the Hindu mystic Bhaduri Mahasaya, who was known as the "levitating saint".[26] If levitation seems incredible, its shock fades in comparison to the accounts of the mystic's ability to become invisible. This is related to us in the biography of Padre Pio, who was said to be able to become invisible at will.[27]

Other forms of extraordinary bodily control are the mystic's ability to bring about self-anesthesia—much the same as is possible today by means of hypnosis[28]—and the ability to survive on little or no food.[29] Yogananda relates a story of a woman yogi who took no food or water, but had no ill effect on her body. The yogi's name was Giri Bala.

> "I know Giri Bala well," Sthiti Babu told me. "She employs a certain yoga technique which enables her to live without eating. I was her close neighbor in Nawabganj near Ichapur. I made it a point to watch her closely; never did I find evidence that she was taking food or drink. My interest finally mounted so high that I approached the Maharaja of Burdwan and asked him to conduct an investigation. Astounded at the story, he invited her to his palace. She agreed to a test and lived for two months locked up in a small section of his home. Later she returned for a palace

22. Cf. Carty, *Padre Pio: The Stigmatist*; Sophrony, *A Monk of Mt. Athos*; Yogananda, *Autobiography of a Yogi*.

23. Carty, *Padre Pio: The Stigmatist*, 169.

24. Ibid., 20, 72, 159.

25. Ibid., 59.

26. Yogananda, *Autobiography of a Yogi*, 78.

27. Carty, *Padre Pio: The Stigmatist*, 61.

28. Ibid., 15; Underhill, *Mysticism*, 359

29. Carty, *Padre Pio: The Stigmatist*, 17; Yogananda, Autobiography of a Yogi, 460.

visit of twenty days; and then for a third test of fifteen days. The
Maharaja himself told me that these three rigorous scrutinies
had convinced him beyond doubt of her non-eating state.[30]

Even in death Yogananda gives us another illustration of the mystic's
control of the body. Yogananda had been able to control his body to the extent of being able to slow the decay process in death. There are many stories
of yogis being able to feign death, being buried for periods, or immersed
in water for long periods of time. But the words of the mortuary director
where Yogananda's body lay before burial gives an even more astounding
picture of the mystic's ability.

> The absence of any visual signs of decay in the dead body of
> Paramhansa Yogananda offers the most extraordinary case in
> our experience. . . . No physical disintegration was visible in his
> body even twenty days after death. . . . No indication of mold
> was visible on his skin, and no visible desiccation (drying up)
> took place in the bodily tissues. This state of perfect preserva-
> tion of a body is, so far as we know from mortuary annals, an
> unparalleled one. . . . He looked on March 27th as fresh and as
> unravaged by decay as he had looked on the night of his death
> [March 7th]. On March 27th there was no reason to say that
> his body had suffered any visible physical disintegration at all.[31]

The same is documented with the Christian saints, Padre Pio and St.
Teresa of the Little Flower. When their bodies were exhumed decades after
their deaths it was discovered that the state of decay was negligible.

The bodies of many mystics are also know to emanate a perfumed, or
incense-like odor.[32] Not only is the mystic able to control his or her own
body, but also the elements of nature. Yogananda tells us of mystics he knew
who could create objects seemingly out of nothing, or cause fire to occur.[33]
Stories still circulate from South India of the guru Sai Baba who in the palm
of his hand was able to create a mystical grey powder out of nothing which
he gave to his devotees to consume.[34] Padre Pio was able to command cater-
pillars to leave a tree they were infesting,[35] and to prevent rain from falling
in the specific vicinity of a friend of his.[36]

30. Yogananda, *Autobiography of a Yogi*, 461.

31. Ibid., 2.

32. Carty, *Padre Pio: The Stigamatist*, 30; Yogananda, *Autobiography of a Yogi*, 47.

33. Ibid., 318–21.

34. Brooke, *Riders of the Cosmic Circuit*.

35. Carty, *Padre Pio: The Stigmatist*, 122.

36. Ibid., 57.

Some of the other outstanding abilities attributed to mystics are their ability to speak and understand languages that they had not formally learned[37] and the ability to prophesy, or speak forth what they heard from the Absolute.[38] But probably the most unbelievable, yet documented, ability is that of bilocation: the ability to be in two places simultaneously. This can be physically in body, in voice, or in felt presence.

Bilocation was a common attribute of Padre Pio's life. He was seen to become physically present as far away as Milwaukee, Wisconsin, while it was also witnessed that he was still in his monastery of San Giovanni, Italy. There are also the instances of persons hearing his voice, or smelling his perfumed presence about them. Paramhansa Yogananda relates an incident in his own life that well illustrates the phenomena of bilocation. Yogananda had gone to a certain swami in order to find help in locating a friend of his father. The swami agreed to help and this is what followed:

> Abruptly terminating our conversation, the saint became grave-ly motionless. A sphinxlike air enveloped him. At first his eyes sparkled, as if observing something of interest, then grew dull. I felt abashed at his pauciloquy; he had not yet told me how I could meet Father's friend. A trifle restlessly, I looked about me in the bare room, empty except for us two. My idle gaze took in his wooden sandals, lying under the platform seat. "Little sir, don't get worried. The man you wish to see will be with you in half an hour." . . . [M]y watch informed me that thirty minutes had elapsed. . . . I heard somebody coming up the stairs. An amazed incomprehension arose suddenly. . . . "How is it possible that Father's friend has been summoned to this place without the help of a messenger? The swami has spoken to no one but myself since my arrival!" . . . "Sir, how do you happen to come here? [Yogananda asked his Father's friend]. . . . "Everything is mysterious today! [he responded], less than an hour ago I had just finished my bath in the Ganges when Swami Pranabananda approached me. . . . 'Bhagabati's son is waiting for you in my apartment,' he said. 'Will you come with me?' I gladly agreed." . . . This explanation only increased my bewilderment. . . . "Did you meet him in a vision, or did you actually see him, touch his hand, and hear the sound of his feet?" [asked Yogananda]. . . . [The friend] flushed angrily. "I am not lying to you. Can't you understand that only through the swami could I have known you were waiting at this place for me?" . . . "Why, that man,

37. Ibid., 21, 121.

38. Ibid., 23–24.

Swami Pranabananda, has not left my sight a moment since I first came about an hour ago." I blurted out the whole story. . . . "Why are you stupefied at all this?" [asked Pranabananda]. "The subtle unity of the phenomenal world is not hidden from true yogis. I instantly see and converse with my disciples in distant Calcutta. They can similarly transcend at will every obstacle of gross matter."[39]

From these examples, we see that many extraordinary and unbelievable abilities are attributed to those persons who follow the mystic way, whether that way be in Christianity, Hinduism, or some other religious system. Though such events as bilocation, sustenance without food, levitation and the like, all seem more like the wild imagination of a disciple than a reality, these events have all been documented to one degree or another. But, whatever the phenomena may be, it is merely a benefit along the mystic way, and not the goal the mystic desires. The early Hindu writer, Patanjali, has said that one must renounce these powers if one desires to continue along the path to enlightenment, lest a person become enamored of the powers and so quit the path. This is the true test of a mystic, for the mystic gains powers that the magician desires, only the mystic will renounce these powers, surrendering them with the self, in order to gain the goal of the Absolute.

39. Yogananda, *Autobiography of a Yogi*, 23–25.

4

A Christian View: Possession by Evil

P ossession in the Christian world takes on two forms: possession by evil, in the form of the Devil or his demons, and possession by the Holy Spirit. Both forms of possession are rare when compared to the total number of persons claiming to be Christians, yet there has been a resurgence in both forms over the past few decades.[1] We will begin our study of the Christian view of possession with a look at demonic possession.

Conversation regarding possession and the demonic is no more heatedly discussed than in the theological community itself. This is probably because the person who does not believe in the Christian assertions can, with a seemingly clear conscience, reject such speculation as superstition. But for Christians, the excesses of the medieval period and of the seventeenth-century witch hunts have left tender spots in their psyches. Truly, these excesses of the past have left the present generation of Christians defensive, tainted in regard to the discussion of the demonic and possession. The generations following that of the excesses have "inherited the sins of their fathers," or as the prophet Jeremiah said, "their fathers ate sour grapes, and their children's teeth were set on edge."

Thus, to attempt to discuss a Christian view of possession, or of the demonic, with which all Christians will agree, is difficult. There exists today no consistent belief in the demonic to which all Christians will ascribe. A typical example is found in a debate within the Church of England a few decades ago. In response to a court case where the defendant was claiming innocence due to possession, many respected churchmen—and psychiatrists—began to take a closer and more believing look into the possibility of the demonic. Yet the hierarchy of that same church vehemently spoke against the rising tide of superstition and medievalism, claiming that they were now more rational and should avoid such outmoded models.

1. Quebedeaux, *The New Charismatics II.*

34

This controversy is not confined to the Church of England but is consistent throughout most of Christendom. It is, therefore, difficult to set forth a common doctrine from which we will be able to glean some commonalities with which to explore the phenomena of demonic possession in today's world. Even so, there are groups that cross denominational lines and still do maintain a belief in the demonic and in possession. One such group is that of the neo-Pentecostals. Because of the consistency of belief exhibited by neo-Pentecostals, a consistency that even crosses denominational doctrinal lines, it is upon them that we will focus for our understanding of the phenomena of possession.

To understand the Christian view of possession we first need to understand the Christian concept of the human being, as well as of health and sickness in general. Much about this view will be further discussed when we examine Rollo May's and C. G. Jung's view of possession, but for our purpose here we need to understand that the Christian doctrines maintain a view of a tripartite person: a view of a person composed of a body, a soul, and a spirit. These, though, are not absolutes. They are not perfectly independent and discrete entities found within a person. Rather, they are descriptive of processes that can appear discrete, but which in actuality overlap and interrelate within the ontological dimension of the complete, or whole, human being.[2]

Throughout the Bible the body is referred to in two manners. The early Hebrews did not speak of the human body as a whole, but spoke more of the individual organs and parts of the body. The closest connotation of a whole body is found in the Hebrew word *basar*, which means flesh. This was picked up in the Septuagint (the Greek Old Testament) and in the New Testament by the Greek word *sarx*, which also means flesh. Up to this point, then, the concept of the body was comprised of the physiological organism, that portion of the person that directly encountered the outer environment.[3]

However, in the New Testament the body began to take on a more extended meaning. In the writings of St. Paul there came a differentiation between the concept of the body as flesh (*sarx*) and the body as the total person (*soma*). There are other interesting manners in which St. Paul uses these words, such as the clarification between *sarx* as the physical flesh of a person, or as the universal Flesh, which subjects humans to the sin of the world. *Soma* is also used to describe the corporate unity of a group. Yet these meanings are peripheral to our present discussion, which is interested only in the individual person.

2. Come, *Human Spirit and Holy Spirit.*
3. Pederson, *Israel: Its Life and Culture.*

St. Paul's use of the word *soma* is at times very similar to what we will
see as Jung's use of the word Self. Because of this it clouds our understanding, since the word spirit also seems to correlate well with Jung's use of Self.
But if we move away from the exegesis of the biblical passages, and look at
today's usage of the word, we can see that when most people speak of the
body—as distinct from the soul or the spirit—they are actually referring to
the *sarx* element of the person; the flesh, the physiological organism.

The soul is distinct from the body in that it does not directly relate with
the environment but only does so through the mediation of the body. The
origin of the soul is seen to be the conjunction of the body and the spirit,
and as such can also be seen to carry on a mediating function between the
body and the spirit. The soul is the seat of knowledge, will, desire, affections,
and the senses. It is here that imagination is found. The soul also acts as
the gate-keeper, determining what the person will perceive and what will
be ignored. In all of these ways the soul truly corresponds to our present
understanding of the psyche, which itself is the Greek word for soul.

A difference between our present understanding of the psyche and
the biblical concept of the soul is that in many ways our present understanding has also collapsed the previous understanding of the spirit into the
psyche, and so our present-day understanding of this area of functioning is
confounded in regard to the past understanding of the soul. Also, the past
understanding incorporated a greater community context than does today's
very individualistic view of the psyche.[4]

The Hebrew idea of the soul (*nephesh*) was not merely a self-contained
unity, but was equally the product of the company one was keeping. The
soul of one person would unite with the soul of others, with the common
center of gravity being within the group rather than being within a person.
Thus the Hebrew could speak of the soul of a people. Consequently, the
Hebrew would also be concerned with whom he or she was relating, for to
keep company with an evil person was to take that evil into oneself, since
their souls had, in essence, united. From this viewpoint it is easier for us to
understand the biblical prohibitions, and fears, of coming into contact with
prostitutes, or persons not of the community.

The soul, then, is seen as the inner person. It is not sharply defined
by space or by time, as is the body. It is a realm of potentiality and change,
as is the body, but in distinction from the spirit. It is the human being as
a personal, individual, responsible creature, as well as a member of the

---

4. Cf. Pederson, *Israel: Its Life and Culture*.

community. It is in many ways what we see as the psyche in all of its conscious, unconscious, and interpersonal aspects.[5]

The spirit is the realm of self-transcendence and of awareness of the transcendent reality. It is the motivating power of the body and the soul. Whereas the soul may function in a potential manner the spirit is structured in actuality. The spirit is the source of individual meaning and of freedom. It is the motivating force behind the move toward self-realization, full self-consciousness, and the completion of the whole human being. It is the principle of power and life and is the part of the human being transcendent of nature. The spirit is truly the whole human being as well, for it is the unity of body and soul. In more existential terms, the spirit is the ground of one's being.

Even though the soul may exhibit volition, the motivating force behind what the soul can will is found in the spirit. The soul may direct the course of the person much as a helmsman does a ship, but the spirit is the captain that gives the helmsman the course. The spirit is that transcendent function, the source of what is often collapsed into today's understanding of the psyche and so called para-psychological.

By being the source of meaning and freedom in a person's life, the spirit is the giver of life. Thus, a loss of meaning, or a loss of freedom, is truly a spiritual problem; one which can mean eternal life or eternal death.

So far the person has been described as consisting of three seemingly independent functions: the body, the soul, and the spirit. These functions are not independent; rather, they are intimately *inter*dependent. The body transmits stimuli from the environment to the soul, which then senses these and either knows them or explores them. The soul directs the body by means of will. But the soul finds the source for this volition in the meaning given it through the spirit. Thus, in a diagrammatic sense the spirit is the center of the human being, affecting all human life as it touches the soul and interacts with the soul. The soul also affects the spirit by the contacts it makes in the environment, and so can limit the freedom in the spirit, or change the sense of meaning. Likewise the spirit affects the body through the soul. No one part works on its own, but all are interconnected and necessary to the others for a person to be a whole human being.

Just as the person is tripartite, so too can illness then be seen to be a sickness in one or more of these functions. Francis MacNutt in his book, *Healing*, has laid out this differentiation quite nicely.

A sickness of the body can occur due to a multitude of reasons, most common of these being diseases or accidents. Such sickness calls for medical

5. Cf., Come, *Human Spirit and Holy Spirit.*

treatment, and most Christians have no problem with the use of medicine, for it is seen as a God-given method of healing the body. Of course, prayer for healing is also an acceptable manner of healing in the Pentecostal and neo-Pentecostal communities, but, as MacNutt stresses, this need not be to the exclusion of good medical help.

Sickness of the soul can be the result of the malfunctioning of one of its processes. Thus we can see such soul-sickness as one of the many psychological disorders that we know today. The list of neurotic, psychotic, and character disorders that are described in the psychological literature are good indicators of what is meant by a soul-sickness. The cure for such a sickness can be prayers for inner emotional healing, as well as counseling and psychotherapy.

The sicknesses of spirit need to be divided into two categories. First, there can be a spiritual sickness because of personal sin: the person has gone against the law of God and so has lost the directing power toward wholeness that the spirit can give to the soul. The second type of spiritual sickness is due to the demonic, and it is this type with which we are most concerned.[6]

Both types of spiritual sicknesses will engender what might be called existential neuroses. One with a spiritual sickness may feel the loss of freedom, or the loss of meaning in life, and so approach life with a sense of futility and boredom.[7] When the cause of the sickness is personal sin, what is needed for the cure is repentance and forgiveness. Here enters the whole area of the need for the grace of God and for the forgiveness of others. When the cause is demonic what is needed is deliverance or exorcism.

Growth in personal holiness has also been a manner of ridding oneself of the demonic, though such growth is often quite difficult when one is in the sway of the demonic. Since all of the functions of the human being are interrelated, any illness in one function can affect the others. Thus, a spiritual illness may also have been seen to affect the willing of the soul, or an illness of the soul may affect the actions of the body. Almost any combination of effect can be imagined.

Demon-induced sicknesses can be further divided into two categories. Tanquerey[8] has described these two forms as obsession and possession, though obsession might more properly be called oppression since it deals more with what is done *to* a person than the present psychological meaning of obsession. Demon-obsession occurs when the Devil "besieges the soul

---

6. Cf., MacNutt, *Healing*.

7. Come, *Human Spirit and Holy Spirit*.

8. Tanquerey, *The Spiritual Life: A Treatise on Ascetical and Mystical Theology*.

from without by assailing it with horrible temptations."[9] Such an obsession "consists in a series of unusually violent and persistent temptations. It is called external when the temptations affect the exterior senses by means of apparitions, and internal when they stir up sensations or emotions." But Tanquerey goes on to say that obsessions are rarely purely external, though "there have been Saints who, though obsessed from without by all sorts of phantoms, preserved an unruffled peace of soul."[10]

The Devil is seen to act upon the external senses by means of appearing to sight in either repulsive or seductive forms, the former to frighten the person and so turn that one away from virtue, and the latter form in order to lead the person into sin. He can act upon hearing by causing obscene words or songs to be heard, and upon the sense of touch by delivering blows and wounds to harm the person, or by embraces to once again tempt the person to sin.[11] A patient with whom I was working a few years ago claimed such an experience of being pummeled by a spirit. He explained that he had come home to find his wife unconscious across their bed, and a "luminous, sparkling entity" hovering at the side of the bed. A mixture of fear and anger came over him, and with a bit of both in his voice he yelled at the "spirit" to get out of there. The spirit then retreated in a circular fashion around the room, picked up speed and coming straight toward him slugged him and knocked the wind out of him. The patient claimed that there was a discernable bruise that others would attest to if I didn't believe him. Certainly such occurrences as beatings and bruises were documented in the life of Padre Pio.

The Devil can also act upon the interior senses of the imagination, the memory, and the passions in order to excite them. This may seem to indicate a psychological obsession and not demonic activity; Tanquerey does warn his readers to be discerning and not to see all such excitation of the internal senses as the work of the Devil. "In order to keep the golden mean, we must follow the rule of accepting as diabolical only such phenomena as point, because of their extraordinary nature or because of the sum-total of circumstances, to the action of the Evil One."[12] It is only when "the temptations are at once violent, persistent and hard to account for by natural means, [that] one may conclude that it is a special intervention on the part of the devil."[13]

9. Ibid., 718.

10. Ibid., 718.

11. Ibid., 719.

12. Ibid., 718.

13. Ibid., 719.

When it is discerned (or diagnosed) that a person is obsessed—or as I prefer, oppressed—by the demonic, what is called for is a deliverance. The difference between deliverance and exorcism is one of degree. What is referred to today in many Pentecostal and neo-Pentecostal circles as deliverance was what the Roman Catholic Church has referred to as informal exorcism. It was believed that since the Devil had not taken possession of the person, that a less forceful means than formal exorcism was needed to be rid of the Devil's actions.

Possession is seen as a much more serious state of affairs, for in possession two elements are present: (1) the Devil (or a demon) is present, controlling the body of the possessed; (2) dominion is exercised by the Devil or demon over that body and through it over the soul of the person. Tanquerey describes two states during the possession: the crisis and the calm. The crisis consists of a violent attack in which "the devil manifests his tyrannical sway."[14] The calm is a period when nothing actually discloses the presence of the evil spirit, except possibly the presence of a chronic infirmity which baffles all the efforts of physicians. We might add to this the sense of meaninglessness or of being bound.

The causes of possession are also frequently debated. Some say that the possessed have no part in being possessed, but rather they were chosen by the Devil for some unknown reason. This would fit most closely with a literal concept of involuntary possession. But most people see that the person who becomes possessed did have some part in it, though this part may have been unconscious or merely naive. The person did not desire to become possessed, but did so only because of some other action or actions that led to the final loss of freedom.[15]

One of the most common explanations for possession today lies in a person naively approaching evil, or the arcane powers of the universe. Many people who are seen to be either oppressed by demons, or to be possessed, have also taken part in some aspect of the occult or have been involved in meditation techniques in worship of a Hindu, Tibetan, or some other god.[16]

Whatever the cause of possession, and whatever the explanation utilized to understand it, there are certain common phenomena that we can study objectively. It is to these that we now turn our attention.

The phenomena that are found described in possessions can be placed into three categories. The first category is made up of the parapsychological

14. Ibid., 721.

15. Martin, *Hostage to the Devil: The Possession and Exorcism of Five Living Americans.*

16. Cf., Koch, *Occult Bondage and Deliverance*; Koch, *Christian Counseling and Occultism.*

occurrences that surround a possession, and is the one that receives the most attention in the literature. The second category is that of the objective behavioral phenomena of the possessed person that is observed by those around that person. The final category can be defined as the impact upon others in the vicinity of the one who is possessed. This last category is made up of the subjective impressions of others that can be used as diagnostic indicators, much as when a therapist may experience feelings of inexplicable anger and begin to question whether or not the patient is suffering from a borderline personality condition.

Of all the phenomena associated with possession, the parapsychological occurrences are probably the most spectacular and most celebrated. They are also the most indicative of a possession. Traditionally, the Roman Catholic Church—which is very careful in its diagnosis of possession—calls for the presence of some of these before they will consider a person to be other than mentally ill.

The phenomenon of understanding a language that the person could not possibly have known, or speaking a language to which he or she has never been exposed, is one of the Roman Catholic Church's criteria for possession.[17] The Catholic Church is usually very careful to not immediately presume that a case of speaking or understanding a foreign language is a possession, but first looks to the psychological explanations by taking an extensive history of the patient to see if that person had ever been exposed to the language sometime during his or her life, attempting to discern whether the language is actually the return of some unconscious perception from the past.

Clairvoyance, or knowledge of distant and hidden things, is another of the criteria used for a possession.[18] Closely allied with this is the telepathic ability of the possessed. This is especially seen in regard to what the possessed knows about those who are attempting to perform an exorcism. The possessed at times can speak to the most hidden aspects of the lives of those present, much to the embarrassment of the participants in the exorcism. Malachi Martin in his book[19] warns of this danger, and that one should be prepared to hear the possessed during an exorcism reveal those embarrassing or discrediting things that one has never told anyone else. These abilities are primarily centered about religious or moral matters, but clairvoyance

17. Cf. Koch, *Christian Counseling and Occultism*; Tanquerey, *The Spiritual Life: A Treatise on Ascetical and Mystical Theology*; Weller, *The Roman Ritual*.

18. Ibid.

19. Martin, *Hostage to the Devil*.

has been known to work to the benefit of the possessed in his or her ability to discern secrets which could help financially or in other matters.

The telepathic or clairvoyant abilities of the possessed are also exhibited in another manner. Tanquerey[20] discusses the interesting occurrence of the possessed either flying into a violent fury or dissociating into a trance when exorcism or prayer for the possessed is performed, even without the knowledge of the person. Likewise if a holy object is in the presence of the possessed person, but hidden, such behavior may still result. I have spoken with a priest who related to me that once, while he was speaking to a person whom he believed to be possessed, he began to pray silently to himself while they were talking. As he began to pray the person suddenly jumped up and began contorting her body into actions mimicking eastern meditation practices.

The third major criteria used by the Roman Catholic Church is the presence of strength out of proportion to the person's age or situation in which the strength is exhibited.[21] These are the three main criteria used by the Roman Catholic Church, yet there are many other parapsychological phenomena associated with possession. Poltergeist experiences may occur in the vicinity of the possessed. The tearing of fabric;[22] the constant opening and slamming of doors;[23] moving furniture; objects moving or flying across the room; or the flipping or moving of Christian articles or pictures[24] are all possible occurrences during a possession. Teguis and Flynn,[25] in their study of the psychosocial dynamics of paranormal occurrences, documented the parapsychological happenings during a supposed possession of an eleven-year-old girl. "The paranormal events involved a number of religious objects moving, changing positions, flipping off walls, laying on their sides—not just crucifixes, but pictures of Jesus and biblical scenes, and statues of religious figures associated with the family's traditional religious upbringing." Teguis and Flynn attempt to explain these occurrences as the child's "unexpressed hostility toward her mother . . . discharged on an unconscious level through psychokinesis." What seems odd about this explanation is that they do not speak about any non-religious objects being

20. Tanquerey, *The Spiritual Life: A Treatise on Ascetical and Mystical Theology.*

21. Koch, *Christian Counseling and Occultism*; Tanquerey, *The Spiritual Life: A Treatise on Ascetical and Mystical Theology*; Weller, *The Roman Ritual.*

22. Lechler, *The Distinction Between Disease and the Demonic*; Martin, *Hostage to the Devil.*

23. Martin, *Hostage to the Devil.*

24. Teguis, *Dealing with Demons: Psychosocial Dynamics of Paranormal Occurrences.*

25. Ibid.

affected by psychokinesis, nor any articles specifically associated with the mother, which one would expect if this was a case of unexpressed hostility towards the mother. Rather, the psychokinetic phenomena were all directed at articles that belonged to the entire family, and specifically were articles that concerned the Christian religion and Jesus Christ. This fits with one of the criteria of possession that we will soon come to, which is that the possessed person will avoid religious objects and will have difficulty speaking the name of Jesus or encountering an object considered holy—thus the traditional use of holy water and holy oil during exorcisms. Teguis and Flynn's explanation of why only religious articles were affected is wholly unsatisfactory, and seems to be an attempt to rationalize the data they found rather than an attempt to evaluate the data objectively:

> It is conceivable that the girl, heavily influenced by traditional, punitively-oriented religious beliefs, called on God or Jesus to help her deal with her manifold problems and her circumstances. If one calls for such help and it does not come, one feels betrayed, and it thus becomes interesting that symbolically, and in reality through psychokinesis, the pictures of Jesus are flipped upside down or turned around on walls, and other religious objects fall or are otherwise moved. Such patterns symbolic of the rejection of Christ and God and religion in general are very common in other instances of paranormal occurrences. It is also interesting that if the personage or deity to whom one is praying is regarded as all-seeing and all-knowing, if the paranormal agent has any guilt feelings about what is happening, having Jesus' face turned around so he cannot "see" is symbolic of preventing him from witnessing what is going on.[26]

Though the explanation for the phenomena may seem inadequate, the phenomena themselves do concur with much of what has been known for centuries. During a possession, the possessed tends to reject Christianity and Jesus, is repulsed by the presence of Christian objects, and will either attempt to get rid of them or to destroy them.[27]

Another form of parapsychological occurrence concerns the individual's relation to gravity. Both levitation and "possessed gravity" have been observed. Possessed gravity is the inability to move a possessed person, as if that person is extremely heavy. Additionally, there is the seeing

---

26. Ibid., 71.

27. Lechler, *The Distinction between Disease and the Demonic.*

of apparitions, especially dark figures, by both the possessed and others in the vicinity.[28]

Finally, there is the hearing of voices: once again, this can be by both the possessed and those around him or her. The voices that the possessed person hears are different from those encountered in schizophrenic disorders. Whereas in schizophrenic disorders the voices may be incoherent, filled with neologisms, or maintaining a running commentary on the behavior of the person, the voices heard by the possessed are usually coherent and speak about religious or moral matters. That is, they usually speak in a derogatory manner about God and those who are attempting to be moral.[29]

The behavioral phenomena that are encountered in a possession can be seen to fit into two categories of their own: the phenomena directly associated with the body and those associated with the individual's attitude. If we examine the attitude of the possessed person, we will find that he or she avoids all mention of demons or the Devil, or only mentions them in a very quiet and concerned manner.[30] This in itself is a diagnostic criteria. If a person is continually complaining about an assault by demons, or is loudly proclaiming that he or she is possessed, then the evidence points to the person being mentally ill, and not possessed. The theological reasoning behind this assertion is that the demonic works best in secret and in the dark. Thus, the demon will attempt to stay hidden: to allow the person to go about proclaiming its presence would defeat its purpose. Those who do so, then, are most likely not possessed but have a mental disorder.

As we already began to discuss in regard to the parapsychological phenomena, the possessed person exhibits a revulsion to religious objects and conversation. This can be seen in the person's attempt to avoid or destroy religious objects and in a difficulty mentioning the name of Jesus. When it comes to the mentioning of the name of Jesus we can begin to get a measure of the degree of demonic activity present in a person's life. The greater the difficulty, the more intense the state of demonization.

As well as the aversion to things religious, the possessed person will also put up a struggle against prayer.[31] At first this struggle is not evident, for the afflicted one may actually come and request prayer or deliverance, but once the prayer has begun a visible struggle goes on in the person

28. cf., Lecher, *The Distinction between Disease and the Demonic*; Martin, *Hostage to the Devil*; Tanquerey, *The Spiritual Life: A Treatise on Ascetical and Mystical Theology*.

29. Ibid.

30. Berends, *Biblical Criteria for Demon-possession*; Koch, *Christian Counseling and Occultism*; Lechler, *The Distinction between Disease and the Demonic*).

31. Scanlon, *Deliverance from Evil Spirits*.

that indicates the discomfort that the possessed is experiencing during the prayer.[32]

If the possessed person him- or herself attempts to pray then a feeling of being choked may occur.[33] Many times when prayer or other religious activity is occurring around the afflicted person, he or she may fall into a feverish agitation, accompanied by bodily contortions, outbursts of fury, and blasphemous utterances, which the person expresses without remorse or guilt. All of these may then be followed by a period of dissociation and a seeming trance state. These actions may also occur in other circumstances, along with screaming, cursing, raving, violence, and the grinding of teeth.

Various other bodily manifestations are: exaggerated secretions and eliminations saturated with inexplicable wracking; distortions of the face with either abnormal tightening of the skin or grimaces; reflexes may be sporadic or abnormal, they may even cease for a time; heartbeats are sometimes hard to detect; there may be disturbances of sleep with the afflicted person being awakened many times during the night; there may also be physical pains in different parts of the body associated with possession.

A possessed person may also seem to have more than one personality present in his or her body. Along with this are the extreme variations or alterations in the person's voice, from very deep throaty sounds to shrill, nasal vocalizations.

Finally, the possessed are commonly afflicted with sudden and violent temptations, obsessions, and compulsions. These really cannot be distinguished from the obsessions and compulsions encountered in other anxiety disorders exhibiting obsessive-compulsive symptoms, or in schizophrenia. They are distinguished as due to a demonic element mainly because they are viewed in conjunction with some of the other possession symptoms.

Not only is the possessed person afflicted by the demonic but so are those that attempt to help him or her. The feelings and subjective perceptions of the helper can also be indicators of whether a true possession is occurring or not.

Some of these perceptions are sensory. There may be a general stench in the vicinity of the possessed, especially an acrid stench. The feeling of coldness, even freezing temperatures, may also be experienced when in the presence of one who is possessed.[34]

Those around the possessed person may also encounter poltergeist phenomena such as discussed earlier. Along with these, or even on its

---

32. Cf. Basham, *Deliver Us from Evil.*

33. Lechler, *The Distinction between Disease and the Demonic.*

34. Martin, *Hostage to the Devil.*

own, a person working with a possessed patient may begin to feel an alien presence lurking in some unknown place, and a subsequent discomfort regarding this feeling. Correlated with the possessed person's feeling of being weighted down, or possessed gravity, the helper may experience the feeling of a suffocating pressure that may induce the helper to leave the possessed person's presence.

One of the feelings that is most indicative of the spiritual nature of possession is that the possessed person has lost a human quality: the helper feels as if he or she is in the presence of something inhuman or that the possessed person is empty and alienated from him- or herself.[35]

If any of these feelings or experiences are encountered when with a person that is exhibiting other signs of possession, the validity of the presence of possession is considered of little doubt.

Phenomena Attributed to Demonic Possessions from the Christian View

Parapsychological Phenomena

- Poltergeist phenomena
- Tearing of fabric in vicinity
- Constant opening and slamming of doors
- Footsteps, noises
- Moving furniture
- Moving or flying objects
- Flipping, moving of religious objects
- Possessed gravity
  - Unable to move person
  - Levitation
- Telepathic powers, especially regarding religious matters
- Clairvoyance: knowledge of hidden and distant things
- Seeing apparitions, especially dark figures
- Hearing voices

35. Ibid.

- – Voices that are coherent
- – Voices that speak about religious or moral matters
- Speaking or understanding an unknown language
- Strength out-of-proportion to age or situation
- Use of exorcism, holy object, or prayer without the knowledge of the possessed produces a fury or dissociation in the possessed person

Behavioral Phenomena

- Avoids the mention of demons
- Struggles against prayer
- Repulsed by religious objects and conversation
- Difficulty in using the name of Jesus
- Destroys religious objects
- Sudden, violent temptations, obsessions, compulsions
- Exaggerated secretions and elimination saturated with inexplicable wracking
- Distortions of face
- Reflexes may be sporadic or abnormal, may even cease for a time
- Heartbeats are sometimes hard to detect
- Feverish agitation
- Bodily contortions
- Outbursts of fury
- Blasphemous utterances
- Dissociation
- Variations or alterations of voice
- Presence of other personalities
- Possessed may feel as if choking if trying to pray
- Screaming, cursing, raving, grinding teeth, violence
- Sleep disturbances
- Physical pain in different parts of the body

Phenomena Affecting Others

- General stench; acrid stench
- Feeling of coldness; lowered temperature; freezing temperatures
- Experience of poltergeist phenomena
- A feeling of an alien presence
- A feeling of suffocating pressure
- A feeling that the possessed has lost a human quality; that the possessed is empty or alienated from him- or herself

5

A Christian View: Possession by the Holy Spirit

M any Christians recognize not only the reality of possession by evil spirits, but also realize the potential for being "filled" with the Holy Spirit. Though much of the Christian community does not recognize such a possession by the Holy Spirit as a valid "Christian" phenomenon, there has been a growing movement within the Christian world to manifest the power of the Holy Spirit. This power becomes manifest once a person has been "baptized in the Holy Spirit," or has allowed the Holy Spirit to work through him or her.[1] Throughout this section we will be referring to the possession by the Holy Spirit by the phrase "baptism in the Holy Spirit" primarily because the Christian tradition has referred to this phenomena as such since its beginnings in the first century A.D.

The history of the baptism in the Holy Spirit begins with the day of Pentecost in the first year after the death and resurrection of Jesus Christ, in the first century A.D. It was on this day that the Holy Spirit came down and dwelt within the disciples of Jesus to give them various abilities and powers in order to enable them in their ministries.

> When the day of Pentecost arrived, they were all together in one place. And suddenly there came from heaven a sound like a mighty rushing wind, and it filled the entire house where they were sitting. And divided tongues as of fire appeared to them and rested on each one of them. And they were all filled with the Holy Spirit and began to speak in other tongues as the Spirit gave them utterance. . . . But Peter, standing with the eleven, lifted up his voice and addressed them. . . . Let all the house of Israel therefore know for certain that God has made him both

---

1. Bennett, *The Holy Spirit and You*; Quebedeaux, *The New Charismatics II*.

49

Lord and Christ, this Jesus whom you crucified." Now when they heard this they were cut to the heart, and said to Peter and the rest of the apostles, "Brothers, what shall we do?" And Peter said to them, "Repent and be baptized every one of you in the name of Jesus Christ for the forgiveness of your sins, and you will receive the gift of the Holy Spirit. For the promise is for you and for your children and for all who are far off, everyone whom the Lord our God calls to himself." And with many other words he bore witness and continued to exhort them, saying, "Save yourselves from this crooked generation." So those who received his word were baptized, and there were added that day about three thousand souls. And they devoted themselves to the apostles' teaching and the fellowship, to the breaking of bread and the prayers. And awe came upon every soul, and many wonders and signs were being done through the apostles.[2]

Throughout this biblical book, The Acts of the Apostles—which documents the beginnings of the Christian church in the first century—there are many more recorded instances of speaking in tongues, healings, and inspired preaching all due to the Holy Spirit working through the followers of Jesus. However, as the centuries wore on, the baptism in the Holy Spirit and its ensuing gifts seems to have declined and faded into relative oblivion in the Western world. St. Augustine, one of the most influential of the early theologians of the church, set the tone for the next seven hundred years by his statement that:

In the earliest times, "the Holy Ghost fell upon them that believed: and they spake with tongues," which they had not learned, "as the Spirit gave them utterance." These were signs adapted to the time. For there behooved to be that betokening of the Holy Spirit in all tongues, to shew that the gospel of God was to run through all tongues over the whole earth. That thing was done for a betokening, and it passed away.[3]

It was not until the eighteenth century and the Wesleyan revivals—which later become Methodism—that the phenomena of possession by the Holy Spirit would once again be introduced on a large scale into the Western world. During these revivals people would be stirred by John Wesley's powerful preaching to the point of ecstasy and trance which resembled a possession by the power of God. The revivals continued throughout the

2. Acts 2:1–4, 14a, 36–43.

3. Kelsey, *Tongue Speaking: An Experiment in Spiritual Experience*, 40.

eighteenth and nineteenth centuries, calling for a return of the power of God in a person's life, and in social reform.[4]

In the nineteenth century, Wesley's movement expanded into what became known as the Holiness movement, a movement that taught that personal holiness was more important than social needs—though social needs were never totally ignored nor considered unimportant—and that there was the need for a second baptism, subsequent to one's baptism into the church.

> The Holiness sects, already committed to individual conversion and constant, intense efforts to become sanctified, were led naturally to the third tenet: the "second baptism" of the Holy Spirit, which would render the first two doctrines more meaningful and possible. The movement differed from orthodox Protestantism in three basic ways: (1) it was fundamentalist, holding to literal translation of the Bible and denial of Darwin's theories; (2) it insisted on the necessity of individual conversion, by contrast with the doctrine of Christian nurture which taught that a child raised according to Christian ideals would ipso facto be a Christian; and (3) it emphasized the moral perfection of the individual as the mission of the church, rather than social reforms.[5]

The Holiness movement gave birth to the beginnings of a new movement in the Christian church, a movement that would introduce on a grand scale the phenomena of possession by the Holy Spirit. Out of the Holiness movement came Pentecostalism. Pentecostalism differs from the Holiness movement in one essential way: it emphasizes the need for a person's baptism in the Holy Spirit and their subsequent speaking in an unknown language, or tongues.[6]

Though influenced by the preceding Welsh Revival, American Pentecostalism was born in 1906, when a Methodist minister named Charles Parham began preaching in an old building on Azusa Street in Los Angeles. His influence spread to many other ministers who, even after Parham's death and the demise of the Azusa Street mission, brought Pentecostalism to people in what are known as the Assembly of God, Church of God, and Full Gospel denominations, to name a few. In the beginning of the Pentecostal movement, most of its followers were of lower class status. Many of the followers were black, in a period where being black generally meant

4. Ibid.
5. Kildahl, *The Psychology of Speaking in Tongues*, 19.
6. Ibid.

being poor and oppressed by the powers of the society.[7] This has given rise to many of the misconceptions that people today hold regarding those who are baptized in the Holy Spirit. Yet, in today's society there are actually three dominant forms of Pentecostalism practiced. First, there are those groups that are comprised of persons primarily from the lower classes of society and which have practices such as snake-handling and other seemingly odd behavior.[8] This group is by far the smallest in number, relative to all who claim to have been "filled with the Holy Spirit."[9]

The second form is Pentecostalism proper, which is exemplified by the Assembly of God Church, which is predominately white, and the Church of God in Christ, which is predominately black. These are the largest Pentecostal denominations and the most structured. Together these denominations number members well into the millions and they are still growing.[10]

The third form is what is now being referred to as neo-Pentecostalism, or the Charismatic Renewal. The Charismatic Renewal is a growing force within the traditional mainline churches. In the Roman Catholic Church it is known as Catholic Pentecostalism. Though it was present to some degree in almost all denominations, the formal beginning of this movement is traced to St. Mark's Episcopal Church, in Van Nuys, California, where, in 1960, then-rector Dennis Bennett announced that he, and others in the church, had been baptized in the Holy Spirit and that they now "spoke in tongues."[11] Today, neo-Pentecostalism is known in almost every major Christian denomination with formal groups in many.

Except for the first form of Pentecostalism, the persons involved are generally a cross-section of society. They are primarily persons in either the middle or upper economic classes, and come from all racial backgrounds. They also are generally a cross-section of the denominations in which they are found.[12] The difference between neo-Pentecostalism and traditional Pentecostalism is that the neo-Pentecostal, remaining a part of a formal tradition (whether it is Anglican, Presbyterian, or the like), maintains the doctrine, teachings, and liturgy of the denomination while supplementing

7. McDonnell, *Charismatic Renewal and the Churches*.

8. Sargent, *The Mind Possessed: A Physiology of Possession, Mysticism and Faith Healing*.

9 For a comprehensive discussion of Pentecostal, Charismatic, and neo-Charismatic understandings of evil and possession refer to Anderson, "Deliverance and Exorcism in Majority World Pentecostalism," in William K. Kay and Robin Parry, eds. *Exorcism and Deliverance: Multi-Disciplinary Studies*.

10. Poloma, *The Charismatic Movement: Is There a New Pentecost?*

11. Quebedeaux, *The New Charismatics II*.

12. McDonnell, *Charismatic Renewal and the Churches*.

these with the baptism in the Holy Spirit. The neo-Pentecostal does not see this as a conflict with the traditions of the church but rather as an addition that helps to make these traditions—and their present Christian work— more alive and powerful.[13] Whatever the background the Pentecostal or neo-Pentecostal comes from, or whatever the doctrinal beliefs each holds, one thing ties them all together: all believe in the validity of the baptism in the Holy Spirit and the power and enablements obtained because of it. These enablements are in three basic forms: the gifts of the Holy Spirit, the fruits of the Holy Spirit, and also the phenomena of "Resting in the Spirit," or being "Slain in the Spirit."

Before we begin to look at these three forms, we first need to look at the extreme forms of behavior practiced by certain persons who believe themselves possessed by the Holy Spirit. This behavior is exemplified by the poisonous snake-handling of certain sects in the American south.

Much of what happens in these revivalistic meetings in the south re-semble what happens in other forms of possession the world over, especially in Voodoo practices. William Sargant, an investigator of the physiological effects of possession phenomena, visited one such meeting and gives us the following report.

> The Zion Tabernacle at Durham was a small hall. The preacher occupied a square space in front of the platform where excited participants could surge towards him as the meeting got under way. Behind him on the platform stood a choir, singing and rhythmically clapping hands. The box containing live poison-ous snakes, mostly rattlesnakes and copperheads, stood on the platform. Pastor Bunn and his converts feared to handle these poisonous snakes until certain recognizable signs proved that the Holy Ghost had descended on the meeting and possessed the congregation, so as to protect them from harm. The signs came when some of the people present exhibited what were called "exercises of the Spirit." These were in fact hysterical jerk-ing and twitches of the body and limbs, which usually occurred fairly soon after the harmonium and accordion began playing, and it was only after this that it was considered safe to open the box, take out the snakes and hand them round. As soon as the snakes were produced, the group excitement mounted tre-mendously, and it was obvious that the pastor could control the excitement by slowing down or accelerating the rate of rhythmic

13. Bennett, *Nine O'Clock in the Morning*; Office of the General Assembly, *Report to the Special Committee on the Work of the Holy Spirit to the 182nd General Assembly: The United Presbyterian Church in the United States of America.*

hand-clapping. . . . As the congregation became excited or possessed by the Holy Ghost, they would flock into the pastor's small square and there dance in states of semi-trance or complete trance. The official snake-handler would give the snakes to the pastor, who would then distribute them among the faithful who had handled them before.[14]

The rationale behind such a practice is based on the biblical promise that those who believe in the gospel and are filled with the Holy Spirit will be able to "pick up snakes with their hands."[15] We need not go into the theological arguments against this practice, but let it suffice to say that the exegesis of this passage by no means supports snake-handling as part of an assembly's regular worship or liturgy.

Much of what we see in Sargant's account of this practice is seen nowhere else in the Pentecostal, or neo-Pentecostal, movement. Rather, this account would easily fit into the description of a Voodoo ceremony, with only the names of the Holy Spirit and that of *Dambala*, the Voodoo snake deity, being exchanged. Therefore, even though this form of practice is attributed to the possession by the Holy Spirit, it so differs from the practices of the predominant Pentecostal and the neo-Pentecostal churches, that we can sensibly place it in another category altogether.[16] Nowhere else do we find people attempting to handle poisonous snakes. Also, the invoking of a trance-state is rare in the neo-Pentecostal practice, though it is encountered to some extent in the Pentecostal church service. Yet, even in these services, a formal trance is not entered, but the person enters more of a euphoric state.[17] The true ecstatic trance is encountered in only one aspect of this movement, and that is in the phenomena of resting, or being slain, in the Spirit. We shall look at this, and other forms of trance, in more detail as we discuss the phenomena of the more predominant beliefs and practices of Pentecostalism, neo-Pentecostalism, and the baptism in the Holy Spirit.

The first group of phenomena, which occur commonly in the Pentecostal and charismatic movements, are referred to as the gifts of the Holy Spirit. Dennis Bennett, in his book *The Holy Spirit and You*, has classified

14. Sargant, *The Mind Possessed: A Physiology of Possession, Mysticism and Faith Healing*, 183–84.

15. Mark 16:18.

16. Cf. Bennett, *Nine O'Clock in the Morning*; Bennett, *The Holy Spirit and You*; Bennett, *Moving Right Along in the Spirit*; McDonnell, *Charismatic Renewal and the Churches*; Poloma, *The Charismatic Movement: Is There a New Pentecost?*; Quebedeaux, *The New Charismatics II*.

17. Sargant, *The Mind Possessed: A Physiology of Possession, Mysticism and Faith Healing*.

these gifts according to three functional groups: (1) the inspirational or fellowship gifts, which enhance the individual's speaking abilities; (2) the gifts of power, which enhance the person's performance of tasks; and (3) the gifts of revelation, which enhance the person's knowledge.[18]

The inspirational gifts comprise the gift of tongues, the interpretation of tongues, and the gift of prophecy. The gift of tongues is the most studied of all the phenomena surrounding the baptism in the Holy Spirit. This is probably because it is the most commonly observable and the most controversial of the manifestations of the Holy Spirit. The gift of tongues is better known to the scientific community as glossolalia and xenolalia. Glossolalia is a "spontaneous utterance of uncomprehended and seemingly random speech sounds," while xenolalia is the spontaneous speaking of a language previously unknown to the speaker.[19] Both glossolalia and xenolalia have been known to occur while a person is "speaking in tongues."[20]

Speaking in tongues is said, by Bennett and other early Charismatic leaders, to be one of the initial manifestations of the Holy Spirit in the believer's life. Anyone who has been baptized into the name of Jesus Christ has the Holy Spirit. The Spirit makes this ability to speak in another tongue available to all, therefore Bennett argued that all baptized Christians could speak in tongues. Those who do not have simply not tried.[21]

There are two forms of speaking in tongues: the gift of tongues proper, and the manifestation of tongues. The gift of tongues is a speaking of another language—either glossolalia or xenolalia—in the assembly of believers in order to bring a message to the gathering. Then, for the message to be understood, the gift of interpretation is necessary. This gift allows another person, or the speaker, to get an impression as to the meaning of the utterance in tongues. This is not a translation, but rather an interpretation.

The manifestation of tongues is a private prayer language given to the individual in order that the person may better pray to God and so be built up spiritually. This form of speaking in tongues differs from the gift of tongues only in that the gift of tongues is meant for the edification of the assembly and thus needs to be joined with the gift of interpretation of tongues, while the manifestation of tongues needs no interpretation; it is seen as the Holy Spirit edifying the individual's spirit directly through the act of prayer.

The combination of tongues and interpretation leads to prophecy. The gift of tongues is seen as the Holy Spirit inspiring the individual's spirit to

18. Ibid., 83.

19. Kelsey, *Tongue Speaking: An Experiment in Spiritual Experience*, 1.

20. Bennett, *The Holy Spirit and You*.

21. Ibid.; Robertson, *Answers to 200 of Life's Most Probing Questions*.

speak forth the thoughts and intentions of God. When these are interpreted
for all to understand, then prophecy, or the speaking forth of the word of
God, has taken place. Yet this is not the only manner in which prophecies
come to the individual. They also come through the gift of prophecy, the
third form of the gifts of inspiration.

Prophecy is not fortune-telling. The Bible strictly forbids the use of
any method of fortune-telling, including astrology, and divination, thus
the Christian is to avoid all such works. Yet prophecy is not a form of
fortune-telling—which is actually a form of foretelling the future—but
rather is a forth-telling of the word of God.[22] At times this may take the
form of indicating what is to happen in the near future, but not in a fatal-
istic manner. It is usually more in the manner of saying what will happen
in the future if a certain action is or is not taken. We see this when we
read most of the writings of the Hebrew prophets. But prophecy may also
indicate what is happening presently to a person or a congregation, or
acts that God would have these disciples perform. The gift of prophecy
is not delivered in an unknown language, as is the gift of tongues, but is
delivered and heard in the vernacular.

The second group of gifts is that of power. This includes the gifts of
healing, the working of miracles, and the gift of faith. The first of these, gifts
of healing, is the only one of the gifts of the Holy Spirit referred to in the
plural. This is probably because there are actually many different types of
healing possible and so a multitude of gifts. Thus, one person may have a
greater facility in healing persons with arthritis, while another person may
do better with backaches. The former would be considered to be utilizing
the gift of healing arthritis while the latter a gift of healing backaches. It
is considered, therefore, that for each disease that can afflict a person, or
animal, that there is a corresponding gift of healing.

The gift of miracles includes such things as controlling the elements,
raising the dead, and even certain forms of healings. Weather patterns can
be altered to either create rain in a drought or to deter inclement weather.
Pat Robertson relates two incidences of just such a control of the elements.
First, he tells the story of his experience of praying that a hurricane would
not hit his fledgling Christian Broadcasting Network, but would stop its
progress and go back into the ocean. At that very moment the weather service noted that the hurricane had stopped its forward motion. After a time
of remaining stationary in the Atlantic, the hurricane turned around and
went back into the deep Atlantic. Robertson also relates the story of a man
named Norvell Hayes, a Florida orange grower. Just as Hayes was preparing

22. Bennett, *The Holy Spirit and You.*

to harvest his oranges, a "killer frost" hit his section of the state. Hayes, though, prayed and commanded the frost not to touch his oranges. The next morning his orange grove was in perfect condition, while the farms just across the road had been severely damaged.[23]

The gift of miracles can also be manifested in such phenomena as levitation or being transported spiritually from only place to another. Bennett relates a story concerning just such an occurrence.

> David du Plessis, perhaps the best-known witness in the charismatic renewal, tells of such a miracle in his earlier ministry. He and some other men were gathered in the garden outside a friend's home, praying for another man who was lying in bed, seriously ill, about a mile away. "As we prayed," says David, "the Lord said to me: 'You are needed at that man's bedside right away!' I snatched up my hat and rushed 'round the house and out the front gate, but as I took one step out of the gate, my next step fell on the front steps of the house a mile away, where our sick friend was! It startled me greatly of course. I know that I was carried that mile instantly, because some fifteen minutes later the rest of the men I had been praying with came puffing down the road. They asked me: 'How did you get here so fast?'"[24]

Miracles and healing will, at times, overlap. This is especially seen in what are considered the creative healing miracles. These are such things as the lengthening of a leg that is shorter than its partner, the growing of a new eye in a previously empty socket, or the appearance of new teeth where none were before. All of these occurrences have been documented to have happened after the person has received prayer. The difference between the gifts of healing and the gift of miracles in this case is that healings are seen to accelerate the normal healing processes, while miracles work to "override or contradict the so-called laws of nature."[25]

The final gift of power is the gift of faith. This is an enablement for the individual to believe in the power of God even in extremely adverse circumstances. "An example of an acted gift of faith is found in the familiar incident in the life of the prophet Daniel. Daniel was 'framed' by some jealous associates, and sentenced to be thrown into a den of hungry lions. Daniel said no word, but simply trusted God, and the lions did not hurt him. Even for as great a man as Daniel, it likely took a special surge of faith

23. Robertson, *Beyond Reason*.
24. Bennett, *The Holy Spirit and You*, 128.
25. Ibid., 124.

for him to go through this frightful experience."[26] Thus, the gift of faith is an ability to trust beyond normal limits.

The final grouping of gifts is that of the gifts of revelation. These are the gift of discernment of spirits, the "word of knowledge," and the "word of wisdom".

These last three are called revelation gifts because they consist of information supernaturally revealed from God. They might be simply understood as the "mind of Christ being manifested through the Spirit-filled believer." Each of these gifts is the God-given ability to receive from Him facts concerning something, anything, about which it is humanly impossible for us to know, revealed to the believer so that he may be protected, pray more effectively, or help someone in need.[27]

The first of these, the discernment of spirits, refers to the believer's ability to understand the motivation of a person, or situation. He is able to determine what is behind it, whether this is a motivation given by God, by an individual's own inclinations, or by an evil spirit.

The word of knowledge is a "supernatural revelation of facts past, present, or future which were not learned through the efforts of the natural mind."[28] This differs from foretelling the future in that the person is not told that "you will marry a dark-haired man," as she might be told by a fortune-teller, but rather is given indications of actions to be taken in the present because of the future, such as "do not go to such-and-such a place." The person who follows that indication may later learn that the plane she would have taken to the place crashed, and that through the word of knowledge she had been saved from disaster.[29] This action of the person in the last example is actually a combination of a word of knowledge with a word of wisdom. The word of wisdom is a "supernatural application of knowledge. It is knowing what to do with the natural or supernatural knowledge God has given . . . [that is it is] proper judgment for action."[30]

Not only is the person who is baptized in the Holy Spirit supposed to be able to manifest these supernatural gifts, but this person is also to begin to show a change in personality. The person who is filled with the Holy Spirit is to become more and more like Christ and manifest what are referred to as the "fruits of the Holy Spirit." These fruits are listed in the Holy Bible in the letter of Paul to the Galatians. These fruits are: love, joy,

26. Ibid., 135.

27. Ibid., 140.

28. Ibid., 155.

29. Cf., Robertson, *Beyond Reason*.

30. Bennett, *The Holy Spirit and You*, 155.

peace, patience, gentleness, kindness, faith, humility, and discipline. These fruits of the Spirit indicate the possession aspect of the Holy Spirit most clearly, because it is believed that the longer a person has the Holy Spirit within him or her, the more one will be conformed to the Spirit, which is becoming like Jesus Christ.

Those who belong to Jesus, and who live for Him, begin to be more like Him. It is as if Jesus were sitting for a portrait, and the Holy Spirit were painting that portrait inside the person. The manifestation of the fruit of the Spirit in a life is the tangible evidence that a person is being changed into the nature of Jesus Christ.[31]

As we saw with mysticism, and as we will see with other forms of possession, the ecstatic state was of utmost importance to the manifestation of possession phenomena. But this is not true in the Holy Spirit possession of the predominant forms of Pentecostalism or mainline charismatics. None of the above gifts or fruits of the Holy Spirit seem to need an ecstatic state present in order to be made manifest. Actually, Bennett has found that extreme emotionalism and ecstasies can inhibit these manifestations. Many researchers have looked into the ecstatic nature of speaking in tongues specifically,[32] but Dennis Bennett gives us a clear account of his experience with speaking in tongues that illustrates the control that the individual has over the action.

> John suggested, "Father Bennett, why don't you and I go in the back room and pray some more about this [speaking in tongues]." It was okay with me. I was still very much interested [in speaking in tongues], and really intrigued by my experience of [it] Saturday afternoon. We sat down on opposite sides of the room and began to pray. Again there was no attempt to "work me up," no emotionalism or excitement. Once more I prayed very quietly and cautiously, and this time, after only about three or four minutes, words began to come in another language, the same language, I noted, that I had spoken on the previous Saturday—at least it sounded like it. Again, I was in no way compelled to speak this new tongue. It was something that I could do if I chose. I was in no strange state of mind whatsoever, and was in full possession of whatever wits I normally had! The dynamics of the new language were entirely under my control: whether I spoke or not, whether I spoke loudly or softly, fast or slow, high or low. The only thing that was not under my volition was the

31. Robertson, *Answers to 200 of Life's Most Probing Questions*, 67.

32. Cf. Sargant, *The Mind Possessed: A Physiology of Possession, Mysticism and Faith Healing*; Kildahl, *The Psychology of Speaking in Tongues*.

form of the words. After all, how could I formulate words in a
language I didn't know? It was like playing the work of a famous
composer on the piano. I could play—loudly, softly, fast, or slow;
and was free to play the whole thing an octave higher or lower,
if I chose; but as long as I was playing, say Bach, or Chopin, I
couldn't be playing my own notes. I was playing their notes, not
because I was compelled to, but because I chose to. So it was
with speaking in tongues.[33]

Thus, ecstasy and compulsion are not normal occurrences of the
manifestation of the Holy Spirit in the lives of the practitioners. Yet there is
one form of behavior that is a form of ecstatic trance practiced by some of
these persons: resting in the Spirit.

Resting in the Spirit—as it is called by Catholics—or slaying in the
Spirit—as it is referred to by most others—occurs when a person is said to
be "overcome" by the Holy Spirit and so swoons into a restful, trance-like
state.[34] Most often, this phenomenon occurs in the context of a healing
ceremony. When an individual comes to a person to be healed, the minister
may place his or her hand on the individual's head at which point this person falls to the ground in a trance. "Most people describe this phenomena
as giving in, submitting to God or the Holy Spirit. Sometimes they speak of
being scared and cold, even feeling 'goose bumps' as a hand touches them,
while many others feel warmth flowing through them. Either way they generally describe a sense of holy power or energy flowing in, which makes
them relax and fall, bringing peace and joy."[35] Unlike some of the induced
trance states in other forms of possession, or the ecstatic states of the southern snake-handlers, resting in the Spirit is a quiet, peaceful, phenomenon.
Though in the past this slaying in the Spirit might have led to persons con-
vulsing or rolling about on the floor, today they usually do not show signs
of jerking or spasms, neither is there a total loss of consciousness. Rather,
there is experienced a certain "haziness [as] in a petit mal seizure.[36] Kelsey
further quotes Father George Maloney as describing the feeling during the
phenomenon as a floating sensation.

A "floating" effect accompanies the falling to earth, filling the
receiver with a sense of deep peace and joy. The whole body,
soul and spirit seem to "let go" under an invisible power. This
state of relaxation on all levels, with the body in a very loose

33 Bennett, *Nine O'Clock in the Morning*, 22.
34. Kelsey, *Discernment: A Study in Ecstasy and Evil*.
35. Ibid., 17.
36. Ibid.

condition, accounts for falls with rarely any physical mishaps accompanying them.[37] Be-

Unlike the gifts and fruits of the Holy Spirit which we were discussing a few moments ago, there is no direct reference to this phenomenon in the Bible, though it is alluded to in certain contexts, such as when John in the Book of Revelation saw the Son of Man and "fell at his feet as one dead". Because of this lack of scriptural foundation it has become suspect in many of the Pentecostal and charismatic circles. David du Plessis, who has by many been called "Mr. Pentecost," and who was the representative of classical Pentecostalism to the Second Vatican Council, has warned the neo-Pentecostals to avoid this experience. Du Plessis, in a conversation with a Catholic priest who was renowned for his ability to minister this experience to others, told this priest to stay away from slaying others in the Spirit.

> As this priest wrote, "[du Plessis] told me unequivocally to stay clear of slaying in the Spirit entirely—that in all of his years of Pentecost all over the world he had never seen it build up the Church but rather cause discredit to the classical Pentecostals. It was one reason for the derisive name "holy rollers." He also said that he had the same reservations about people who practiced it, especially if they made slaying in the Spirit the focus of their whole ministry. In a fatherly way he beseeched me to leave it alone. He also added the very sobering admonition that he felt strongly that the Spirit was not calling Catholics to imitate classical Pentecostals—much less their mistakes—but to be authentic Catholics who are open to the Spirit. He said it was important for us to discover the Spirit within our own traditions![38]

The leadership of the neo-Pentecostal movement is skeptical in regard to any phenomenon that tends to reduce a person's ability to maintain self-control. Even speaking in tongues is regarded as being under the control of the speaker. Thus, the ecstasies of the southern snake-handlers and of those slain in the Spirit is questioned by the neo-Pentecostal community; the former, though, more than the latter. Slaying in the Spirit seems to be accepted as an action that actually can be beneficial to the individual by giving that one a deep sense of peace and rest in God, but it is not seen as helpful to a congregation as a whole. Because of this it is not totally disregarded, but it is advisably not used as the central point of an assembly of believers.

Throughout this discussion we have been describing the experienced phenomena using the names given to them by the Pentecostal and

37. Ibid.
38. Ibid., 23.

neo-Pentecostal movements. Except for "slaying in the Spirit," these names are those derived from a biblical description of the phenomena. In summary, though, we have seen that trance and ecstasy do have a role in the experience of Holy Spirit possession, even though it is minimal, especially in comparison to other possession states. Those possessed with the Holy Spirit may find themselves speaking a previously unknown language and being able to understand other previously unknown languages. Speaking forth the thought and direction of another, presumably God, is also an experience of these persons. They are able to perform extraordinary feats such as controlling the elements and healing the sick. They have seemingly clairvoyant abilities enabling them to discern the motivation of others, see facts in the past, present or future and know how to act in relation to these facts. The only difference between these experiences and true clairvoyance is in the believed origin of the experience. Clairvoyance is more often believed to be a natural psychic phenomenon while the gifts of the Holy Spirit have nothing to do with the natural abilities of the person, but are the thoughts and actions of Jesus Christ working in the person through the Holy Spirit.

6

Possession States in Voodoo

"Certain exotic words are charged with evocative power. Voodoo is one." So Alfred Metraux begins his book, *Voodoo in Haiti*,[1] and he is correct. The mention of Voodoo conjures in our minds thoughts of zombies, secret murderous cults, poisonous brews and black magic. Yet, Voodoo is much more than these. In fact, the Voodooist sees these as perversions of Voodoo, and not the true practice.

Voodoo is no longer viewed as merely a perverse cult or a superstitious folk-belief, but can be seen as a true form of religion.[2] It is made up of priests, priestesses, a liturgy, and an elaborate system of belief, similar to other recognized religions. For many outsiders, Voodoo has seemed to be an odd conglomeration of African superstitions, animist folk-beliefs, and Catholicism. Yet, as research has progressed, Voodoo has come to be seen more and more as a fairly reliable transplant of certain West African religions, especially that of the Fon people of Dahomey.[3] Voodoo came to Haiti with the slaves, beginning in the sixteenth century, and not only to Haiti but to the other areas where slaves were taken. With the influx of African slaves, Voodoo spread to Cuba, the islands of the Caribbean, and to South America. In Brazil especially, forms known as Umbanda and Macumba are still popular.[4]

The proponents of the slave trade used to say that they were importing only the dregs of African society as slaves, helping these African societies to be rid of their undesirables. But the complicated theology and the ritualized form of the Voodoo practices, which closely resemble their origins in

1. Metraux, *Voodoo in Haiti*, 15.

2. Devillers, *Haiti's Voodoo Pilgrimages: Of Spirits and Saints.*

3. Courlander, *Religion and Politics in Haiti*; Metraux, *Voodoo in Haiti.*

4. Sargant, *The Mind Possessed: A Physiology of Possession, Mysticism and Faith Healing*; Valois, *The Integrative Aspects of Possession Trance.*

63

Africa, speak to the fact that many priests and those of the higher tribal classes were brought to the New World as slaves. Once in this new land, the priests began practicing their religious beliefs and worshiping their spirits in the old ways. But the old ways could not be totally incorporated into this new life, because, as slaves, these people were no longer only with people of their own tribe, but were forcibly mixed with persons of other tribes. Thus, the various spirits of the various tribes were blended in a curious syncretism that began the development of Voodoo as it is known today. However, the prominent forms of the Dahomey and Anago religions of Western Africa are still quite discernable in the Voodoo ceremonies.[5]

Voodoo is centered on the worship of a multitude of spirits, or *loa*. *Loa* is the most commonly used word to describe the spirits and is from the Bantu word for deity. Voodoo and the worship of the *loa* is more than the temple ritual, though. "It is an integrated system of concepts concerning human activities, the relationship between the natural world and the supernatural, and the ties between the living and the dead."[6]

To catalog and understand all the various *loa* in Voodoo theology is nearly impossible. One can get an idea about the major spirits, but the number of minor spirits changes regularly, according to the changes in the folk-beliefs and the number of adherents to a certain *loa's* worship. The major *loa* are similar to the gods of the original West African tribes, but there are also many minor *loa*: the Voodooist holds animistic beliefs, which adds a multitude of *loa*, for all of nature is populated by spirits. Thus, there are spirits in the trees, rivers, waterfalls, and even in the center posts of the Voodoo temple. The spirits of Voodoo are therefore not merely the African gods transported to the Haitian environment, but also are the spirits of the surrounding environment, as well as the spirits of those who have died and the spirits of twins. The cult of the twins is quite powerful in Voodoo, and the presence of twins, living or dead, is a sign of supernatural power.

What makes Voodoo difficult for many to understand is the manner in which Catholic Christianity has been incorporated into the Voodoo theology and practice. Since the beginning of slavery in Haiti, the Catholic Church has been attempting to stamp-out the Voodoo rituals and beliefs. Finally in 1941, the Church and the Haitian government instituted an anti-superstition campaign in an attempt to destroy Voodoo. During this campaign many of the temples and places sacred to Voodoo were destroyed, and the practices of Voodoo outlawed. Yet, even this did not dissuade the Voodooists. Voodoo is still very much alive, only its practitioners are more

5. Courlander, *Religion and Politics in Haiti*.
6. Ibid., 12.

careful to hide their participation in it from their local priests and Christian religious workers. They do so by going to other towns for their Voodoo celebrations, but later return for the Catholic Mass. So the Haitian seems to live a double life. On the one hand, he or she practices Voodoo, and on the other hand, Christianity. Yet to the Haitian the two go hand-in-hand. Many of the Catholic saints have merely been incorporated into the Voodoo pantheon. This is understandable. Since Voodoo was already a melding of various African tribal religions, the addition of another religion, Catholicism, should not have been too monumental a task. The saints of the Christian Church were incorporated into Voodoo and understood through the eyes of Voodoo. Because Saint James the Elder is portrayed in many paintings carrying a sword, the Voodooist sees him as representing the warrior spirit, *Ogu*. Since St. Patrick is commonly portrayed with the snakes he mythically drove out of Ireland, he is seen to represent the powerful *loa*, *Damballah-wedo*, the serpent spirit.

This combination of beliefs can be vividly seen in many of the Voodoo festivals. An example is the celebration of *Vyej Mirak*, or the visitation of the Virgin of Miracles. This festival takes place on the 16th of July each year. It is a commemoration of the appearance of a vision of the Virgin in a grove of palm trees on Haiti, near the beginning of the twentieth century. The story of this vision goes as such, as told to Carol Devillers:

> "It started long before I was born," says local lawyer Stanislas Jeannot, now in his 70s. "My father told me that a man named Fortune, searching for a lost horse, came to a palm grove. Dazzled by a flash of light, he looked up and saw the Virgin nestled in the palms. He notified the authorities." Word of the vision spread. Stories were told of the blind and the deaf miraculously restored to sight and hearing. Soon Saut d'Eau became a center of devotion for Christians and Voodooists alike. As pilgrims swarmed in, superstitions multiplied. Food offerings mingled so often with votive candles that the church decided to put a stop to what seemed more like idolatry than Catholic religious fervor. That was during the American occupation, between 1915 and 1934, when U.S. Marines were sent to restore order in a country wracked by anarchy. "I was an altar boy at the time," recalls Jeannot. "The French priest at Saut d'Eau asked a couple of Marines to help get rid of what he thought to be a mere superstition. They took pistol shots at the vision. It simply moved to another tree. They shot again, yet the vision remained." Finally, they had townspeople cut down the grove. As the palms fell, the vision changed into a pigeon and flew away. It never

returned." "Actually," adds another villager, "the pigeon fell into the nearby waterfalls for which Saut d'Eau is named, thereby blessing them."[7]

It is not just the Virgin of Miracles that the Voodooist sees in this apparition, but also the presence of the great *loa*, Ezili Freda, the spirit of love. Each July people flock to the waterfalls at Ville Bonheur—or Saut d'Eau (fall of water) as it is also called—to stand in the stream of water and be blessed. This is a vivid illustration of the combination of animistic beliefs, beliefs in *loa*, and Catholic religious fervor; for within the waters of Saut d'Eau is believed to live a spirit, and that spirit is at the same time both Ezili Freda and the Virgin of Miracles.

Voodoo theology is not merely a ritual of worshiping spirits, it is also a way of living life, of gaining wealth, prosperity, and healing. It is also a manner to get even with one's enemies. Magic is an integral part of Voodoo, and though the Voodoo practitioner will say that true Voodoo is only white magic, black magic is still pervasive in Haiti. Magic is the realm of the Voodoo priest and priestess, otherwise known as the hougan and the mambo, respectively. True, respectable hougans and mambos only practice what is considered white magic; that is making potions to heal, causing prosperity without harming others, and bringing down the blessing of the *loa*. But these magicians also need to know black magic in order to combat the curses and illness places upon people by evil sorcerers. A sorcerer is merely a hougan or mambo that is double-faced, practicing the Voodoo ritual on the one hand and performing black magic on the other. It is to black magic, and the work of evil *loa*, that most misfortunes and illnesses are attributed. One of these illnesses is possession.

Possession is central to both Voodoo ritual and to black magic. Possession is "the means by which *loa*, or deities, interact with mankind. Through possession of congregants the *loas* enter the Haitian world to punish and reward them and to treat their ills and worries."[8]

In the ritual of Voodoo, possession is something to be coveted. To be possessed is to be shown special favor by the *loa*. Before a *loa* can possess a person, it must first drive out of that person one of his or her two souls. In Voodoo belief, a person is comprised of three entities: the body, the *gros bon ange* (good big angel), and the *petite bon ange* (good little angel). Similar to what we saw in Christian theology, these three correspond to a physical organism, a soul—or vital force—and a spiritual force, respectively. The *gros bon ange* is the vital force within all of life, it is that force that gives

---

7. Devillers, *Haiti's Voodoo Pilgrimages: Of Spirits and Saints*, 400.

8. Kiev, *The Psychotherapeutic Value of Spirit-Possession in Haiti.*

life to the body. The *petite bon ange* is the spiritual force that differentiates the human being from the rest of life, by giving the human an intellect and reason.[9] When a person is possessed, it is their soul, or the *gros bon ange*, that is first driven out of the person's head by the *loa*, which then takes its place. This is what is seen to be responsible for the trembling and convulsions common to the opening stages of the possession.[10] Once the possession has occurred the *loa* is then present with the congregation and can communicate with the people, by expressing itself through the voice and movements of the possessed person. The possessed is usually amnesic in regard to what happens during this time, a length of time that can last from a few seconds to weeks.[11]

If possession is central to the Voodoo ceremony, the drumbeat is central to the entering of the possession trance. "The drum on which the rhythms are beaten out for the dances symbolizes Voodoo. 'Beating the drum' in popular speech has come to mean 'celebrating the cult of the *loa*'."[12] As we shall see later, drumbeats with a rhythm between eight and thirteen beats per second can produce a trance state in the brain, and the Voodoo beats which tend to be conducive to possessions are in the eight to nine beats per second range.[13] Thus, "a musician who has not got all the rhythmic formulae at his fingertips will certainly throw dances into confusion and directly hamper the epiphanies of the *loa*."[14]

There is more to the cause of these possessions than just the drumbeat rhythms, for it seems logical to think that anyone who would be in the collective mood of the ceremony and was experiencing the beat long enough would enter the trance state. However, this is not the case. Collective delirium is not a common occurrence in these ceremonies.[15] Collective possession does occur at times, especially if the drummers are to redouble their efforts, and as the possessed performs some spectacular feat, such as jumping within and over flames.[16] But, once again, if it were the drumbeats and the spectacular feats that elicited possessions, then it could be expected that the drummers should become possessed. The drummers do seem to

9. Douyon, *Voodoo in Haiti*.

10. Metraux, *Voodoo in Haiti*, 120.

11. Ibid., 123.

12. Ibid., 177.

13. Walker, *Ceremonial Spirit Possession in Africa and Afro-America*, 18.

14. Metraux, *Voodoo in Haiti*, 178.

15. Ibid., 138.

16. Ibid., 130.

enter some stage of trance, yet they are not considered to be possessed, nor do they enact the later stages of possession.

The tambouriers (drummers) are endowed not only with a delicate sense of rhythm and a vast musical memory but also with exceptional nervous stamina. For nights on end they make their instruments speak with a passionate violence that at times attains frenzy. To see them with their eyeballs turned back, their faces taut, to hear the rattling gasps in their throats you might easily suppose them to be possessed. But their delirium is not the work of a god. In fact, only very seldom are drummers possessed by *loa*.[17]

Once possessed the person begins to act like the *loa*, and begins to resemble the mythical personage.[18] As a matter of fact, the identity of the spirit is known only by the behavior of the possessed.[19]

A distinction is made between possession by *loa* and possession by an evil spirit. Where the former is sought after and prized, the latter is frightening and morbid. Possession by a *loa* can bring blessing, but possession by an evil spirit, or *baka*, will cause illness, misfortune and death.

Possessions by evil come about by at least three means: angering a *loa* by neglecting its observance, by black magic, or by selling one's soul to a *baka*. The remedy for these is to find a hougan or mambo to counter the magic or gain the blessing of a more powerful *loa*.

A sorcerer will cause the possession of a person, or the death of a person, for two explicit reasons. One, if someone pays him or her to do so. Second, to feed the evil *loa*, or *baka*, human blood. The *baka* feed on human blood and will continually ask for it, so the sorcerer must feed the *baka* with whom he or she is in league or pay the consequences of probably being eaten him- or herself.

It seems that the Faust myth is quite alive in Haiti. A sorcerer will sell his or her life to an evil *loa* for certain benefits, or he or she will promise other lives to the *loa* for special rewards. In Haiti, this is referred to as acquiring a "hot point."

> The possession of a "hot point" is only obtained at great risk. Once you are "committed" to him, a *baka* never lets you go. You think you are its master, only to discover you are its slave. Always thirsting for human blood, a *baka* keeps asking, every time it opens its mouth, for fresh victims. Nothing can bend its will.

17. Ibid., 178.

18. Ibid., 127.

19. Devillers, *Haiti's Voodoo Pilgrimages: Of Spirits and Saints*, 403.

> Sooner or later it ends by killing its partner who, tired of giving
> it human beings, tries to get out of his commitment.[20]

Like Faust, the sorcerer who thinks he is gaining power is actually possessed by the evil he wishes to control, and in the end this evil totally overcomes the sorcerer.

There are two other forms of possession attributed to black magic in Voodoo: the zombie and the werewolf. In Haiti, the werewolf is actually the name for a female vampire who kills small children by drinking their blood.[21] It is the counterpart of the Middle Eastern Lilith. Becoming a werewolf is a form of possession, for the woman is under the spell of an evil hougan, or mambo, who is paying off the baka with whom he or she is dealing.

> The state of werewolf . . . often proceeds from the penalty-clause
> in a contract. In other words, it is often the "pay off" for the
> advantages derived from the acquisition of a "hot point." The
> boko [sorcerer] who "commits" a woman to evil spirits gives
> her a ring or any other object which has first been "drugged"
> (drogue). This talisman is a pledge of luck, but it also has the
> power of turning the bearer into a werewolf. In the early stages
> of their career werewolves commit their crimes without know-
> ing it. Night excursions, cannibal meals are for beginners no
> more than nightmares which haunt their sleep. Then, gradually,
> the terrible truth dawns on them—but by now it is too late to
> stop: the taste for human flesh which these unfortunates have by
> then acquired, has become an uncontrollable vice.[22]

Though the identities of the werewolves in the community seem to be common knowledge in the Haitian village, still little can be said about the validity of this belief, except that the same form of belief in female vampires is also encountered in various tribes of West Africa.

Unlike werewolves, more validity is being given to the belief in zombies. "Zombi are people whose decease has been recorded, and whose burial has been witnessed, but who are found a few years later living . . . in a state verging on idiocy."[23] Zombies are the "living dead."

In 1980, a man named Clervius Narcisse began to tell about his two years as a zombie. In 1962 he was declared dead of malignant hypertension and pulmonary edema at Albert Schweitzer Hospital in Deschapelles,

---

20. Metraux, *Voodoo in Haiti,* 289.

21. Ibid., 300.

22. Ibid., 301.

23. Ibid., 281.

Haiti. In actuality he was paralyzed.[24] Despite this paralysis, Narcisse claims he was completely conscious during his burial. He says he heard himself being pronounced dead, saw the lid close on his coffin and felt himself being lowered into the ground. He was also fully aware during his resurrection. Narcisse was taken from the ground, beaten, bound, and given a zombie name. He was fed a paste containing daturas, hallucinogenic plants known in Haiti as "zombie cucumbers," which induced disorientation and probably amnesia. In this state he was packed off to the bocar's plantation and enslaved.

Wade Davis, then a Harvard ethnobotany graduate student, investigated certain mixtures said to make zombies and found common to all tetrodotoxin, a substance derived from puffer fish. This drug mimics death by first causing hypothermia, nausea, respiratory difficulties, hypertension then hypotension, and finally absolute paralysis. These symptoms resemble those experienced by Narcisse before his "death."[25] The whole process takes about six hours to complete.

Besides tetrodotoxin, Davis sees the formula for creating a zombie as containing parts of toads, sea worms, lizards, tarantulas and human bones. This has the appearance of dry black dirt and is then rubbed on the body of the proposed zombie and soon the effects begin.[26] The maintenance of the zombie condition may be both psychological and pharmacological. It is not clear how control was maintained over Narcisse during his captivity, but Davis thinks the "set and setting," including the pronouncement of death, the graveyard revivification and the presence of other zombies, coupled with Narcisse's belief that zombies exist, would have been sufficient to keep him in a zombie state, completely in the thrall of the bocar. It is possible that the zombies were kept insensate with regular doses of daturas. By whatever manner control over Narcisse was acquired and maintained, it is clear that the creation of zombies entails an extremely sophisticated melding of the sciences of pharmacology and psychology. Thus, in the case of zombies, possession is the result of the interaction between drugs, the existence of a supporting belief system, and extreme trauma. Trauma can also be seen as the cause of other forms of possession.

> Possessions also occur in ordinary, daily life. In fact it is in lay surroundings that the psychological function of possession becomes clear. Trance sometimes amounts to an escape-mechanism in the face of suffering, or simply fatigue. Dr. Louis Mars

24. Jordon, *What's in a Zombie?*
25. Ibid.
26. Del Guercio, *Zombie's Secret: Voodoo Myth is Uncovered.*

witnessed an attack of *loa* which took place in someone under-going an operation; it broke out at the very moment when the pain was at its sharpest. On another occasion he saw two people become possessed just after a motor bus accident in which they had been involved.[27]

Whether or not we attempt to explain possession as a dissociative de-fense mechanism against suffering, we can clearly see that some form of severe trauma may result in a possession state.

A final form of possession that we need to discuss is that of possession by the dead. Here it is that the spirit of a dead person is understood to enter a living person causing madness and illness. If the spirit of a dead drunken vagabond is unleashed against someone, then the living person will become a drunk.[28]

The dead do not possess on their own, but are conjured up by black magic to afflict a person. So, it is not only the "dead" that must be fought in such a possession, but the evil hougan or mambo as well, if a healing is to occur.[29]

Possessions in Voodoo hold to certain common patterns and phe-nomena. In a ritual, or ceremonial possession, the possessed will go through two stages: the opening stage of possession and the possession proper. During the opening stage of possession the person will exhibit mild trembling throughout the body. Respiration will increase and the person will being to pant. Drops of sweat will become visible on the brow. A sleepy condition, or a vague languor, will then set in and the person will become semi-conscious. The person's face will take on a vacant, anguished expres-sion. The individual's hands will begin to flutter and the body will continue to twitch and tremble. This beginning stage can last for many minutes in the novice being possessed. Those adept at possession will pass quickly through these phenomena, sometimes to the point where this opening stage is hardly noticeable.[30]

The opening stage gives way to the true possession. The opening symp-toms are attributed to the *loa* driving the *gros bon ange* out of the person's head. After this is completed the *loa* enters the person's head. This entry is de-scribed by the participants as the *loa* "mounting his horse," for the possessed then begins to act as a wild horse might when first mounted by a rider. The

27. Metraux, *Voodoo in Haiti*, 131.

28. Ibid., 275.

29. Ibid., 276.

30. Cf. Kiev, *The Psychotherapeutic Value of Spirit-Possession in Haiti*; Metraux, *Voodoo in Haiti*.

possessed person begins to jump about, making chaotic leaps and gestures. He or she may roll about on the ground as well. Self-control by this time is lost. The possessed person's eyes are fixed and estranged. The person describes this period of being possessed as a time of darkness engulfing the brain. There is no memory of any of the occurrences during the time of possession; there is total amnesia associated with this period.[31] The possessed will later describe the feeling at the time as a sensation of total emptiness.

Once the convulsions diminish the person will take on a new personality. In many ways this is very theatrical, but the person is not play-acting a part in the Voodoo ceremony, he or she actually is the part.[32] The personalities taken by the person may be many, and may change rapidly. These may have the person melancholy or irritable at one moment, and excited and playing the clown at the next. For a while the possessed may be tyrannical, and then without warning be capricious. He or she may show rage, prophesy or give instructions to the congregation about matters pertaining to worship of the *loa*, or how to cure someone. During each change in personality the individual's voice may change, as well as his or her gestures, facial expressions and body movements.

Some other bodily manifestations of possession are extreme twisting of the neck, hanging out of the tongue, and general distortions of the body. Finally, people may just faint, falling into a deep trance from which the hougan or mambo must attempt to rouse the person.

During a possession a person may manifest masochistic tendencies as well as exhibit glossolalia, or the speaking of a language unknown to others or the person. Among the more spectacular aspects of possession are the feats of agility, and access to increased energy, that the possessed person displays. During a possession he or she may be able to perform in a manner that they could not, at least consciously, perform before the possession. For example, Metraux tells the stories of sailors whose survival in a death dealing situation was enhanced due to possession, and of a woman who gained the energy to complete a pilgrimage because a spirit gave her new energy.

> People who have to make some exceptional effort sometimes ask a spirit to help them—in other words they hope their task will be made easier if attempted in a trance state. Stories are told of shipwrecked sailors who were able to reach land thanks to the god *Agwe* entering into them. In the course of a pilgrimage to the Balan cave, in the neighborhood of Port-au-Prince, mambo Lorgina who was moving over stony ground slowly, because of

31. Metraux, *Voodoo in Haiti*, 120–23.
32. Ibid., 127.

rheumatism, was suddenly possessed by *Legba*: instead of limping and pausing every few seconds as she had been till then, she went on her way with a resolute step and without apparent weariness.[33]

Possessed persons also perform other spectacular feats. "Some people, when possessed by *Damballa*, the snake god, perform extraordinary feats of agility, such as climbing down tree trunks head first. Others hold hot irons in their hands, chew broken glass, or walk bare-footed over hot coals."[34]

Possession by evil can take more varied forms than the ceremonial possession of the Voodoo ritual, yet some of the same phenomena happen in the possession by evil as happen in the ritual possession. As we have seen, a person possessed by the dead can take on almost any aspect, depending on the attitude and behavior of the dead spirit. Likewise, suicide is seen to be the result of magic and possession, and not the choice of a person. Finally, a person possessed by evil will begin to grow thin, spit blood, and finally die.[35]

33. Ibid., 131.
34. Ibid., 136.
35. Ibid., 273–75.

7

Possession States and Shamanism

We turn now to one of the most ancient forms of religion still practiced in the world today: shamanism. To be more precise, shamanism is not actually a religion but rather a "technique of ecstasy."[1] It is a method by which certain persons in a society enter the spiritual realms in order to bring to that society the knowledge and power contained in these other worlds. In this regard the shaman is more a mystic than a practitioner of the society's cultic religion.[2]

In support of this view is the observation that shamanic practices coexist with cultic and sacrificial religions, and with the priests of these religions.[3] But, where the role and expertise of the priest is in appeasing the gods, the role of the shaman is in encountering and personally dealing with these gods and the spirits. Both priest and shaman act as intermediaries between the society and the supernatural, but the shaman does so in a state of ecstasy, or possession, which makes his or her action much more personal.[4]

For this reason, possession, or ecstasy, is absolutely central to the role of a shaman. This ecstasy is of a specific nature, for it is composed of what is called the shamanic journey. "Hence," in Eliade's opinion, "any ecstatic cannot be considered a shaman; the shaman specializes in a trance during which his soul is believed to leave his body and ascend to the sky or descend to the underworld."[5]

Though there are similarities between the ecstasy, or trance, of the shaman and those of a Voodoo practitioner, the shaman does not experience this state as a possession. During the trance, the shaman is seemingly in

1. Eliade, *Shamanism: Archaic Techniques of Ecstasy*, 4.
2. Ibid., 8.
3. Ibid., 5
4. Ibid., 7
5. Ibid., 5

control of him- or herself, and also is not manipulated by the spirits against his or her will. Rather, the shaman works with the spirits and can actually be said to be more the possessor of spirits than possessed by them.[6] Thus the shaman's state of ecstasy is thought to be different from that of other trance-like states commonly seen as possession. For this reason Michael Harner, author of *The Way of the Shaman*, prefers to call it the "shamanic state of consciousness."[7] Whether this distinction is accurate, or necessary, is a question to which we will return in due time.

The shamanic state of consciousness is not only the distinguishing feature of a shaman, it is also the prerequisite experience to becoming one. "A shaman is not recognized as such until after he has received two kinds of teaching: (1) ecstatic (dreams, trances, etc.) and (2) traditional (shamanic techniques, names and functions of the spirits, mythology and genealogy of the clan, secret language, etc.)."[8] Thus, the call to the role of shaman is both spontaneous and learned. The future shaman may exhibit trances, epileptic-like seizures, dreams or visions, but these alone do not constitute a shaman's existence; they are only the precursors of a shaman's life. Those who do exhibit these phenomena will be taken into training to be shown how to use these ecstatic states, and how to control them for the benefit of the clan.[9] So, the shamanic state of consciousness is not merely the trance state, "but [is] also a learned awareness of shamanic methods and assumptions while in such an altered state . . . the learned component of the [shamanic state of consciousness] includes information about cosmic geography of nonordinary reality, so that one may know where to journey to the appropriate animal, plant, and other powers."[10]

Once the shaman has achieved the ability to enter the trance state, and has learned how to behave while in it, she or he is ready to begin serious shamanic journeying. The shaman's journey consists of travelling through a tunnel into one of the other cosmic zones. Shamanic cosmologies are commonly composed of three cosmic zones: the earth, the sky, and the lower-world. These zones are connected by a central axis, the axis mundi. This axis—which is variously symbolized as a tree, a mountain, or a pillar—passes through each cosmic zone. It is at this point, where the axis mundi passes through the zones, that there is a space through which the shaman

---

6. Ibid., 6

7. Harner, *The Way of the Shaman: A Guide to Power and Healing*, 26.

8. Eliade, *Shamanism: Archaic Techniques of Ecstasy*, 13.

9. Ibid., 15.

10. Harner, *The Way of the Shaman*, 26.

can travel. This space is commonly experienced as a tunnel leading into the supernatural realms.[11]

The shaman's journey is not undertaken frivolously, or on the spur of the moment, but is accompanied by a ceremonial ritual, and usually occurs at night. As we saw in Voodoo, the drum is also an essential feature to the shamanic ceremony. The shaman's journey begins with the beating of the drum, is maintained by the drum's rhythm, and ends with a rapid increase in the drumbeat.[12] The drumbeat is accompanied by the use of rattles as well. Though the drum is common to most all shamanic practices, Harner does not see it as essential to the entering of the trance. Rather, it is an ability to relax and clear the mind of ordinary perceptions that is important, the drum and rattle only assisting with this ability.[13] The journey begins with the shaman travelling down a dark tunnel. In the tunnel he or she may encounter creatures or people, although this usually occurs at the end of the tunnel. When the shaman does reach the end of the tunnel he or she enters a completely new world. It is a world populated by many of the same animals and plants as those in the ordinary world, but there is more as well. This world of the shamanic consciousness also contains dragons, demons, and other creatures mythical to the ordinary world but quite real to the world of the shaman. Even those plants and animals that are seemingly common in ordinary reality take on a new spiritual significance in the shaman's nonordinary reality. It is in this world that the shaman travels with the assistance of his or her guardian and helping spirits, both known as power animals.[14]

While the shaman is travelling within these other zones, the onlookers in the ordinary reality can catch glimpses of what is happening by means of the shaman's voice and actions. At the beginning of the ceremony the shaman, and the shaman's assistant, begin the drumming and rattling. Soon the shaman will enter into a trance. There may be shaking and seizures associated with the entry into the trance, much as there were in the preliminary stages of Voodoo possession. The shaman may begin to speak a new language, the language of his or her power animals. The shaman may relate to the onlookers what he or she is seeing or doing. He or she may begin to dance, to imitate the flight of a bird, or the swimming of a seal, for in the shamanic state of consciousness the shaman actually has become a bird, seal, fish, or other animal. As the journey draws to a close, the shaman will signal his or her assistant to increase the rhythm of

11. Eliade, *Shamanism*, 259.

12. Ibid., 174; Harner, *The Way of the Shaman*, 67.

13. Harner, *The Way of the Shaman*, 38.

14. Ibid., 73ff.

the drumming in order to assist in a quick return to the ordinary reality. During this return the shaman experiences coming back to the entry of the tunnel (or some new, but similar exit) and journeying back up the tunnel to the earthly cosmic zone.[15]

Once the shaman has learned to traverse these other cosmic zones, she or he is ready to perform the societal functions of a shaman. Then the shaman becomes healer and psychopomp (the guide of the dead).

The societies in which shamans function can view illness from many aspects: physical, psychological (or soulish), and spiritual. Yet, the kind of illnesses brought to the shaman are essentially four-fold: illness due to the loss of one's soul; loss of one's power animal (or guardian spirit); bewitchment; and power intrusion (or possession by evil spirits).

It is believed in societies holding shamanic practices, that a person can become ill because one's soul has left, or been taken from the body of the individual. If this is what has occurred then the shaman will be paid to undertake a journey in search of that soul. The journey can be dangerous and the shaman may have to use all his or her wiles to get the soul back. When the shaman does find the person's soul—which is often found in the form of a fly or a bee—he puts the soul under his arm, or in his hand, and begins the journey back through the tunnel to the ailing person. Once back he replaces the soul into the person by putting it in the person's head, mouth, fingers or big toe.[16] A person can also be ill, or "dis-spirited," because his or her guardian spirit (or power animal) has wandered off. Once again a shaman will be employed to journey to find this wandering spirit. Once in the other cosmic zones the shaman will search for an animal that shows itself four times, in four differing manners. When this happens the shaman knows that this is the spirit for which he is searching. He then grabs the spirit under his arm and journeys back to the ordinary reality. There he blows the spirit back into the body of the sick person, first through the chest, then through the soft spot on the back of the skull.[17]

With both bewitchment and power intrusions, we come to the aspect of illness closest to the form of possession by evil spirits. Though the initiation of the illness may differ, the results are the same: the person falls ill because there is an object, or spirit, within that is causing the illness. The object can enter because a sorcerer supernaturally places it there, or because a demon or one of the dead has done so.[18] When this happens, the shaman

---

15. Eliade, *Shamanism*, 190ff; Harner, *The Way of the Shaman*, 38ff.

16. Eliade, *Shamanism*, 256.

17. Harner, *The Way of the Shaman*, 98.

18. Eliade, *Shamanism*, 331.

is called in to suck out the harmful intrusion. To do so is also dangerous for the shaman because he or she can become possessed in the process.

> The struggle against the evil spirits is dangerous and finally exhausts the shaman. "We are all destined to fall before the power of the spirits," the shaman Tusput told Sieroszewski, "the spirits hate us because we defend men . . . ." And in fact, in order to extract the evil spirits from the patient, the shaman is often obliged to take them into his own body; in doing so, he struggles and suffers more than the patient himself.[19]

To prevent becoming possessed, the shaman secretly places into his or her mouth two objects similar to those believed to be intruding in the person's body. One is placed near the front of the mouth and one near the rear. Then the shaman begins to suck the intrusion out of the patient's body, using either the mouth directly, or sometimes a type of straw or tube applied to the patient's skin. As the sucking progresses the spirits are believed to come out of the patient's body and enter the shaman's mouth. The objects in the shaman's mouth now come into play. They are believed to be the abodes of the shaman's spirit-helpers which will capture the evil spirits as they enter his or her mouth. If the intruding spirit makes it by the first spirit-helper then the one near the rear of the mouth will absorb it. If the intruding spirit makes it by both spirit-helpers then the shaman will be possessed and need to find another shaman to now suck these out of him or her. If the spirits are captured, the shaman will then remove the objects from the mouth and act as if these had actually been in the body of the patient. A shaman does not see this as trickery but as the manner by which common folk can understand the process. Those assembled about the shaman will believe that it is the physical object that caused the illness, but the shaman will know that it was the spirit of the object that was the villain.[20]

The shaman is not only a healer, but is also the one who is in charge of guiding the dead to their place of rest: the shaman is also a psychopomp. The ceremonial manner in which this is done varies according to the society in which it is found. For instance, there are various durations between the time of death and the date the shaman takes the soul to the other cosmic zones. There are also various ideas of how many souls there are in a person and which of these is guided to the nether regions. But common to all is the manner by which the shaman escorts the dead. The shaman will go into a trance, find the soul of the dead person—often still in the vicinity of the family or village—and take this person through the

19. Ibid., 229.

20. Eliade, *Shamanism*, 331; Harner, *The Way of the Shaman*, 148.

cosmic tunnel to the other zone where the dead abide. The shaman will then return and inform the family and onlookers that this person has successfully made the trip to the place of the dead. If the shaman is unsuccessful, though, the village and family could be in for a time of haunting by a frustrated and angry spirit. Then a stronger shaman must be found to succeed where the former had failed.

The phenomenology of the shamanic experience is two-fold: it comprises the subjective cognitive experience of the shaman, and the observed phenomena experienced by the ceremony's onlookers. Unlike the Voodoo possession where the possessed individual returns to ordinary reality amnesic, the shaman returns from the trance to relate the whole journey to those assembled. The cognitive experience of the shaman depends upon the level of reality with which he or she was dealing: the ordinary reality common to all of us, or the dream-like experience of the nonordinary reality of the shamanic state of consciousness. "Whichever the reality, the shaman thinks and acts in the ways appropriate to it, and has as his objective the mastery of both his nonordinary activities and his ordinary activities."[21] We have already seen some of what the shaman may experience while in the nonordinary reality of the shamanic journey. While in this state much of what we see as mythical will become reality for the shaman. The shaman may encounter dragons, mythical humans, and speaking animals. He or she will be able to see the spiritual aspects of all nature, and not merely the corporeal nature we see in ordinary reality. Anyone who has dreamed will have had a taste of what the shaman experiences, yet the shaman experiences these in an even more pronounced manner. It is this that is the essence of the shamanic consciousness: the "seeing" of the spiritual nature of the world.

While the shaman may be "seeing" this other reality, those around the shaman are observing other manifestations of the trance. During the trance the shaman will at times become like a wolf, or some other creature or being. While in the shamanic state of consciousness the shaman experiences this transformation as an actual change into the animal—he has become that animal—while those in ordinary reality may see him imitating this animal-spirit's actions—acting like the animal.[22] He may begin to move his head like that of the spirit-creature,[23] make diving or flying motions like a seal or bird,[24] or imitate the noises of the animal he has become.[25] If

21. Harner, *The Way of the Shaman*, 59.
22. Eliade, *Shamanism*, 335.
23. Ibid., 225.
24. Ibid., 243.
25. Ibid., 93, 191ff, 324.

the shaman has taken a dive into the depths of the sea he or she may arise gasping for breath.[26] If the spirit that the shaman is imitating happens to be human and is drinking, the shaman may begin to act as if he were drunk, even hiccupping when the spirit does.[27] The shaman may even begin to speak in a different manner when a spirit has taken over: his voice may change into a falsetto as if a dead person or a spirit was speaking through his or her body. Here possession is an accurate term to use, since the soul of the shaman is believed to have left his body at this point, as we see in an excerpt from a Tungus séance.

> When all these things [ceremonial preparations] have been done, the audience gathers in the wigwan. The shaman begins drumming, singing, and dancing. He leaps higher and higher in the air. His assistants repeat the refrain of his song in chorus with the spectators. He stops for a moment, drinks a glass of vodka, smokes a few pipes, and resumes dancing. Little by little he excites himself to the point where he falls to the ground inanimate, in ecstasy. If he does not return to his senses, he is thrice sprinkled with blood. He rises and begins to talk in a high voice, answering the sung questions addressed to him by two or three interlocutors. The shaman's body is now inhabited by a spirit, and it is the spirit that answers in his stead. For the shaman himself is now in the lower regions. When he comes back everyone utters joyful cries to greet his return from the world of the dead.[28]

This excerpt begins to illustrate some of the physical reactions and actions that the shaman may exhibit while in the trance state. The leaps into the air, the rising excitement and vigorous actions and dancing, and finally the collapse into a cataleptic trance.[29] This falling into a trance takes the form of fainting or a state of lethargic sleep in some regions.[30] The bodily excitement is exhibited in diverse ways as well, with shaking and nervous tremors.[31] There may also be nervous yawning and hysterical hiccupping.[32] Vomiting is a common method for expulsion of spirits, and so the sight of

---

26. Ibid., 296.
27. Ibid., 335.
28. Ibid., 239; cf. 209, 230, 255.
29. Ibid., 195, 197, 241.
30. Ibid., 53.
31. Ibid., 82ff, 230.
32. Ibid., 230.

the shaman vomiting near the end of a ceremony, or whenever a spirit has entered his mouth, is a common sight.[33]

Though we have seen that the shaman may speak in a different voice according to which spirit he or she has become, this is not the only change in the shaman's speech that is encountered. In order to speak with the spirits, the shaman has to acquire a new spirit-language. This may be the language of a certain animal species or a spiritual language of some other sort. Whichever it is, those present at the shamanic séance will experience the shaman conversing with the unheard spirits in a language incomprehensible to themselves.[34]

Not only does the shaman acquire a new language, she or he may also exhibit exceptional cognitive abilities. Some shamans have exhibited telepathic and clairvoyant abilities. Others have also been seen to have divinatory abilities such as predicting the weather, or the fate of a season's crops.[35] In some cases the shaman may act as a prophet. As we have already discussed, prophecy needs to be distinguished from divination, but this differentiation is worth repeating here. A prophecy is a speaking forth of a message from a spirit or god. Divination is the foretelling of the future. Both of these can be encountered in a shamanic séance.

Incredible feats and abilities are attributed to shamans in every region in which shamanism is found. Shamans have been seen to stab themselves deeply without pain or issue of blood,[36] or to cut others with like results. They are renowned for their abilities to operate, with seemingly magical capacity.

Often they undertake an "operation" that still preserves all its shamanic character. With a ritual knife, duly "heated" by certain magical exercises, the shaman professes to open the patient's body to examine his internal organs and remove the cause of illness. Bogoras even witnessed an "operation" of this kind. A boy of fourteen lay naked on the ground, and his mother, a celebrated shaman, opened his abdomen; the blood and the gaping flesh were visible; the shaman thrust her hand deep into the wound. During all this time the shaman felt as if she were on fire and constantly drank water. A few moments later the wound had closed, and Bogoras could detect no trace of it.[37]

---

33. Harner, *The Way of the Shaman*, 155.

34. Eliade, *Shamanism*, 82, 96, 291.

35. Ibid., 184, 197, 296, 310.

36. Ibid., 244.

37. Ibid., 256.

In the past, shamans were reported to be able to both predict the weather and to control it,[38] as well as have a multitude of magical abilities. They are credited with the power to make a grain of wheat germinate and sprout before the eyes of the audience; to cause pine branches to come from distant mountains in the twinkling of an eye; to make rabbits and kids appear, feathers and other objects fly. They can also throw themselves from heights into small baskets, produce a living rabbit from a rabbit's skeleton, and transform various objects into animals.[39] But most common to shamans the world over is their power over fire: they are masters of fire.

> Like the devil in the beliefs of the European peoples, shamans are not merely "masters over fire"; they can also incarnate the spirits of fire to the point where, during séances, they emit flames from their mouths, their noses, and their whole bodies. This sort of feat must be put in the category of shamanic wonders connected with the "mastery over fire," of which we have given many examples. The magical power involved expresses the "spirit condition" obtained by shamans. . . . Such "fire" and mystical "heat" are always connected with access to a certain ecstatic state—the same connection is observed in the most archaic strata of magic and universal religion. Mastery over fire, insensibility to heat, and hence, the "mystical heat" that renders both extreme cold and the temperature of burning coals supportable, is a magico-mystical virtue that, accompanied by no less marvelous qualities (ascent, magical flight, etc.) translates into sensible terms the fact that the shaman has passed beyond the human condition and already shares in the condition of "spirits."[40]

This mastery over fire is seen in various observable forms. Shamans can walk on, and handle, red-hot iron, or burning coals without pain or incurring burns.[41] Likewise, they may place these hot items in their mouths and even swallow them.[42]

> Closely allied in incredulity are the psychokinetic exhibitions of the shamanic séance. Objects have been seen to move during the shaman's trance such as the report that a "shaman's clothes—which he had taken off before the séance—[had] come

38. Ibid., 299.

39. Ibid., 315n.

40. Ibid,. 373, 335.

41. Ibid., 219, 244.

42. Ibid., 299, 316n.

to life and [started] flying about the house over the heads of the audience."[43]

Finally, another phenomenon that is encountered during the shamanic séance is the distinct odor of decay around the shaman while he is in the trance. An odor described as the smell of death.[44]

These subjective and objective experiences of the shamanic ceremony are common to cultures throughout the world. It is this commonality that draws many people to believe in the common roots of shamanism. As we look at the phenomena exhibited in the shamanic ceremony it becomes clear that there is little difference between what is found here and what is found in other forms of possession. Yet, the argument against shamanism as a form of possession lies in the shaman's own experience.

Shamans do not see themselves as possessed by spirits, but rather as the possessors of spirits. The shaman is not out-of-control, but rather controls the spirits.[45] However this may be only a Faustian argument. For like Faust, it is questionable who is the possessor and who ultimately the possessed. The shaman possesses a "power animal" in order to gain power, yet the shaman must continually "feed" this spirit-animal by dancing its dance, drinking tobacco water, or taking a certain drug. If this is not done, the power animal will wander off from the shaman causing the shaman to become dis-spirited: illness ensues and possibly even death.[46] This actually appears no different from the Voodoo sorcerer's need to feed his evil *loa* in order to maintain his power. Shaman and sorcerer both fall into the Faustian pit of believing themselves to be in control, while slowly losing more and more of themselves to the spirit which they need to feed, for if it is not fed they must deal with the spirit's retribution, which is illness or death. I believe that to see shamanism as a true form of possession does no harm to the concept of shamanism, but rather may enhance its understanding.

43. Ibid., 295.
44. Ibid., 83.
45. Ibid., 6.
46. Harner, *The Way of the Shaman*, 73.

8

Spiritualism and Possession

S pirtualistic phenomena have been in humanity's experiential knowledge since humans were first able to conceive a realm of the supernatural. Yet Spiritualism as a religion—or a method of study—is relatively new,
arising as recently as the early nineteenth century.

Spiritualism as a religion needs to be distinguished from other forms of
mediumistic activities, some of which we have already encountered in Voodoo and shamanism. Mediumistic cults are widespread in the world, being
found on all continents and in all strata of society. In the Western world it
can be found in the various forms of Spiritism and what has been referred
to as New Age religions that have sprung up since the early 1960s. In the
East it is encountered in the still active ancestor cults of the Chinese and
the corresponding Chinese spirit-medium cults. Yet, many of these New Age
religions, and the Chinese spirit-medium cults are actually more forms of
shamanism than they are forms of what is presently falling under the rubric
of Spiritualism.[1] Spiritualism differs from these other forms by means of a
subtle distinction: Spiritualism sees spirit manifestations as based on natural
law, whereas mediumistic cults view spirit manifestations as miraculous or
supernatural.[2] Unlike the shaman, who sees his ability to enter a trance and
communicate with the spirits as a gift from the gods, the Spiritualist sees
his or her mediumistic abilities as a natural gift which is due more to one's
constitution than to one's being favored by a god or spirit.[3]

Spiritualism also differs from the scientific study of parapsychological
phenomena. Both of these are interested in the existence of these phenomena, and the human potential to utilize them, but the Spiritualist unequivo-
cally accepts the validity of spirit communication and the other paranormal

1. Elliot, *Chinese Spirit-Medium Cults in Singapore*, 15.

2. *Spiritualist Manual*, 74.

3. Ibid., 184.

events, and even searches how to apply these to daily life in a religious manner; the scientist is more interested in the cause and nature of these events.
Arthur Conan Doyle, an early proponent of parapsychological studies and
of the Society for Psychical Research, has related to us the following quote
in regard to the difference between the scientific approach of the Society for
Psychical Research and the Spiritualist:

> [T]here is a sharp line of distinction between the Society for
> Psychical Research and the Central Association of Spiritual-
> ists. The Spiritualists have a settled faith—nay, more, a certain
> knowledge—in regard to facts about which the Society for Psy-
> chical Research would not yet profess to have any knowledge
> whatever. The Society for Psychical Research are busy with phe-
> nomena only, seeking evidence of their existence; . . . to them
> the idea of spirit communication, of sweet converse with dear
> departed friends—so precious to Spiritualists—has no present
> interest. We speak of them, of course, as a Society—not of indi-
> vidual members. As a Society they are studying the mere bones
> and muscles, and have not yet penetrated to the heart and soul.[4]

Even though there seems to be a sharp distinction between the scientific approach to paranormal phenomena and the religious approach, the
Spiritualists still see themselves as a science, as well as a philosophy and a
religion. The National Spiritualist Association of Churches has defined Spiritualism as "the Science, Philosophy and Religion of continuous life, based
upon the demonstrated fact of communication, by means of mediumship,
with those who live in the Spirit World."[5]

> "Spiritualism Is a Science" because it investigates, analyzes and
> classifies facts and manifestations demonstrated from the spirit
> side of life. "Spiritualism Is a Philosophy" because it studies the
> laws of nature both on the seen and unseen sides of life and
> bases its conclusions upon present observed facts. It accepts
> statements of observed facts of past ages and conclusions drawn
> therefrom, when sustained by reason and by results of observed
> facts of the present day. "Spiritualism Is a Religion" because it
> strives to understand and to comply with the Physical, Mental
> and Spiritual Laws of Nature, which are the laws of God.[6]

Even though the Spiritualists see themselves as scientific, the distinction still remains that the scientific studies of parapsychology (as exemplified

4. Doyle, *The History of Spiritualism*.

5. *Spiritualist Manual*, 37.

6. Ibid.

by the early studies of the Society of Psychical Research) are more objective and less value-laden than the studies of the Spiritualists. Spiritualists already accept as a fact that the phenomena they experience come from spirits and only wish to research what the communications mean for their lives. Parapsychologists have no such a priori acceptance of spirits. Finally, Spiritualism needs to be distinguished from occultism in general. Occultism is a term that is not easily definable, nor has it been pinned down to one or another set of variables or phenomena. Generally, though, it refers to the whole gamut of paranormal, or magical, events and practices. Marcello Truzzi[7] has attempted to define the parameters of the occult and has done so by categorizing it into five forms.

The first form he refers to as proto-scientific occultism, of which parapsychology is an example. This form attempts to validate paranormal events through use of scientific methods, but as of yet has not been generally accepted by the majority of the scientific community.

The second form is the quasi-scientific, a form which pays "lip service" to scientific criteria and methods, but in actuality does not utilize them. Astrology is an example of this. Here also, the scientific aspect of Spiritualism fits.

The third form is the pragmatic occultism of the magician. This form relies primarily on the outcome of the occult practice. Thus, if a certain potion is seen to bring about a certain result, then the magic works. If the potion does not work, then it is no good.

The fourth form is that in which the Spiritualist religion mostly lies: shared mystical occultism.

> Like pragmatic occultism, this form of belief centers on some personal demonstration of truth but without the possibility of empirical or truly intersubjective validation. Here one experiences a personal, essentially mystical truth, but this is in part communicable to another through language and others are told that they too can experience this same subjective truth if they perform appropriate acts.[8]

The final form is that of private mystical occultism. This form consists of "purely private forms of occult validation. Here the believer must have a direct . . . experience of his 'truth,' and this is self-validating."[9] Much of what is practiced in the occult today falls into this category. Most casual

---

7. Truzzi, *Definition and Dimensions of the Occult: Towards a Sociological Perspective.*

8. Ibid., 250.

9. Ibid.

practitioners of divination, or fortune-telling, do it with only a few others or by themselves. The interest in Tarot, card laying, Ouija-board use, casting Runes or the I Ching, is mostly of a private nature and not organized as in other forms of occult practice.

Spiritualism can be seen to fit into certain aspects of these five categories. Aspects of Spiritualism are quasi-scientific, pragmatic and shared, yet it is distinguished from the occult in general for it is not proto-scientific, nor would the casual occultist be considered a Spiritualist.

Spiritualism as a specific form of religion and belief can first be seen in the beginning of the eighteenth century, and grew into a force during the nineteenth century. It was at this point in history that Emmanuel Swedenborg (1688–1772) came on the scene.

Swedenborg was one of the first true Spiritualists.[10] In the beginning of the nineteenth century the Spiritualist movement expanded to the United States with the Shakers and the Fox sisters. It is usually from the Fox sisters' experience on March 31, 1848 that modern Spiritualism dates its birth, but this is primarily because it was the Fox sisters who essentially founded the present Spiritualist Church.

The Fox family had recently moved to a house in Hydesville, New York in the year 1847, when they started hearing rapping, or knocking sounds. This did not seem to alarm the family, until, in March of 1848, the sounds increased.

> Finally, upon the night of March 31 there was a loud and continued outbreak of inexplicable sounds. It was on this night that one of the great points of psychic evolution was reached, for it was then that young Kate Fox challenged the unseen power to repeat the snaps of her fingers; . . . the child's challenge, though given with flippant words, was instantly answered. Every snap was echoed by a knock. . . . Mrs. Fox was amazed at this development, and at the further discovery that the force could apparently see as well as hear, for when Kate snapped her fingers without sound the rap still responded.[11]

Later, after they had grown, Kate Fox, and her sister Margaret, began giving public séances and demonstrating spiritual, or psychic, phenomena to the general populace. Interest in the phenomena grew in both America and also back in England. Later, these followers of the Foxes would set up the Spiritualist Church.

---

10. Doyle, *The History of Spiritualism, v.1.*

11. Ibid., 62–63.

Central to the function of Spiritualism is mediumship. "A Spiritualist is one who believes, as the basis of his or her religion, in the communication between this and the spirit world by means of mediumship and who endeavors to mold his or her character and conduct in accordance with the highest teachings derived from such communication."[12] A medium is an intermediary between the spiritual world and this world, and the mediumistic activity usually occurs during a séance of some sort.

> During séances the medium falls into a trance; his spirit escapes and his body gives shelter to wandering spirits of the "astral plane" who speak through his mouth and act in a way that effectively shows a new personality. Impressive to the uninitiated, especially when accompanied by clairvoyance or materializations, these phenomena are too similar to phenomena of possession not to be immediately classed by psychologists among the forms of personality division.[13]

Thus, possession is not merely central to Spiritualism, Spiritualism *is* possession. The list of phenomena associated with the Spiritualistic possession reads like a compendium of parapsychological occurrences.

> The Phenomena of Spiritualism consist of Prophecy, Clairvoyance, Clairaudience, Gift of Tongues, Laying on of Hands, Healing, Visions, Trance, Apports, Levitation, Raps, Automatic and Independent Writings and Paintings, Voice, Materialization, Photography, Psychometry and any other manifestation proving the continuity of life as demonstrated through the Physical and Spiritual senses and faculties of man.[14]

There are degrees of mediumship experienced by the Spiritualist. Not all mediums achieve a state of complete unconsciousness. Some only enter what the Spiritualist refers to as an "abstracted consciousness" or a "partial or intermittent entrancement."[15] During such a trance the medium may exhibit the speaking forth in a "spirit voice," perform healings, or other forms of Spiritualist phenomena. Others enter into a full state of trance, losing all self-consciousness. These mediums are referred to as "trance-mediums," and the trance medium is believed to be a more pure conduit through whom the spirits may work.[16]

12. *Spiritualist Manual*, 37.
13. Sudre, *Parapsychology*.
14. *Spiritualist Manual*, 37.
15. Ibid., 154.
16. Ibid., 153.

The Spiritualist's trance differs from others in that this medium seems to pass from the conscious state into the trance with only a few nervous or muscular twitches.[17] The spirit-medium exhibits little of the muscular excitability, convulsive movements, and cataleptic symptoms of many trance states.[18] Thus, the Spiritualist medium is similar to those persons in both Voodoo and shamanism who are experienced in entering into the possession, or trance, state.

While in the trance the medium may meet old friends, or walk in the spirit-world for a time. The medium may also be able to recollect these experiences of the trance, yet he or she will not be able to recollect the message given by the spirits during the séance. The medium is amnesic in regard to the event of the séance, much as the Voodoo practitioner is amnesic of the actions and speech of the possessing *loa*.

The mediumistic phenomena has been placed into four groups by the Polish researcher Lebiedzinski.[19] These groupings are (1) a change in the physical or mental state; (2) supernormal perception; (3) supernormal action of the mind on its own body; (4) supernormal action of the mind on matter and energy outside its own organism.

Into the first of these fall the trance states of the medium, the ability to speak other languages, the speaking in different voices and the like. Into the second, the phenomena of telepathy, clairvoyance, clairaudience, and prophecy fall. Telepathy is the ability to acquire knowledge from others without the use of the senses; essentially mind-reading.[20] Clairaudience is the ability to hear without using the sense of hearing. Clairvoyance, literally meaning "clear seeing," is the ability to gain knowledge of distant or unknown events without the use of any of the known senses.[21]

Spiritualists further sub-divide clairvoyance into six sub-categories: subjective clairvoyance, objective clairvoyance, X-ray clairvoyance, cataleptic clairvoyance, trance-control clairvoyance, and telepathic clairvoyance. The first two have to do with the seeing of spiritual beings or objects. With subjective clairvoyance the medium "sees" a mental picture of the being or object, while in objective clairvoyance a person can objectively see beings or objects outside of him- or herself that others do not see. The clairvoyant with X-ray clairvoyance "is able to see physical objects through intervening physical matter, can perceive the internal parts of the

17. Ibid., 151.
18. Sudre, *Parapsychology*, 65.
19. Ibid., 51.
20. Koch, *Christian Counseling and Occultism*, 56.
21. Ibid., 60.

human body, diagnose disease and observe the operations of healing and decay."[22] Cataleptic clairvoyance is a blending of subjective and objective clairvoyance while in the trance state. The person may be able to travel to remote places "to see clearly what is transpiring in the places it visits and to observe spiritual as well as material things in its environment."[23] Cataleptic clairvoyance is what is commonly referred to as astral projection. In trance-control clairvoyance the physical body of the medium is taken over by a spirit which then informs the listeners of what is happening elsewhere. Finally, telepathic clairvoyance is the reading of thoughts from afar. These thoughts come in the form of pictures.[24] The third form of occult, or spiritualist, phenomena is the supernormal action of the mind on its own body. This can mean such things as stigmata, radiations of energy, projections of doubles (that is bilocation or being in two places at once) and materializations. Materializations are what, in this category, are usually seen in Spiritualist séances. It is the materialization that is commonly portrayed in caricatures of séances: the wispy white and luminous figures of spirits that arrive in the midst of the séance. "In the trance state certain individuals can extract from their own bodies, and probably also from the bodies of nearby people, an unknown substance . . . [which is] capable of imitating all forms of life and of inanimate matter, and of carrying out the greatest variety of mechanical, physical or chemical actions."[25]

The fourth grouping of phenomena, the supernormal actions of the mind on matter and energy outside of itself include such events as healings, levitations, raps, automatic writing and painting, and dematerializations of matter. A very common occurrence during séances is the lowering of temperature and breezes of cold air in the room. During one séance, the room seemed to be filled with cold air and an automatically registering thermometer dropped three degrees of centigrade. This feeling of coldness is also present in many recorded cases of demonic possessions.

As we have been reviewing the Spiritualist phenomena, we have seen that possession in this category is seemingly voluntary, and does not appear to have an adverse effect upon the practitioner. Unlike other possession-beliefs, the Spiritualist does not believe in involuntary possession, nor even in the existence of evil spirits that can so possess a person. The Spiritualist sees evil spirits merely as the spirits of the uneducated dead.

22. *Spiritualist Manual*, 114.

23. Ibid., 115.

24. Ibid.

25. Sudre, Parapsychology, 229.

We believe there are both intelligent and ignorant spirits. No being is naturally "bad"—evil always originates in ignorance.... Those whom you call evil spirits are also the spirits of those who have lived on the earth plane. Many of them through lack of opportunity, want of proper education, and the influence of wrong social conditions have passed through this world and into the Spirit World in absolute ignorance of spiritual laws. They are, however, no worse than mankind has sent them into the Spirit World, and they are still our Brothers and Sisters.[26]

Because of this, the Spiritualist does not believe in the potentially harmful encounter between the spirits and the medium. In fact, the Spiritualist believes that the encounters are actually beneficial.

Many people have erroneously supposed that trance-mediumship causes a loss of individuality or that it is followed by detrimental results to the mentality; but, as a matter of fact, the best trance, as well as inspirational, speakers and mediums, are also the best unfolded otherwise. For these reasons: First: The intelligences acting upon them are almost invariably of a superior character and, therefore, must mold the organism by constant use, for the expression of higher forms of thought. Second: The relation of the medium to the manifesting intelligence is that of pupil and teacher, sometimes that of a child to a wise loving parent, and sometimes both of these relations combined with a subtle and ennobling spirituality. Third: There is always a mutual spiritual relation, even though the medium is not humanly conscious of it; and no one can be a medium for the perfect expression of spirit messages or discourses, who does not consent to the procedure and cooperate with the manifesting spirit. Fourth: As the master-musician improves the instrument he plays upon, so, also a spirit controlling a human organism for the purpose of expressing wholesome thought, imparts a greater power, both to the brain and the spirit of the medium.[27]

This description is obviously one of a person possessed, but of one possessed by what he or she conceives of as a beneficial spirit. Yet, like the Faustian argument we explored with shamanism, it is doubtful as to how beneficial such a possession actually is. Kurt Koch,[28] in his research into the effects of occult and spiritist practices, has found that many cases of such involvement have not been harmless or beneficial.

26. *Spiritualist Manual*, 186–87.

27. Ibid., 153.

28. Koch, *Christian Counseling and Occultism*.

Effects on those who exercise Occult Influence: By this group we mean those occultists who, as spiritist leaders, mediums, practicing diviners and experimenters with magic charms, carry on an active occult practice. The family histories and the end of these occult workers are, in many cases known to me, so tragic that we can no longer speak in terms of coincidence. . . . In many instances we see suicide, . . . fatal accidents, . . . psychoses, . . . or horrible death-bed scenes. Besides the instances recorded in this study, there are numerous other examples of this kind well known to me, e.g., the leader of a spiritist group in South Wuttemberg who hanged himself, and the leader of another group who ended his life in an asylum, . . . a pioneer in the field of psychical research, Crawford, who made experiments with the medium Kathleen Goligher, took his own life in 1920. In the literature of psychical research we continually find reference to such happenings.[29]

The practice of Spiritualism may not be as harmless as the proponents of it wish think. As more and more persons practice some form of Spiritualism in the more loosely organized manner known as the New Age Movement, we also find a rise in the need for therapy for ailments referred to as spiritual crises. Whether this is because certain unbalanced persons are drawn to these practices, and so raise the number of incidents, or if the practices themselves have an effect of such nature on these persons is something that requires more study. However these effects that Koch relates occur across the practice of the occult, and apply to the practice of astrology, divinations, witchcraft and Satanism. It is to the latter two that we now turn our attention.

29. Ibid., 184–85.

9

Witchcraft, Satanism, and Possession

U p to this point we have been dealing with religions and practices with dual forms of possession: those that could be considered either good or evil. In Christianity there was both possession by the Holy Spirit, as well as possession by demons or the devil. In Voodoo and shamanism a person could be possessed by either a good spirit or an evil spirit. In spiritualism one could be taken over by an intelligent or an ignorant spirit. Now we turn to two forms of possession which are essentially only evil, to look at persons who have voluntarily opted to be possessed by what is perverse and destructive in order that they might gain some limited degree of power. We now turn to witchcraft and Satanism.

Before we can begin this study, the parameters which distinguish witchcraft from other forms of magic-working first need to be determined. Jeffrey Russell has come to the conclusion that European witchcraft is a distinctive phenomenon, separable from what is referred to as witchcraft by anthropologists studying non-Western cultures.

I should make it clear at the outset what it is that I mean by witchcraft. I am not referring to the modern amalgam of neo-pagan practices known as Wicca; and I do not use the term as a synonym for sorcery or magic. In spite of the efforts of anthropologists to compare the two, there are only limited analogies between European witchcraft and the sorcery of Africa or Oceania.[1] Sorcery can generally be distinguished from witchcraft in that sorcery is essentially the use of magic potions or formulas to bring about a desired result—usually maleficent—in which there is no invocation of spirits. Witchcraft, on the other hand, has historically been the practice of invocation of the spirits to assist the witch in his or her desired ends. In

1. Russell, *Medieval Witchcraft and Medieval Heresy*, 180.

European witchcraft this invoking of the spirits took the form of diabolism in which the witch called upon Satan, or one of his demons.[2]

Closely akin to invocation, yet distinct from it, is diabolism: deliberate worship of the devil, or of demons. This worship involves a variety of ritual actions, usually occurring at the diabolical assembly, or "synagogue," or "Sabbath". It entails a pact in which the devotee submits himself wholly before the devil, accepting him as lord; it further may involve sexual intercourse with the devil in the human form of an incubus or succubus, receipt of the devil's prick or "mark" on one's body, flight through the air on an anointed stick, transformation into the shape of an animal, and so forth.[3] Though some of this description may sound ludicrous, still the "idea of witchcraft was a reality in the minds of those who practiced as well as those who prosecuted it."[4] Russell describes European witchcraft as arising from four primary sources: folklore, inquisitional fabrication, scholasticism, and heresy. Folklore has contributed the least to the rise of witchcraft, but the ancient stories and fears that the people had who held these beliefs would later be transferred from the folkloric sorcerer, or fairy, and applied to the witch.

More important to the rise of European witchcraft is the Christian church's response to it. "The Inquisition helped increase the magnitude of witchcraft and to fix it firmly in the popular mind."[5] Likewise, the scholastics such as Abelard and John of Salisbury added validity to witchcraft by acknowledging its reality.[6] But the most important factor in the rise of witchcraft, and in the form it has taken, is the heresy trial of witches. It is from these trials that most of the doctrines of classical witchcraft have been derived.[7]

The actions and phenomena associated with witchcraft are various, bringing in, once again, the folk-beliefs of the people along with the theological understanding of evil and of Satan. Witches were believed to have "passed through walls or closed doors, rode through the air, met in secret places at night to hold sexual revels, ritually slaughtered and ate children, had intercourse with the Devil who took various shapes, and offered him

2. Kieckhefer, *European Witch Trials: Their Foundations in Popular and Learned Culture, 1300–1500.*

3. Ibid., 6.

4. Russell, *Medieval Witchcraft and Medieval Heresy*, 180.

5. Ibid., 181.

6. Ibid., 115.

7. Ibid., 182.

obscene homage with ritual kisses."[8] But it is the use of diabolic, or demonic, magic for which the witch is best known.

In order to gain power for performing magic the witch had to first sell his or her soul to Satan, then becoming the possession of Satan. "Making a pact with the Devil is the first function of satanic science. The pact normally involves the exchange of the soul for a devilish favor—be it money, a change of circumstances, attacks against fellow human beings, help with the crops or the performing of some dark miracle. Other motives include the acquiring of honor and glory, invisibility, the gift of tongues, and transportation from one place to another in the twinkling of an eye."[9] The pact made with the Devil was usually a pact of blood, and this practice still continues in many circles today.

> In order to attain power from the Devil the prospective witch would stand within a pentagram, triangle or circle in which some protective name was written. The person would then conjure up Satan with pleas and threats. When Satan did appear he would say: "I am here! What does thou seek? Why does thou interfere with my rest? Give me answer." The person would then respond: "I desire to make a pact with thee, for the purpose of obtaining riches at once. If thou wilt not agree to this, I shall blast thee with the Words of Power of the Key." Then Satan would answer: "I will agree only if thou wilt agree to give thy body and soul to me after twenty [or seven] years, to use as I please." The person then signed in his or her blood a contract with the Devil with the agreed-upon powers and time of relinquishing the soul and body to Satan.[10]

This selling of one's soul to Satan would set at the witches' disposal Satan and his army of demons, and it was the demon or the Devil himself that was the real perpetrator of the magic attributed to the witch. "The witchcraft literature abounds in passing, incidental references to the role of demons as witches' accomplices."[11] Kieckhefer goes on further to say that "Francisco de Toledo defines *maleficium* as 'the art of harming others by the power of a demon'; amatory witchcraft is effected by the devil's use of phantasms and his motion of the imagination, whereas 'venefic' witchcraft is accomplished either by poisons which the demon provides to the witch or else by the di-

8. Ibid., 181.

9. Masters, *The Devil's Dominion*, 125.

10. Ibid., 127–28.

11. Kieckhefer, *European Witch Trials: Their Foundations in Popular and Learned Culture, 1300–1500*, 83.

rect action of the demon in the service of the witch."[12] The magic performed by these witches was manifold, and we shall be looking at it in a moment.

Common to most descriptions of witchcraft is the Sabbath meeting. The first recorded Sabbath meeting of witches dates from the fifteenth century. It was supposedly the gathering of witches to worship Satan and to take part in orgiastic activities. The Black Mass that we know today is a re-creation of some portions of this witches' Sabbath, but as it is performed today it was virtually non-existent in medieval witchcraft.

> The black mass is for the most part a literary invention of the nineteenth-century occultists. . . . [T]he absence of black masses in the Middle Ages is a strong point against those who argue that witchcraft originated as an explicit distortion of Christian rite. Had this been true, the mass, the central feature of Christian worship, would surely have been blasphemously enacted at the witches' conventicles. Here is further proof that witchcraft was drawn from heresies which, however gross, lacked this ultimate outrage.[13]

The black mass, though not a true historical artifact, would later arise in satanic witchcraft and Satanism to be of central importance.

In many other ways, though, witchcraft has not significantly changed over the past few centuries. The only major difference is a decrease in today's societal apprehension in regard to witchcraft, and what many who practice it perceive as the origins of witchcraft. Historical witchcraft was commonly associated with Satan worship, but today's modern witch is more eclectic, believing witchcraft to be a folk tradition of magical beliefs.[14] Yet, this belief is unfounded, and is rather a modern creation.

> Still less do I mean to dignify modern occultists by adopting the Murrayite view that witchcraft is an ancient religion that has preserved a marvelous continuity to the present day. Such a continuity is indeed marvelous to the historian, who knows there is no evidence for it.[15]

Today's practice of witchcraft ranges from the casual practice of solitary persons to the devoted ritualistic endeavors of the Satanic covens. Generally, though, witches can be divided into two groups: (1) the solitary

---

12. Ibid., 83.

13. Russell, *Witchcraft in the Middle Ages*, 253.

14. Truzzi, *Witchcraft and Satanism*.

15. Russell, *Medieval Witchcraft and Medieval Heresy*, 180.

witches who practice their art either individually, or in loosely organized groups of friends, and (2) the groups of well-organized witches, or covens.[16]

The solitary witches can be further classified according to the manner by which they enter into the practice of witchcraft.

1. represents those who, having learned the secrets of the art through some special kinship-relation to another solitary witch, practice witchcraft as a culturally inherited art from kin;

2. the other represents those who, having invented their own techniques or having obtained their practice from occult literature, practice witchcraft as self-designated witches.[17]

This second group of solitary witches is where the vast majority of today's witches are to be found.

The organized groups of witches can also be divided into two forms: the covens of white witches and the covens of black witches. Each of these is determined by the type of magic that is utilized by those in the coven.

> The alleged difference between so-called white versus black magic is one major distinction discussed in much of the occult literature. While white magic is supposed to be the use of magic for socially beneficent ends, black magic is supposed to be the use of magic for malevolent ends. Even though some ritual forms of black magic clearly involve calling upon such malevolent forces as the Devil or his demons, most magicians basically view magic as a value-free "technology-of-the-supernatural" (or super-normal, a term preferred by many magicians). They believe that their own motives really determine whether their use of magic is for good (white), or for evil (black). . . . The distinction between black and white magic is essentially a matter of user's intent rather than of his technique.[18]

Whether witches who view magic as value-free are possessed is a matter for further argument. That there is actually a difference between white and black magic is also questionable. Kurt Koch has stated that white magic "has the same character as black magic, except that it appears in a religious guise."[19] He can say this because he has viewed a similar reaction to each.

---

16. Truzzi, *Witchcraft and Satanism.*

17. Ibid., 216–17.

18. Ibid., 215–16.

19. Koch, *Christian Counseling and Occultism,* 150.

That black and white charms are really essentially equivalent appears first of all from the similar psychological effects attaching to them. Further, the equivalence of the procedures can easily be seen from a simple theological consideration. The charmer who seeks to force a cure, whether by God's help or that of the devil, stands in relation to these transcendent powers as one who would dispose over them. This is clear from ch. 1 of the well-known charm book, the 6th and 7th Book of Moses.[20]

What is not arguable, though, are that the roots of witchcraft, Satanism, and today's Satanic witchcraft are all found in a person becoming the possession of the Devil.

As we saw in the historical initiation into these satanic sciences, the person becomes bound to the Devil by means of a contract signed in blood. But blood pacts are not only found in witchcraft. The urge to form a blood-signed pact with Satan also seems to arise when a person is searching for a way to gain control in a situation in which he or she seems powerless. These persons differ from witches proper in that they do not desire to continuously practice magic, but ask only for a favor. For an example, Kurt Koch tells the story of a refugee girl who sold her soul to the Devil.

> A refugee girl who was without country, parents or livelihood drifted, in her emotional distress, into disreputable ways. During the night hours she earned herself a morsel of bitter food. One day she was caught in a police raid, and was committed to the Office of Health and Welfare, which established that she had infectious skin-disease. She spent a few weeks in detention. In her cell an unusual idea struck her. She took a sheet of paper, cut her finger, and with her blood wrote a pact with the devil. The conditions of this pact were as follows. If the devil would advance her to a respectable life, she for her part would give him her soul.[21]

Blood pacts and the giving of one's self to the Devil is one of the many commonalities between witchcraft and today's Satanism. Satanism, like witchcraft, has many forms, from the solitary Satanist to the devoted Satanic church-goer. Truzzi[22] has categorized four types of Satanism: (1) groups viewing Satan as an angel to be worshiped; (2) those grouped into certain sado-masochist clubs or flagellation societies; (3) groups arising out of what he called the "acid culture," of which the Charles Manson group was

20. Ibid., 136.
21. Ibid., 153.
22. Truzzi, *Witchcraft and Satanism.*

an example; and (4) the dominant form of group Satanism, the Church of Satan originating in San Francisco. The Church of Satan may no longer be the dominant group form since Truzzi's writing, however, it is still indicative of the type of public Satanic worship that is now also seen in other groups such as the Temple of Set. A fifth type of Satanism that seems to be growing in popularity is Satanism as practiced by sole individuals.

The becoming of a Satanist, or the entrance into a Satanic group, entails the giving of oneself to Satan, as illustrated in the following excerpt from an initiation ceremony where a married couple by the name of Kordiev was taken into membership.

> After a few drinks, the Kordievs were asked to strip. They also had to pay an initial subscription . . . for robes and apron. Once inside the ceremonial room they were given black satin aprons to wear, which had as a frontal decoration an orange eye and triangle. The color scheme of the room was in red, black and white. There were black tiles on the floor over which a white pentagram had been superimposed. Heavy red carpeting was hung around three walls while on the fourth a gigantic mural showed a chained and horned monster, surrounded by flames, about to attack a naked girl. Beneath this dramatic illustration was placed an altar with six black candles and, below it, a marble slab. Lighting was provided by a glowing brazier and surrounding it were half a dozen robed and hooded figures. The initiation ceremony began with one of these figures declaiming: "Brothers and sisters, on this occasion two strangers pray for admission to our fold, and it is for you, Disciples of the Prince of Darkness, to say now whether you have or have not any objection or reason why these two persons should not be received into our circle." This solemn pronouncement was rather anti-climaxed by the tape-recorded bleating of a goat. However, impetus was soon restored by a naked man covered in red oil who stood by the altar. He wore a black Devil mask and was accompanied by two young female acolytes who were wearing black robes. The Kordievs were then told to kneel before the "master" and some form of mild narcotic was thrown onto the brazier, giving off a thick, perfumed smoke. The Kordievs were then asked to promise eternal homage to Satan and to sign the pledge with their own blood. They were then given . . . satanic names . . . then the master placed his hand on the Kordiev's genitals and they felt a tingling sensation . . . a back-to-back dance followed, with which the ritual was complete . . . .[23]

23. Masters, *The Devil's Dominion*, 162–63.

This excerpt also illustrates some of the paraphernalia common to Satanic practice. Black, hooded robes with white and red linings are common. Black candles, goat heads, horned monsters, darkened rooms, and sexual rituals are all common. In the above example the officiate only grabs the two initiate's genitals, while in other ceremonies copulation between the high priest and a female member is an expected ceremony.[24] But most important to our present study is the historical tradition of giving oneself eternally to Satan, for it is this that indicates the person's voluntary possession by this personality of evil.

Many witches and Satanists may balk at the concept that they are possessed. Much as in our discussion of shamanism, the witch or Satanist may argue that it is they who control the demons rather than the demons controlling them. If one is to once again look at the practice of magic conjuring, and at the manner in which Satan is summoned, their argument might look plausible. But the idea that the witch or Satanist is actually still in sole possession of themselves is less credible when one observes the events surrounding a person who attempts to break the pact with Satan, as we will see during the review of the phenomena surrounding these activities.

Before looking at each of the specific phenomena associated with these practices, we need to take a look at the specifically Satanist offshoot of the witches Sabbath: the black mass. The black mass is characteristically a "blasphemous ceremony that exactly reverses everything in the Christian high mass."

> The altar is covered with a black cloth instead of a white one, the crucifix is hung upside down, hymns and prayers are sung and recited backwards, candles are black, the priest is preferably a defrocked one and whenever the name of God or Christ is used, it is spat upon or abused. Satan takes the place of Christ, water replaces wine in the chalice and a turnip or a similar satirical replacement is used instead of the host. Sexual rites are a more modern invention, and although the Devil is seen to be worshiped during the mass, the origins of the ceremony are more likely to be pagan.[25]

It is not only water and turnips that may replace the wine and bread of the Christian Eucharist, but almost any substance that is likely to revolt the partaker. "Some Black masses use urine or menstrual flow in place of the traditional wine in an attempt to evoke disgust and aversion to the ritual."[26]

24. Ibid.
25. Ibid., 112.
26. Moody, *Urban Witches*, 230.

Likewise, the communion wafer has been replaced by human excrement or even human flesh.[27] In recent years there has been more and more discussion surrounding the sacrificing of babies and small children and their being consumed as a part of the ritual. These are all used in an attempt to degrade the power of the Christian religion, and the dominant values of the society, in the mind of the Satanist.

> In many cases the exhortations and teachings of his [the Satanist's] Satanic colleagues are not sufficient to alleviate the sense of guilt and anxiety he feels when engaging in behavior forbidden by Judeo-Christian tradition. The novice may still cower before the charismatic power of Christian symbols; he may still feel guilty, still experience anxiety and fear in their presence. It is here that the blasphemies come into play, and they take many forms depending on the needs of the individuals involved. . . . If an individual can be conditioned to respond to a given stimulus, such as a communion wafer or wine, with disgust rather than fear, that stimulus's power to cause anxiety is diminished. Sexuality is also used. A young man who feared priests and nuns was deliberately involved in a scene in which two witches dressed as nuns interacted with him sexually; his former neurotic fear was replaced by a mildly erotic curiosity even in the presence of real nuns. The naked altar—a beautiful young witch—introduces another deliberate note of sexuality into a formerly awe-inspiring scene.[28]

We can see that the world is a place much different for the black witch and the Satanist, than it is for the typical person. It is a place where much of what is typically seen as good is viewed as bad, what is normally seen as perverse has become desirable. The value-stance of many witches and Satanists is the inverse of the Judeo-Christian society in which it is presently found. This is seen in the black masses, and if it were confined to these perverse ceremonies there might not be much need for concern. However, some Satanists and satanic witches perform other ritualistic activities that are even more disturbing. Among these are murder, kidnapping, child-abuse, child-sacrifice, cannibalism, and necromancy. Though these are the activities of the extreme forms of witchcraft and Satanism, they are still being practiced to a greater extent than one would like to believe.[29] As support groups form for persons who believe themselves to have been the victims

27. Cf., Masters, *The Devil's Dominion*; Smith and Pazder, *Michelle Remembers*.

28. Moody, *Urban Witches*, 230.

29. Cf., Raschke, *Painted Black*; Smith and Pazder, *Michelle Remembers*.

of ritual abuse, more and more stories of horror arise. Even if some of these can be attributed to false memory syndrome, still there are enough stories to make us think twice before dismissing these phenomena as either extremely rare or altogether false.

Kidnapping by Satanist groups occurs for two primary reasons: to bring a child into the cult, or to provide a human sacrifice. If the child is to be inducted into Satanism, then it is abused and forced to take part in the ceremonies which may include ritualistic murder and cannibalism. This is done to destroy the child's belief in God and his or her sense of wrongdoing with regard to what is happening. If a human sacrifice has been made, the body is usually burned and the ashes may then be ingested by those present.[30] Murder is also an activity of Satanists. Murder may take place for a variety of reasons, but usually it has some ritualistic overtones. Now infamous examples are the Tate-La Bianca killings performed by the Charles Manson cult and the Los Angeles "Night Stalker" case of Richard Ramirez.[31]

Necromancy is an activity of satanic witches. This is the attempt to gain control over the dead, and the actual practice of this magical activity involves the exhuming of bodies from the grave and the using of parts of these bodies in the spell to be cast.

Necromancy leads us to the magical activities of witches and some Satanists. As we have seen, witches are supposed to employ demons in order to perform their magic. Even the supposedly white witches of today, who deny any converse with demons, still employ archaic magic spells which are actually invocations of demons or the devil. The spells are used for such endeavors as divination and the seeing of the past and the future; making oneself invisible and maintaining youth; as well as the more malicious controlling of others and even murder by magic.[32]

Witches and Satanists have also been seen to develop mediumistic abilities. They have reported seeing spirits, especially during their black masses.[33] Clairvoyance has been seen as a common occurrence.[34] Soul excursions, or spirit travel, have also been recorded. In medieval times, the witches were said to travel to their Sabbath by two manners: either they physically secreted themselves off to a secluded grove there to meet other witches, or they would enter a trance, and fly to a visionary Sabbath. The

30. Raschke, *Painted Black*; Smith and Pazder, *Michelle Remembers*; Sakheim and Devine, *Out of Darkness: Exploring Satanism and Ritual Abuse*.

31. Raschke, *Painted Black*; Truzzi, *Witchcraft and Satanism*.

32. Masters, *The Devil's Dominion*, 130; Truzzi, *Witchcraft and Satanism*, 232.

33. Ibid., 134.

34. Koch, *Christian Counseling and Occultism*, 186.

latter type is reminiscent of the shaman's journey, for the witch will return and be able to relate the flight and the occurrences at the Sabbath.[35]

Mediumistic activity is said not only to be procured by the witches, or Satanists, for themselves, but this activity is also transferable to future generations.[36] This has been seen both in folklore and in the experience of ancestor possession. The British psychiatrist R. K. McAll[37] has also observed this in work with his patients. He has found that for many of his patients, a relative had been in some way connected with an occult practice. This may have contributed to the present patient's problem, for when the patient renounced this ancestor's activity, or took Holy Communion for that person, it was then that the patient's pathology ceased. Hauntings and poltergeist phenomena are also said to have been experienced in houses where witches have lived, and where Satanists have held their ceremonies.[38]

Some of the greatest evidence for the witch and the Satanist actually being possessed is encountered in cases where the person attempts to break the blood pact, for it is here that negative phenomena—from the witches' viewpoint—begin to happen. Such things as suicide, mental illness, depression, compulsions, poltergeist activity, and maniacal laughter with no known source, may occur.

Earlier, as we were investigating Spiritualism, we saw that suicide, fatal accidents, psychoses, and horrible death-bed scenes were all encountered, and the same is true in the lives of witches and Satanists, to a degree greater than chance. Anthony Masters relates an incident which is not uncommon for those who attempt to break away from witchcraft and Satanic activities. It is an incident which includes the same couple we earlier witnessed being initiated into the Satanic group. After observing a ceremony they disliked they left the group, and hardship followed them.

> The Kordievs attended a black mass, of which they strongly disapproved. A young girl member of the circle had been accused of betraying confidences. Because of this she had to form a naked altar while the black mass was said over her. Eventually the master had sexual intercourse with her and a wax dummy which had particles of nail and hair from the "outsider" [the one to whom she had betrayed the confidences] was placed on the altar. A black cock was sacrificed and members of the circle were

35. Koch, *Christian Counseling and Occultism*, 212; Seligmann, *The Mirror of Magic*, 244.

36. Koch, *Christian Counseling and Occultism*, 187.

37. McAll, *Healing the Family Tree*.

38. Koch, *Christian Counseling and Occultism*, 189.

obliged to drink its warm blood from a chalice. Later Kordiev discovered that the outsider was a prominent businessman, and that he had died of a heart attack on the same evening as the black mass ritual had been carried out. Before their "confirmation" ceremony took place the Kordievs decided to leave the circle. But this was not so easy. Their financial luck turned, and Kordiev's wife came near to breakdown. They moved to remote Romney Marsh in Kent but serious misfortune followed them. A huge toad appeared on the doorstep, maniacal laughter echoed through the house, and much of the interior of the building was mysteriously wrecked. . . . Worse was to follow: Despite forming a white magic coven, misfortune still occurred in Kordievs' lives. Then, in 1971, the breakages began again, and there was considerable poltergeist activity. Anne Kordiev appeared to be the center of these disturbances. For a while she seemed possessed and then threw herself from the bedroom window, breaking both legs. Against her will, Serge Kordiev put the house on the market. His wife told him that she would never leave it. Her prophecy was all too correct and a few months later she was dead.[39]

This type of occurrence is commonly reported by those who have taken part in Satanic activities.[40] Therefore, even though it may seem that the witch is in control of the demons, or that the Satanist is being especially blessed by Satan—merely because he or she worships the Devil—it soon becomes apparent who is actually in control when the person attempts to do that which is contrary to the blood signed agreement. It becomes quite clear that these persons are possessed.

---

39. Masters, *The Devil's Dominion*, 163–65.
40. Koch, *Christian Counseling and Occultism*.

10

The Compatibility of Possession States

To superimpose the forms of possession we have been studying on one
another is to view a phenomenon of almost singular regularity. Whether
it is mysticism or witchcraft, Voodoo or Shamanism, the phenomena found
in each are very similar.

Common to all these forms of possession, whether voluntary or involuntary, was a loss of self-control. This loss of self-control could occur in
conjunction with violent bodily reactions, such as trembling, convulsions,
twitches, and the like, or it could come on quickly and quietly. The loss of
self-control was predominately in the form of trances, these being either
ecstasies, raptures, or mediumistic in nature. The ability to recollect what
occurred during the trance varied with the type, with Voodoo and Spiritualism being the main forms that exhibited amnesic reactions.

Other forms of control loss were in the obsessions and compulsions
experienced by the individuals involved. These were usually seen in the
involuntary forms of possession such as demonic possessions in Christianity, werewolf possession in Voodoo, and in certain aspects of witchcraft
and Satanism.

Common also to these various possession states was a change of some
type in the speech of the possessed. In almost all forms the possessed person might acquire an ability to speak a previously unknown language, or to
understand a previously unknown language. Likewise, during the trance-
state of the possession, the voice of the individual involved might fluctuate
widely, with a common phenomenon being that the person's voice would
attain a falsetto. To most, this was an indication of the spirit speaking directly through the medium. The person was then taking on more of the
qualities of the spirit which was in possession. It was not only in voice that
the person would become more like the possessor, but in action and attitude
as well. In Voodoo, the practitioner might gain abilities similar to that of the

snake god that possessed him, or in shamanism the shaman might begin to act like the bird he or she had become in spirit. In most forms of possession these changes in personality would only remain during the trance. But in mysticism and Christianity the changes were more gradual and more long-lasting. The mystic would develop to become more and more removed from his or her own personality and become more like the Absolute which was his or her goal. Likewise, the Christian possessed by the Holy Spirit would gradually grow in the fruit of the Holy Spirit to become more and more like the personality of Jesus Christ.

Changes in the abilities of the possessed were common in all forms of possession. In most forms, the person was able to perform some incredible feat, such as walking on hot coals, cutting himself or others without pain, other forms of self-anesthesia, or becoming incredibly heavy. Bilocation—the ability to be in two places at once—or spirit-travel were found in most forms. The ability to heal oneself and others was also a common occurrence, as was the ability to control the spirits and nature. Levitation was common to many, but the need for little or no food was only reported in cases of mysticism.

The perceptions of the possessed were also changed. The ability to read others' thoughts, to hear without use of the auditory senses, and the ability to see the past and the future were commonly encountered phenomena. So also was the seeing of visions and the hearing of voices. These visions and voices were experienced both externally and internally, in corporeal form and in the form of inner visions. When the person would speak forth what he or she had seen or heard, these visions and voices would take the form of prophecy to the communities in which they were found.

Still other common occurrences were poltergeist-type phenomena, such as moving furniture, rapping in the walls, and the destruction of religious objects. Only in the Holy Spirit possessions were these found to be absent. Odors surrounding the possessed were also encountered, with the odor of death or sulfur especially surrounding demonic possession and shamanistic possessions, while pleasant, perfume-like odors surrounded the mystics. A temperature change in the vicinity of the possessed was also encountered; in demonic possessions, Spiritualistic possessions, witchcraft and Satanic possessions the room might become quite cold, and a cold breeze might be felt.

Some more negative aspects are encountered in all forms of possession, except for mysticism and possession by the Holy Spirit. These negative aspects include a tendency toward murder and other anti-social behaviors. Depression, mental illness, suicide, and accidental deaths are reported to be more common in these forms of possession than is typical in society.

When observing only the phenomena involved in these various forms, we may come to the conclusion that there is a universality to the possession state. The difference between these forms seems to lie in the practices and beliefs that surround them. The only form that stands forth as being significantly different from the others is that of the neo-Pentecostal baptized in the Holy Spirit, who does not practice the trance form of slaying in the Spirit. Here no sense of being out-of-control is encountered, nor any of the negative manifestations of possession states.

In this review of possession forms we have been looking only at those which have classically been seen as spirit-possession. Of future interest are other forms of possession that seem to have just as firm a hold on persons. Possession by the spirit of science, the spirit of a nation, or the spirit of humanism seem from the outset to be just as compelling a master as any of these other well-recognized and archaic spirits. Thus, the question may become clearer in the future, not whether possession is a valid phenomenon, but by what spirit is an individual possessed.

11

The Cultural Explanations

P ossession is not merely of historical or theological interest. Belief in possession, and the related phenomena, is still encountered in most cultures in every part of the world today. Belief in one of the forms of possession is common to nearly every society that has not embraced the rationalism of the industrialized countries. Although some societies, such as many Native American tribes, have not commonly held a belief in involuntary possession, even those usually have an intricate shamanistic culture, abounding with experiences of spirits and voluntary possession, of encounters with sorcery and witchcraft.

The majority of the excursions into cultural explanations of involuntary possession come from the field of anthropology, a field that concentrates primarily on beliefs and behaviors of peoples and the explanations of such in the context of the social milieu. Anthropology concentrates on the "what" of a belief and the individual's or group's behavior, as well as on the "why" of such events and attitudes in relation to the culture's needs and values. As we look at the various cultural explanations of involuntary possession, we find four dominant factors used by the anthropologist to explain the possession phenomenon.

First among these theories is the contention that involuntary possession is a culturally acceptable way of expressing illness, whether it be physical or mental.[1] One manner by which this is made manifest is in the reduced responsibility assigned by the society to the afflicted person for the manifested abnormal behaviors, as well as a consequent diminishing of the

1. Alland, *Possession in a Revivalistic Negro Church*; Kapferer, *Mind, Self and Other in Demonic Illness: The Negation and Reconstruction of Self*; Maduro, *Hoodoo Possession in San Francisco: Notes on Therapeutic Aspects of Regression*; Walker, *Ceremonial Spirit Possession in Africa and Afro-America*; Ward, *The Psychodynamics of Demon Possession*; Yap, *The Possession Syndrome: A Comparison of Hong Kong and French Findings*.

guilt felt by the one afflicted.[2] Erika Bourguignon has pointed out that "according to Opler in North India deviant, disrespectful behavior is explained as due to spirit possession, for this is the only way in which such breach of custom can be accounted for."[3]

Not only does the possession explanation reduce the guilt incurred by the afflicted person, it is also likely to gain for that person greater group support than if he or she were thought to be ill.[4] Due to the relative enigma of mental illness in most cultures—and fear of severe physical disease—the person labelled as ill is more likely to be ostracized from the group. Unlike this is the fate of the possessed person, who, on revealing a belief in the possibility that he or she is possessed, has the group gather around for support and for a culturally sanctioned healing ceremony or exorcism and the concomitant reinitiation into the society.[5] Finally, involuntary possession seems to relieve the afflicted person from the cognitive disorganization and perceptive disorientation associated with psychosis, since the event of a possession casts the afflicted one into what is another culturally sanctioned role: the role of the possessed.

Obeyesekere[6] has put forth three prime criteria which constitute the psychological dimensions of abnormality. These are: (1) A cognitive disorganization where the individual's cognitions are private and incommunicable. (2) A perceptive disorientation where the individual is perceiving the world in a manner that the remainder of the culture finds abnormal. (3) An affective disorientation where the afflicted individual's affect is in marked contrast to the others in the society. Obeyesekere observed that the person who is defined as mentally-ill in a society may fall into the above three categories and so be alienated from the remainder of the society, whereas the possessed person by being possessed—rather than ill—was able to avoid the first two of these criteria and so remain a member of the social group.

The afflicted person was able to ward off the cognitive disorganization since the demonic forces with which he or she was in contact were not culture-alien. Thus, if a person were to meet a tree-spirit on the streets of a middle American city that person would be perceived as being cognitively disorganized, and at least temporarily removed from the society, because tree-spirits are culture-alien in the society of twentieth-century America.

2. Maduro, *Hoodoo Possession in San Francisco: Notes on Therapeutic Aspects of Regression*; Ward, *The Psychodynamics of Demon Possession*.

3. Bourguignon, *Possession*, 7.

4. Ward, *The Psychodynamics of Demon Possession*.

5. Obeyesekere, *Psychocultural Exegesis of a Case of Spirit Possession in Sri Lanka*.

6. Obeyesekere, *The Idiom of Demonic Possession*.

Yet such an interpretation would not be made by the culture of an aboriginal group living along the upper reaches of the Amazon River. Rather, this latter group would accept the person's visitation and instead of isolating and rejecting the person, they would gather to the afflicted one and probably show that person more than normal attention. Fear of the demonic, where culture-alien, leads to a perception by society of the afflicted individual as being cognitively disorganized. Yet, demonic fears that are culture-bound inflict no societal penalty on the fearful individual, but may actually turn out to be advantageous.

Likewise, in a culture that has no demons, to see a demon is considered a hallucination or a perceptive disorientation. However in a culture maintaining a belief in the independent personal demonic, the seeing of a demon is not to be considered an idiosyncratic fantasy, but—from the non-belief point of view held by Obeyesekere—a culturally-constituted fantasy: a fantasy that allows the individual to maintain his or her ties to the group.

A second class of cultural explanations for possession is formed by those proposals that possessions are culturally acceptable manners of acting out forbidden behaviors within the society. This class of explanations may at first seem to fit more precisely into the psychological explanations of possession rather than the cultural, since we are here referring to such phenomena as catharsis and overcoming strict repressions. Yet, the cathartic acting-out is not viewed as socially reprehensible when it is done as a form of possession rather than as a psychopathology or a mere social rebellion. To express socially unacceptable hostility, or other socially unacceptable affect while in a state of spirit-possession will allow the person to so act-out while simultaneously remaining a part of the society, whereas psychopathology tends to alienate the individuals from the society.[7]

Langley provides us with an example from Malaysian society which illustrates this point as well as those of the previous class of explanations:

> As in many Islamic societies, Kelantan custom strongly discourages direct confrontation between individuals. Open hostility upsets the delicate fabric of the community, in particular the extended family. And as a result, there is undoubtedly much emotional repression in the society, especially within marriage. Moreover, a wife's role is restricted both in the home and in the mosque. Her role within marriage is unstable. Kelantan has one of the highest divorce rates in the world, and although Islamic law recognizes the rights of alimony these are rarely given. And

7. Langley, *Spirit-Possession, Exorcism and Social Context: An Anthropological Perspective with Theological Implications*; Obeyesekere, *Psychocultural Exegesis of a Case of Spirit Possession in Sri Lanka.*

as it is not considered proper to initiate a direct confrontation, all the repressed anger, jealousy and indignation concomitant with an imminent divorce is transferred to the spirit world. In this neutral and socially acceptable realm, latent hostility can be acted out. By a displacing of the real causes of the illness into a third force, the drama can be revealed in a non-disruptive way. Admission of guilt can be publicly announced without loss of face; and in the cathartic release of emotions . . . repressed feelings can be brought to the surface, but without absolute accusation. Moreover, all the important members of the patient's family are present, and both in viewing the proceedings and in having paid for the costly ritual, they are reaffirming their desire to see her reintegrated. [This] provides the patient with a theater in which she can at the same time act out her emotions and come to terms with her role in society. No blame is incurred since the illness is blamed on the spirit, and this helps diminish any sense of guilt that the patient might have in causing such an expensive affair to be held.[8]

This illustration also contains the seeds of two other commonly used modes of explanation: a conflict between the sexes and the role of social oppression. The concept of involuntary possession as the cathartic acting out of a conflict between the sexes arises primarily from the observations of the Zar possessions of eastern Africa and the Middle East.

Zar is a term used in Egypt, the Sudan, Ethiopia, and the Arabian Peninsula to refer to belief in possession by spirits and the ceremonies associated with this belief. The central theory of the Zar is the spirit-possession manifested by illness which can be alleviated by propitiating the spirits through ceremonies that consistently include dance and trance behaviors. Other features which the Zar shares with similar possession cults are that the spirits are peripheral to the major religious belief of the society and that the participants are predominantly women.[9]

The Zar has also been found in other areas of the Middle East and seems to be a concomitant of the Islamic societies in which it is found. In general, Islamic society is strongly patrilineal and male-dominated. Women are to be submissive to their husbands and are not allowed full participation in their religion. Divorce is easily obtained by men, but almost impossible for women. It is a society where for a woman to express her wants and needs in anything but a weak and submissive manner would

8. Langley, *Spirit-Possession, Exorcism and Social Context: An Anthropological Perspective with Theological Implications,* 227–28.

9. Saunders, *Variants in Zap Experience in an Egyptian Village.*

lead to her being punished harshly. Into this milieu falls the Zar possession of the women. During a possession a woman can express herself emotionally and sexually as well exhibit her power over men of the society without fear of severe retribution.

When such a possession is discovered a woman shaman and the friends of the patient gather for an elaborate ceremony. During this ceremony there is frantic dancing and release of affect culminating with the belief that the Zar spirits arrive and have intercourse with the women.[10] The ceremony of exorcism has then been completed and the patient has been reintegrated into the society.[11]

It seems obvious that in such a society the outlet of spirit-possession may be a necessity for these women. "When [women] are given little domestic security and are otherwise ill-protected from the pressures and exactions of men, women may thus resort to spirit-possession as a means of both airing their grievances obliquely, and of gaining some satisfaction." Langley also quotes the following story from Lewis that illustrates this phenomena:

> The wife of a well-to-do official was feeling out of sorts one morning and sitting morosely in his house, where there happened to be fifty pounds of ready cash belonging to her husband. An old woman who was a [zar] specialist came to visit her and soon convinced her that she was possessed by a [zar] spirit and would need to pay a lot of money for the mounting of a cathartic dance ceremony, if she were to recover. The wife readily fell in with the suggestion and the necessary [zar] expert was quickly engaged, food brought, and neighbouring women summoned to join the party. When the husband returned for his lunch at midday he was amazed to find the door to his house tightly barred and to hear a great hubbub inside. The shaman ordered his wife [to] not let him in, on pain of serious illness, and after knocking angrily for some time the husband lost patience and went away to eat his lunch in a tea-shop. When, in the evening, he finally got back from work, the party was over. His wife met him and explained that she had been suddenly taken ill, [zar] possession had been diagnosed and, alas, she had had to spend all his money on the cure. The husband accepted this disturbing news with remarkable restraint.[12]

---

10. Ellenberger, *The Discovery of the Unconscious: The History and Evolution of Dynamic Psychiatry.*

11. Bilo, *The Moroccan Demon in Israel: The Case of Evil Spirit Disease.*

12. Langley, *Spirit-Possession, Exorcism and Social Context: An Anthropological*

In such cases, it is not difficult to explain possession as the female's adaptation to a male-dominated society.

The Zar possession phenomenon can be taken to a more general level in the next explanation of possession. Yap[13] in his study of the possession-syndrome in Hong Kong and France concluded that the combination of three factors would lead to the possession-syndrome in an individual, or a group.

First, the afflicted person, or persons, would need to believe in the possibility of a person being possessed. This agrees with Bourguignon's contention that possession only exists where there is a belief in possession. The person is then confronted with a problem—either personal or instinctual—which she or he sees no hope in solving. Then, if this person is dependent and conforming in character, and occupies a position in society that does not allow a reasonable amount of self-assertion, this person will exhibit the possession-syndrome believing him- or herself to be possessed; as will others in that same group.

Pattison has also concluded that the presence of social oppression and of personal impotence has brought about the phenomenon of involuntary possession and a belief in demons.

> With an understanding of the social conditions which give rise to demonology, it is possible to see that contemporary social conditions are ripe in the Western world for the re-emergence of supernaturalistic belief systems, and even demonology. Society has been perceived as oppressive, trust in social institutions has disintegrated, social protest has been realistically dangerous, and a mood of helpless impotence has emerged. New hope, new meaning, and new purpose can be seen in the myriad of supernaturalistic systems now gaining devotees. So it should not surprise us that the evil [in] society should again be personified and symbolized in demonology. . . . [W]e see that rather than unexpected, it is most consonant with history that supernaturalism and demonology should again appear in our time. The nadir of scientific psychiatry offers least to Western man in terms of meaning, and people turn from the psychoanalyst to the exorcist.[14]

An existential philosophy that breeds hopelessness creates also the experience of impotence. This combined with perceived social oppression

---

Perspective with Theological Implications.

13. Yap, *The Possession Syndrome: A Comparison of Hong Kong and French Findings.*

14. Pattison, *Psychosocial Interpretations of Exorcism,* 9.

or social disintegration may all lead to the belief in and the experience of involuntary possession.

We have so far been discussing explanations of possession that relate to possession as an adaptive behavior that allows an individual to behave in a socially unacceptable manner without incurring social disapproval. Langley has also posited that along with social impotence, social marginality has a large role to play in possession. As he observed Malaysian, Somalian, Kenyan, and Afro-Christian society he noted that it was those persons of marginal identity in the society that tended to be those most afflicted with involuntary possession.

In Malaysia and Somalia women are the primary victims of possession, as well as being "subject to acute stress and deep insecurity associated with their lack of status in society; . . . marginal personages, existing on the margins of society, victims of marginality and its concomitant illnesses."[15] In Kenya those who were the ones afflicted with possession were men who were born to the warrior caste. Yet the warrior now has no functional purpose in Kenyan society. And marginality was also found to be a factor in the Afro-Christian possession cult Langley discusses. So, an individual's marginality within society, as well as the society itself being marginal or liminal—that is, the society being in the midst of change—are both seen as factors in the occurrence of involuntary possession.

Finally, possession is at times the explanation for an illness that does not respond to the ordinary forms of treatment.[16] This belief indicates that those societies that believe in possession do not immediately jump to the conclusion that one is possessed when one becomes ill. Rather, attempts at physical healing may frequently precede the speculation that possession may be present, much as it does in the practice of neo-Pentecostal Americans. "Possession is suspected most often when a person is ill and the condition does not respond to other cures such as herbal remedies, removal of the cases of specific illnesses induced by the evil eye, or removal of the effects of sorcery, and local medical practice."[17] When possession is so defined by a group, it can become the catch-all category for any illness that is unknown or does not respond in an expected manner.

As we have seen, involuntary possession is a phenomenon common throughout times and cultures. Most, if not all, of these explanations we have been discussing have been applied cross-culturally and are believed to be

15. Langley, *Spirit-Possession, Exorcism and Social Context: An Anthropological Perspective with Theological Implications*, 228.

16. Bourguignon, *Possession*; Saunders, *Variants in Zap Experience in an Egyptian Village*.

17. Saunders, *Variants in Zap Experience in an Egyptian Village*, 179.

the explanations for a unified phenomenon described under the rubric of involuntary or spontaneous possession. Whether these explanations actually fit the phenomena is a matter for further discussion. From a cursory review of the various forms of possession, many of these cultural explanations are brought into question. The manner by which these sociological explanations may explain the presence of such phenomena as parapsychological occurrences—mass suggestion or mass illusion—has not proven satisfactory. This form of problem does not negate these explanations, but illustrates their limitation in accounting for the occurrence of possession.

14

The Neuropsychological Explanations of Possession

W e now turn from the interpersonal explanations put forth by the anthropological community to the intrapsychic explanations of psychology. The theories put forth here are just as varied and, in many ways, just as convincing as those of the anthropologist. Most basic of these explanations are the neurophysiological, and so we shall examine them first.

Neurophysiological manifestations of possession states and the subsequent motor behaviors have provided some of the most concrete data observed with these disorders. Unfortunately most of the neurophysiological data that have been collected are in reference to ceremonial, or voluntary possessions, and not to involuntary possession. Therefore, we must immediately question the applicability of this data to our present topic. Yet Walker feels that the "non-ceremonial possession, like ceremonial possession . . . appears to be a basically normal, neurophysiological reaction to some kind of stress,"[1] and so both might exhibit similar patterns.

A major study of the physiological aspects of possession has been done by Sargent.[2] He, using Pavlovian concepts and theories, has attempted to explain the possession phenomena as the individual's physiological response to overstimulation of the sensorium, much the same as his earlier explanation of brainwashing.

> Sargent . . . uses a Pavlovian model to explain phenomena such as brainwashing and intense revivalistic-type religious experiences, which involve mechanisms similar to those involved in possession. His theory of transmarginal stimulation and

1. Walker, *Ceremonial Spirit Possession in Africa and Afro-America*, 25.

2. Sargent, *The Mind Possessed: A Physiology of Possession, Mysticism and Faith Healing.*

inhibition interprets such phenomena as responses of the central nervous system to degrees of stimulation or deprivation of stimulation in excess of that with which the body is prepared to cope. This excess stimulation or deprivation upsets the organism to such a degree that hysteria, collapse, and/or a total disruption of previous conditioning may result. Fatigue, drugs, glandular changes, and other forms of stimulation can help lower the subject's resistance to such a breakdown. The temperament of the individual and the degree of stimulation play a large role in determining the actual form of the response obtained.[3]

Thus, it is the stress associated with overstimulation—or deprivation—that will bring about the resultant "possession," much as this caused a breakdown in Pavlov's dogs.

When the stress became too great for the test dogs one could observe a psychic breakdown. A reduction of the dog's resistance was obtained through exhaustion, starvation, drugs, and forced wakefulness. Sargent was interested in the brain inhibition which occurs under extreme stress, and of which one can discern two stages. One stage is where previously learned responses are erased and the other, which is more important for the psychology of possession, results in the greatly increased susceptibility of the individual to suggestion and conditioning. These breakdowns, which can be explained purely by brain physiology, also apply to humans. One can, according to Sargent, even regard Wesley's violent and lengthy testimonies on the tortures of Hell as so inductive of stress that individuals quite simply collapsed.[4]

Neurochemistry, as well as neurophysiology, may account for some of the supposed cases of possession encountered both today and historically. A neurochemical imbalance is the theoretical etiology of Tourette's disorder, a disorder with a phenomenology closely resembling certain aspects of demonic possessions.

This disorder is named for Gilles de la Tourette, a student of Charcot at Salpetriete, France in the late nineteenth century. There he encountered and worked with persons who exhibited strange movements and tics. Today, these tics are known to develop in childhood, as early as two years or as late as fifteen years of age. Kaplan and Sadock describe the symptoms as a:

3. Walker, *Ceremonial Spirit Possession in Africa and Afro-America*, 10

4. Wikstrom, *Possession as a Clinical Phenomenon: A Critique of the Medical Model*, 95.

repertoire of motor tics that involve not only spasmodic grimacing but also violent stereotyped tics. Spasmodic movements of
the upper part of the body may finally involve the whole body
until the tic-like actions are expressed by hopping, skipping,
jumping, grinding of the teeth, and other sudden motor outbursts that may, nevertheless, also involve a certain amount of
coordination. What gives this syndrome its specific flavor and
what is pathognomonic for it is that the patients are compelled
to utter profanities or obscenities, usually repeatedly calling out
four-letter words. There is compulsive coughing, spitting, blow-
ing, or barking sounds. There also may be echolalia or palilalia
consisting of the repetition of words or short phrases immediately after the patient has heard them. This strange behavior
is exhibited spontaneously and unpredictably, although it may
sometimes be triggered or worsened when the patient is experiencing emotional stress or fatigue.[5]

This description is reminiscent of some of the happenings to the nuns
of Loudun, a historical case of group possession among a religious community.[6] All of these symptoms have occurred somewhere in recorded cases
of possession, and this fact therefore raises the question of whether what
has been seen historically as possession may actually be a form of Tourette's
disorder. As in possession, the Tourette's sufferer exhibits no thought disorders nor abnormal personality characteristics. It is also found more often
in families with a history of the disorder, as is possession.[7] The cause of Tourette's disorder has not been completely determined, but the evidence for
a hyperactivity of the dopaminergic system contributing to the etiology has
grown. It is known that the neurotransmitter dopamine "plays a significant
role in the involuntary regulation of postural and motor behavior."[8]

There may be a good basis for looking at a dopamine imbalance as the
cause of some possession phenomena. Yet, Tourette's disorder itself as an
explanation for many cases of possession is not satisfactory, since the onset
of Tourette's disorder is usually sometime between the ages of two years and
fifteen years, while possessions are first seen at almost any period in the
life-cycle.

Another physiological view of possession has been put forth by Neher.[9] Neher studied the effects of drum-beats on the human nervous sys-

5. Kaplan and Sadock, *Comprehensive Textbook of Psychiatry/IV*, 1229.

6. Huxley, *The Devils of Loudun*.

7. McAll, *Healing the Family Tree*.

8. Kaplan and Sadock, *Comprehensive Textbook of Psychiatry/IV*, 1713.

9. Neher, *A Physiological Explanation of Unusual Behavior in Ceremonies Involving*

tem. He conjectured that it was not a response to stress, such as Sargent advocated, but rather the stimulation of the latent epileptoid tendencies within the individual that resulted in the possession trance.

> According to Neher, most individual brain wave frequencies are from eight to thirteen cycles per second. This is the most effective range for obtaining responses to rhythmic light stimuli. A slightly lower range for sound stimuli is more effective because of slower frequencies in the auditory region of the cortex. Hence one would expect to find most drum rhythms for possession ceremonies slightly below eight to thirteen beats per second. In Africa many dance rhythms have been found with seven to nine beats per second. In Haitian Vodun music agitated behavior occurs when drum rhythms reach eight or nine beats per second. This is neither the fastest rhythm possible nor is it particularly easy for the drummer to maintain.[10]

Because of this difficulty for the drummer it is believed that the rhythm is maintained for the specific purpose of inducing the trance, or altered state of consciousness. "[P]ossession falls clearly within the category to which Ludwig refers as 'altered states of consciousness.'"[11]

Ludwig has defined five types of situations which usually result in an altered state of consciousness. Of these five the stress of overstimulation is only one, thus expanding the possibilities for the physiological causes of the possession phenomena. Walker has summarized these five situations as:

1. Reduction of exteroceptive stimulation and/or motor activity—result of absolute reduction of sensory input, changes in pattern of sensory data, or constant exposure to repetitive, monotonous stimuli—which includes hypnotic trance; [altered states of consciousness] from prolonged social isolation, e.g., mystics, ascetics.

2. Increase of exteroceptive stimulation and/or motor activity and/or emotion—excitatory mental states resulting mainly from sensory overloading or bombardment, which may or may not be accompanied by strenuous physical activity or exertion. Profound emotional arousal and mental fatigue may be major contributing factors. Dance and music trance in response to rhythmic drumming; hyperkinetic trance states associated with emotional mental contagion, often in group

---

Drums.

10. Walker, *Ceremonial Spirit Possession in Africa and Afro-America*, 18

11. Ibid., 11.

or mob setting; religious conversion and healing trance experiences during revivalistic meetings; mental aberrations, associated with certain rites of passage; spirit possession states; shamanistic, divinatory, prophetic, and ecstatic trances.

3. Increased alertness or mental involvement: these result from . . . focused or selective hyperalterness and results of peripheral hyperalterness for prolonged periods; . . . fervent praying; total involvement in listening to dynamic speaker; trance resulting from watching a revolving object.

4. Decreased alertness or relaxation of critical faculties: passive state of mind with minimum of active, goal-directed thinking.

5. Presence of somatopsychological factors: results from alterations in body chemistry or neurophysiology which are deliberate or because of a situation over which the individual has no control . . . drowsiness; dehydration; hypoglycemia from fasting; [hyperventilation]; hormone disturbance; sleep deprivation.[12]

These are the situations that may lead to an altered state of consciousness. Walker goes on to cite Ludwig's description of the characteristic features of altered states of consciousness. These characteristics include:

1. Alteration in thinking: inward shift in direction of attention; disturbed memory, concentration, judgment.

2. Disturbed time sense.

3. Loss of control: may gain greater control or truth through loss of conscious control, e.g., identity with source of greater power.

4. Change in emotional expression: less control, inhibition; more primitive, extreme emotions; may be detached.

5. Body image changes: depersonalization, body-mind schism, dissolution of boundaries between self and others or universe, feeling of oneness or transcendence.

6. Perceptual distortions—hallucinations and pseudohallucinations; content of perceptual aberrations determined by culture, group, individual, [and]/or neurophysiological factors. May represent wish fulfillment, expression of basic fears or conflicts, or phenomena of little dynamic importance.

12. Ibid., 11–12.

7. Change in meaning or significance; attach increased meaning or significance to subjective experiences, ideas, perceptions in such state; often feelings of profound truth, insight, illumination. This feeling of increased significance or importance is one of most important features of religious or mystical consciousness, and is probably a major feature in stabilizing many religious groups.

8. Sense of ineffable; because unique, subjective experience, hard to communicate nature or essence to one who has not undergone it; tendency not to remember.

9. Feelings of rejuvenation, renewed hope.

10. Hypersuggestibility; increased propensity of person to accept and/or automatically respond to specific statements, i.e., commands or instructions of leader, or to non-specific cues as cultural group expectations. The distinguishing feature of these states is the hypnotized subject's emotional conviction that the world is as suggested by the hypnotist rather than a pseudo-perception based on this suggestion. There is also a reduction of the effective range of critical faculties with an attendant decrease in the capacity for reality testing, i.e., an inability to distinguish between subjective and objective reality. This situation creates a compensatory need to bolster such faculties by seeking props and guidance in an effort to relieve the anxiety usually associated with such a loss of control. There is increased reliance on an authority who is seen as omnipotent.

   With the "dissolution of self boundaries," an important feature of ASC's, the subject has a tendency to identify with an authority [in possession this would be the god or spirit, priest, and total community] whose wishes and commands are seen as the individual's own. As a result of all these factors there occurs a monomotivational state in which the person strives to realize in concrete behavior, the thought or ideas he experiences as subjective reality. This subjective reality is determined by the expectations of the authority figure or group as well as by the individual's own wishes and fears. In an altered state of consciousness in which external direction and structure are ambiguous or ill-defined (e.g., panic, acute psychosis) the person's internal mental productions are his major guide in the perception of reality, and thus have a large role in determining his behavior. In this case the subject is more susceptible to the dictates of this emotions and the fantasies and thoughts associated with them than to the directions given by other people.[13]

Finally Walker lists the features of possession as Raymond Prince has delineated them:

1. Induction of possession state frequently achieved by dancing to music with a pronounced and rapid beat.

2. It frequently follows a period of starvation and/or overbreathing; hypoglycemia and overbreathing both cause a slowing of the brain waves, as little as three minutes of the latter being sufficient to effect the change.

3. Onset of possession period marked by brief period of inhibition or collapse.

4. In neophytes collapse may be followed by period of hyperactivity; once experience is acquired, controlled, deity-specific behavior pattern emerges.

5. During state of possession frequent fine tremors of head and limbs and sometimes grosser, convulsive jerks; diminution of sensory acuity may be evident; the initial collapse state, muscular jerks, and fine tremors suggest neurophysiological changes.

6. Return to normal consciousness followed by sleep of exhaustion from which subject awakens in state of mild euphoria.[14]

After reviewing these lists it can be seen that the state of consciousness achieved by a person during ceremonial possession is very similar to the classical categories for altered states of consciousness of all types, whether due to daydreams, drugs, or hypnosis. Also, much of this research can be applied to involuntary possessions as well, although not to all involuntary possessions. An important fact is that the involuntary possession is not induced by either rhythmic dancing or music. Thus, if Neher's theory is to be applied to involuntary possessions, some other means of stimulating the latent epileptoid potential must be discovered.

But the most telling of the problems regarding the neurophysiological approach to possession is also one of the primary problems associated with the behavioristic and positivistic approach to psychology in general: "these theories only concentrate on the biological conditions for the external form

13. Walker, *Ceremonial Spirit Possession in Africa and Afro-America*, 13–14.

14. Ibid., 15.

of possession. What these theories . . . do not discuss is the specific content that the experience has for the individual and the collective."[15] The individual as a gestalt is ignored in these studies in favor of the supposedly objective data of physiology. Yet such "objective data" are always questionable when taken out of the context of the person's experience as a whole.

The study of the neurophysiology of possession is both informative and important in leading us toward an understanding of the phenomena involved. But this is where such a study stops, for it cannot be used as an explanation for possession unless more conclusive evidence is gathered, for these studies do not answer the fundamental question as to whether the neurophysiological state is the cause or the result of possession. The neurophysiological response cannot be assumed to be a cause merely because it is present, concurrent with an individual's certain state of being.

Neurophysiological Mimics of Possession

A commonly held conception is that possession phenomena are merely the historical understanding of now recognizable neurophysiological disorders. This is a reasonable conjecture and many such disorders exhibit the bizarre behaviors typically viewed as possession. We have already looked at Tourette's syndrome as just such a condition. Others may include drug induced behaviors and psychoses. After over fifty years of common recreational drug use, we are all aware of the effects of hallucinogens such as LSD, peyote, magic mushrooms; the debilitating effects of methamphetamines, Ecstasy, and marijuana. We know that a person intoxicated with PCP can exhibit strength beyond normal, so much so that a person so intoxicated casting large police officers aside like rag dolls is no longer a shock. However, most persons exhibiting possession symptoms are not necessarily using a drug. A simple question for a person exhibiting bizarre behaviors is whether they are presently influenced by some drug. If they are not—and this can be determined both by observing common signs of drug intoxication, as well as merely asking them or their friends—then this explanation for the behavior can be ruled out.

The ruling out of intoxication follows the basic principle of all good diagnosis, one which looks for the simplest explanation first. Diagnosis is based on Occam's Razor, which states that amongst competing theories the one with fewest assumptions is likely the best. Guided by this principle, a person

15. Wikstrom, *Possession as a Clinical Phenomenon: A Critique of the Medical Model*, 96.

exhibiting bizarre behavior is first analyzed by blood tests, genetic analysis, and brain scans, to determine any organic origin to the behavior.

Other neurological disorders to rule out are brain tumors, which may result in certain bizarre behaviors—such as ecstatic epilepsy—as will traumatic brain injuries, of which there has been a dramatic increase as a result of war injuries. Ecstatic epilepsy may be mistaken for incubus possessions and attacks because there is a sense of bliss combined with intense sexual feelings and satisfaction. It can even seem beyond sexual by some and may be experienced as deeply spiritual. One fifty-three-year-old teacher described her ecstatic seizure by saying, "The feeling was almost out of this world. This led to a feeling of complete serenity, total peace, no worries; it felt beautiful, everything was great. . . . Maybe the closest sensation that I know would be an orgasm, but what I felt was not at all sexual, . . . it was almost religious."

Anti-NMDA receptor encephalitis is an auto-immune condition that produces bizarre, impulsive behaviors easily mistaken for possession. This brain disorder is 80 percent more prevalent in women and is caused by antibodies attacking the brain, causing swelling and inflammation. The result is a condition where one minute a patient may be acting normally and the next instance develop extreme paranoia and an inability to control their limbs. Some patients even describe their brains as being on fire.

Another demon-possession-mimicking disorder is Othello syndrome, or Lewy-body dementia. It was named after Shakespeare's character Othello—who killed his wife, Desdemona—believing that she was having an affair. Patients develop the same stubborn delusions of suspicion and jealousy toward their spouses and constantly accuse them of infidelity. Some patients experience hallucinations of their spouse having sex with someone else. In the majority of such patients the cause is the disease affecting the right frontal lobe of the brain. In other instances, it is brought on by the use of dopamine therapy for Parkinson's disease at which point merely reducing or stopping the medication may alleviate the symptoms of Othello syndrome. Like Othello, patients can become dangerously violent. Men with Othello syndrome have tried to strangle their wives or start fights with neighborhood men suspected of being their wives' lovers.

Huntington's disease also results in possession-like behaviors. Caused by a mutation in the Huntington gene, Huntington's disease is a rare inherited disorder that breaks down nerve cells in the brain over time, affecting a patient's behavior and movement. Later, in advanced stages, the disease mimics historical descriptions of demon possession as the patient exhibits uncoordinated, jerky body movements and a decline in mental abilities and behavioral problems which generally decline into full dementia.

A final illustration is an interesting mimic known as McLeod neu-roacanthocytosis syndrome. According to Southern Methodist University researchers, McLeod syndrome may have been the real reason Henry VIII of England beheaded two of his six wives. Initially, Henry VIII was strong, athletic, and generous. Then, at around forty years of age, he began to experience weakness and atrophy in his legs, which eventually resulted in immobility. He also descended into psychotic paranoia, ultimately be-heading his wives.

McLeod syndrome is specific to the Kell blood group, which causes difficulty in pregnancy, which may also explain the difficult pregnancies of Henry VIII's wives and mistresses. They were pregnant with at least eleven of his children, but only four lived past infancy. Assuming Henry VIII carried the Kell antigen in his blood, and his wives did not, then they would only be able to have a healthy first child before losing every one thereafter.

McLeod syndrome is a neurological disease that is often first noticed in midlife typified by seizures, muscle weakness and atrophy, involuntary jerking of the legs and arms, grimacing, vocalizations like grunting, men-tal deterioration, depression, anxiety, emotional instability, and lack of self-restraint.

These are merely a handful of neurological disorders that mimic some of the bizarre behaviors encountered in the possession state. However, each is clearly of organic origin and therefore fairly easily distinguishable from true possession phenomena.

13

Possession and the Hypnosis Theory

C losely allied with the neurophysiological theory—by means of its association with studies in altered states of consciousness—is the hypnosis
theory of possession. Due to the significant amount of research independently performed on hypnosis, it shall be considered separately from the
former theory.

According to this perspective, both hypnosis and possession function
by a similar means or process: regression in the service of the ego.[1] This differs from regression proper, in that during regression in the service of the ego
the ego itself remains intact and functioning, while during regression proper
the ego orders reality in a neurotic manner and lessens its ability to function
in a healthy manner. "In regression proper the id, ego, and superego are all
altered, whereas in regression in the service of the ego only part of the ego is
altered and it engages in altered interpersonal relations."[2]

In order to understand how regression in the service of the ego
works, it must be postulated that the ego can have associated to it various
subsystems which can be unknown to the waking ego. These subsystems
have access to repressed materials to which the waking ego does not. In a
regression in the service of the ego, "id-like phenomena are produced by
a subsystem which hallucinates and recalls repressed material, rather than
the total ego system."[3]

Those who hold to this theory of hypnosis believe that it is the subsystem that is being related to while the person is in the hypnotic trance, and
it is the subsystem that is relating to the environment during the trance, not
the total ego system. Thus, the person can speak of repressed material and,
when back in a normal state of consciousness, seem to forget it once again.

1. Walker, *Ceremonial Spirit Possession in Africa and Afro-America*.
2. Ibid., 34.
3. Ibid.

Yet we cannot actually say it was forgotten since the total ego system never actually had access to the material: it was only the subsystem which had such access.

Like hypnosis, it is the temporary assuming of primary control by such a subsystem that can seemingly explain the possession phenomena.

> According to Gill and Brenman's formulations, the most sig-
> nificant element in regression in the service of the ego, in terms
> of personality dynamics, is that a subsystem is temporarily set
> up in the ego to which the ego temporarily relinquishes con-
> trol of the functioning of the organism. . . . This ego subsystem
> is analogous to the personality of the deity in possession. The
> individual's executive faculties are temporarily placed in abey-
> ance as the deity takes over such habitual functions. When the
> possession is ended the devotee is again himself with ordinarily
> no recollection of what has happened.[4]

Other research has shown that these subsystems of the ego can act in a manner significantly unlike that of the waking ego.

> It has been discovered that in hypnotic states, where we know
> that the degree of suggestibility is greater, but also that the bar-
> riers for what is repressed or "dissociated from consciousness"
> are weaker, that so-called alter-personalities can appear. A new
> personality can spontaneously take command. The individual's
> language, diction, sentence rhythm, dialect, voice level, etc., can
> then change. An apparently completely new personality speaks
> through the lips of the person hypnotized.[5]

According to Gill and Brenman, regression in the service of the ego is:

1. more likely to occur as the ego grows more adaptive and less as the ego grows less so,

2. marked by a definite beginning and end,

3. reversible with a sudden and total reinstatement of the usual organization of the psyche,

4. terminable under emergency conditions by the subject unaided,

---

4. Ibid., 36.

5. Wikstrom, *Possession as a Clinical Phenomenon: A Critique of the Medical Model*, 98.

5. subject to occurrence only when the individual judges circumstances to be safe,

6. a state which is voluntarily sought by the subject and, in contrast to regression proper, active rather than passive.

All these factors also characterize traditionally regulated ceremonial possession.[6]

These factors lead us to question whether this theory is as applicable to involuntary possession as it is to voluntary possession or ceremonial possession.

It is true that this theory helps us to understand the involuntary possession research that indicates that the possessed person still functions within the society. But many of the remaining factors are clouded in darkness when it comes to involuntary possession. Involuntary possession may have a definite beginning and end, but it has also been shown to have a gradual onset. It may also be suddenly reversible, and the subject may be able to terminate it, but there has been no evidence to this effect. But the last two factors are what create the most concern regarding the applicability of this theory, for both of these factors call for the voluntary participation of the individual, which is in contrast to our discussion of involuntary possession. Whether regression in the service of the ego can occur against the will of the total ego system is unanswered by the possession research; yet it would seem doubtful, for the research into hypnotic induction has indicated the need for the subject's willing participation for the trance to occur.

6. Walker, *Ceremonial Spirit Possession in Africa and Afro-America*, 33.

14

Possession and the
Dissociative Disorders

The concept that such a subsystem of the ego can take over the individual's functioning without the consent or knowledge of the total ego system is implicit in the theory of the multiple personality or dissociative identity disorder, a disorder that has frequently been the psychological explanation for possession beliefs for it is easily perceived as possession.

Kenny found that "possession and multiple personality are phenomenologically similar."[1] According to Kenny, the distinction between the two is essentially made according to "culture-specific" bias. Those cultures that observe a belief in the spirit-world will understand the phenomena as due to possession while those cultures that do not observe such a conviction may turn to the more rational belief encompassed in the theory of multiple personalities within the individual psyche. Kenny also notes that even though "spirit possession is an anthropological commonplace, adequately reported cases of multiple personality are very few indeed."[2] Yet he once again explains this as due to cultural bias, the views of Western medicine and psychotherapy according little integrity to the "alter-personalities" relative to the ego, which is seen as the "more 'genuine' and integrated self."[3] Though it was true that cases of multiple personality were considered rare when Kenny was writing, this is not the case today. The diagnosis of the dissociative identity disorder—which is the formal designation of this phenomena—has made an astounding comeback. The reasons for this are many. One may be with the rise in the understanding and acknowledgement of child molestation and ritual abuse. Some whose descriptions of

1. Kenny, *Multiple Personality and Spirit Possession*, 337.
2. Ibid.
3. Ibid., 338.

abuse were labeled delusional are now believed to be truly recalling traumas. Previously they were diagnosed as psychotic, but are now seen as afflicted with dissociated memories. Another important reason may coincide
with the wane in the power of the psychoanalytic community within the
psychological world. Classical psychoanalysis and Freud are seen more as
historical artifacts than as patently viable theories by which to understand
human functioning. The plethora of other theories of psychological workings—especially the neurobiological—have taken their toll on the preemi-
nence of psychoanalytic theories. Likewise there has been a significant rise
in the attraction of Jungian-oriented theories and analytical psychology.
Jung's theory is based on a dissociative spectrum of phenomena while
Freud's theory was based on repression. Since repression—or its lack—figures prominently in hysterical conditions and schizophrenia, these pathol-
ogies have had higher rates of diagnostic incidence over the earlier decades
of the twentieth century. If a researcher, or therapist, observes the world
through the repression-oriented paradigm then repression-related explanations will abound. This is merely the result of confirmation bias. Due to
this, hysterical neuroses and the schizophrenic conditions were more commonly recognized. It is like the old adage, "If all you have is a hammer then
everything looks like a nail." If, on the other hand, a dissociative-oriented
paradigm is utilized then the door is reopened to explanations of a dissociative and transpersonal nature such as the multiple personality and the
"spiritual crises" now recognized more frequently.

Multiple personality and possession are similar being that "in each
case an afflicted individual may show alternating and sometimes quite
sharply contrasting traits in relation to the 'normal,' each set of which is
coherent enough to be regarded as a separate personality. Such groupings may become individualized to the point of acquiring proper names
of their own and affirming their own identities by denying knowledge of
their compatriots. . . . Thus, the spirit-possessed person acts out the role of
a specific deity and recalls nothing about having done so; in the same way,
the various phases of a multiple personality identify themselves through
different names and claim to be ignorant of the existence and activities of
their partners."[4]

The process of multiple personality is postulated to be the same as
that of hypnosis and regression in the service of the ego. It is the subsystem
of the ego that takes on the appearance of being an independent—and at
times foreign—personality within the individual. It is the subsystem—or
systems—that become the "other" to the ego's "me."

4. Kenny, *Multiple Personality and Spirit Possession*, 337.

As with hypnosis and possession, the multiple personality disorder is one in which the person's ego does remain intact and relatively functional. "[W]hereas the hysterias could be attributed to a disintegration of higher organization, multiple personalities were relatively functional, with each personality being more or less capable of the tasks demanded in everyday life."[5] Therefore, we can see that possession—as it is related to both the theories of hypnosis and multiple personality—seemingly fits best into the diagnostic category of dissociative disorders. The multiple personality and the possessed do not seem to exhibit marked neurotic functioning; nor would the intactness of ego functioning lend validity to the assertion that "daimon possession [is] the traditional name through history for psychosis" as Rollo May and others would have us believe.[6]

The theories surrounding multiple personality could help us move another step forward in understanding possession. For whereas by the hypnosis theory we could not explain how a person could be made to enter the trance state of the ego subsystem involuntarily, we can see in multiple personality that, in times of stress, the individual may—by an unnamed process—switch from ego-functioning to subsystem functioning.

Yet this theory, too, is lacking in its ability to explain possession as a specific form of psychopathology. Even though we have been able to rule out neurotic and psychotic modes of functioning, still the dissociative disorders do not subsume possession with complete clarity.

The various editions of the *Diagnostic and Statistical Manual* of the American Psychiatric Association have maintained a rather consistent definition of a dissociative disorder. It has stated that the essential feature of the dissociative disorders

> involve a disturbance in the integrated organization of consciousness, memory, identity, emotion, perception, body representation, motor control, and behavior. Events normally experienced on a smooth continuum are isolated from the other mental processes with which they would ordinarily be associated. This discontinuity results in a variety of dissociative disorders depending on the primary cognitive process affected. When memories are poorly integrated, the resulting disorder is dissociative amnesia. If the amnesia also includes aimless wandering, the specifier "with dissociative fugue" is used. Fragmentation of identity results in dissociative identity disorder (DID). Disordered perception yields depersonalization/derealization disorder and, in conjunction with the symptoms

5. Ibid., 340.
6. May, *Love and Will*, 123.

of posttraumatic stress disorder (PTSD), produces its dissociative subtype. Dissociation of aspects of consciousness is also involved in acute stress disorder.

Yet in many of the documented possessions the onset has not been sudden but rather it has been gradual, even occurring over a span of many years.[7] Also, for the possessed person the sense of unreality and the inability to recall events need not be present.

A fifteen-year-old girl I saw in therapy for some months exhibited many of the characteristics of possession. She had been practicing witchcraft since she was six years old and reported that she had developed some psychic abilities because of her witchcraft, primarily psychokinesis and to a limited extent mind-control. She consulted me because she was hearing what she described as externally audible voices that were telling her to kill herself, which understandably frightened her. She described these voices as very deep, deeper than a man's, and that they would laugh at her in a very evil manner. Though this does not immediately indicate a possession the following information does.

She reported that many years earlier she had been possessed by the ghost of an old man. She had seen this ghost sitting in a tree smoking a pipe before it entered her and possessed her. The ghost, upon seeing her, left the tree and entered into her body. From then on she felt the need to watch horror movies and to witness violence which she asserted she might not have done if not driven to do so by the wishes of her possessor—one she referred to as the "Other." The Other craved violence, while she preferred to avoid it if possible. For example, she once spoke about watching a horror movie and being interrupted by a friend. In response to the interruption she told the friend that she would like to go and do something else, but the Other wanted to watch the movie so she too must stay. She felt that if she tried to leave the movie that the Other would get very mad at her, and that he would not allow her to leave, even though volitionally she wished to do so. The movie was filled with scenes of human dismemberment which she said sickened her, however she simultaneously could feel the excitement of the Other.

This episode indicates the problems we encounter when we try to diagnose a possession as a multiple personality or a dissociative disorder in general. This girl had no problem in recalling what both personalities—her own and the Other's—were wanting, feeling, and doing. Neither did she feel a sense of unreality, either of her own identity or the Other's. Rather she experienced these as two separate personalities present within

7. Martin, *Hostage to the Devil*.

the same moment. She also experienced the Other to be a separate en-tity—different from herself—which invaded her body, and not as another part of herself.

Therefore, though it is illuminating to view possession from the per-spective of altered states of consciousness and dissociative disorders, still we cannot limit possessions to these explanatory systems, for there is still more to the possession syndrome than can be construed from these models.

15

Other Disorders to Which Possession is Commonly Attributed

Almost every diagnostic category has been utilized at one time or another in order to demythologize possession. We find that historical possessions are now described as cases of schizophrenia, paranoia, hysteria, obsessive-compulsive disorders, and multiple personality disorder. Quite recently, today's more popular diagnostic labels have been invoked in order to explain historical possessions. Now we may hear theorists describing possession as due to narcissistic or borderline personality formations, or falling back to the description of the possessed as an antisocial personality.

We have already looked at the schizophrenic hypothesis briefly. Many times the possessed can be characterized as having hallucinatory experiences as well as being marginal personages in society, and so seemingly fit the bill as a schizophrenic. Yet we have also seen that in many situations the ego of the possessed is intact and can even be high functioning, thus making us wonder about the schizophrenic diagnosis in particular, and any generalized diagnosis of psychosis for the possessed.

Paranoia has also been used as a method of explanation, though less frequently than that of schizophrenia. Especially when we review the cases of multiple possessions, such as the famous case of the nuns of Loudun, the diagnosis of a *folie a deux*—or the newer name of the shared psychotic disorder—is invoked. Kiraly,[1] in a study of a mother and daughter who both believed themselves to be possessed, came to the conclusion that the daughter was actually suffering from paranoia and the mother began to share her daughter's delusions rather than lose their relationship.

In many ways Kiraly may be correct in the diagnosis, for both are exhibiting an abnormal perception of reality—according to the manner that

1. Kiraly, *Folie a deux: A Case of 'Demonic Possession' Involving Mother and Daughter.*

134

our society tends to define reality—which leads to the paranoid classification. But to be so diagnosed actually says very little about the dynamics of the situation. The paranoid diagnosis is actually a very general one. In a sense, it is a catch-all for what does not seem to fit elsewhere. "What distinguishes the Paranoid Disorders is that they do not have all the symptoms to meet the criteria for other disorders. They simply feature an organized delusional system in an otherwise more or less intact individual."[2]

When we look at the case that Kiraly presents we find that in many ways it fits the criteria for a classical possession, except that the daughter is seemingly more open about discussing the presence of the demonic than is the norm in other suspected possessions. Otherwise many of the symptoms are similar, as well as the presence of a common precursor to many supposed possessions: the delving into the occult.

Thus, to say that this possession may be a form of paranoia may be technically correct, but it does not actually give us any more information about the specific phenomenology found in these cases than does giving it the classical definition of demonic possession. To define it so may allow us access to the literature on paranoia in our search for an understanding of possession, but that is about the extent of help this diagnosis gives us, for it is in many ways merely a renaming of the phenomenon to make us more comfortable with it, rather than a means to understanding.

Two of the common symptoms of possession have been obsessions and compulsions. Because of this the obsessive-compulsive neurosis has, in a common-sense way, been used as the explanation of the possession phenomena. Once again, as with paranoia, this explanation has its merits. Yet the question immediately arises as to whether these symptoms are actually a part of the possession disorder, or if possession is actually an obsessive-compulsive disorder. Though in many cases this circular argument may be unanswerable, in the general case we can discard this diagnosis as viable. Primarily this is true because most possessions exhibit what are classified as hallucinatory activity or marked delusions and thus force the diagnosis toward the psychotic rather than neurotic end of the spectrum. But also we must recognize that the definition of what is obsessive or compulsive is in many ways arbitrary. "Many forms of reaction which today are designated as compulsion neuroses are normal and institutionalized in other civilizations."[3] Thus, even though we may view the seeming obsessions of the possessed, to reduce the diagnosis and treatment of the possessed's disorder to an obsessive neurosis seems uncommonly limiting.

2. Webb, *DSM-III Training Guide*.
3. Fenichel, *The Psychoanalytic Theory of Neurosis*, 586.

The character or personality disorders are also being used as factors in what has previously been seen as possession. Even though the antisocial personality has for quite some time been an explanation, today the borderline and narcissistic character formations are also being examined as possible entries in the contest to diagnose the person formerly classified as possessed.

In his book, *People of the Lie*, the psychiatrist Scott Peck, examined both the phenomena of possession and the possibilities of what he called the evil personality. Peck observed many of the symptoms of the evil personality to be very similar to those of the narcissistic personality, yet more extreme. Thus he has stated that the evil personality may be a sub-class of the narcissistic personality disorder. But how he draws the line between what is narcissistic and what is evil is nebulous. The work, however, appears promising in an attempt to understand those persons who view themselves as "people of the light" and yet whose actions exhibit what others may call evil. Even so, to begin to apply the metaphysical and metapsychological understanding of evil to an individual is dangerous. Since it is so unclear where the demarcation between "normal narcissism" and evil occurs there is the danger of putting a moral judgment on degrees of narcissism. But in this discussion what is most important for us about Peck's conclusions is that this form of pathology is being reconsidered in connection with evil and possession in general.

Likewise, it is not hard to see how the borderline personality disorder could be seen to explain possession. The dissociation from certain portions of the personality and the tendency to view people and things as all-good or all-bad—known as splitting—are predominant in the borderline's functioning and resemble in great detail the possession phenomena of being controlled by something else with that "something else" being all-bad while the person him- or herself is all-good.

The borderline personality disorder explanation could be invoked to explain possession, just as the narcissistic or antisocial character disorder can be. By examining possession in the light of the many possible diagnostic disorders we can see how easy it is to try to understand it by means of these because it seems to fit into so many categories. But as Fenichel has said the "devil neurosis . . . once studied by Freud, could not be fitted into any present diagnostic scheme."[4] The phenomenon of possession seems to fit into many diagnostic schemes and by so doing fits none. Possession seems to be a disorder that needs individual attention; a phenomenon that transcends our current diagnostic categories.

4. Ibid., 586.

16

Possession and Hysteria: A Psychoanalytic View of Possession

Another form of dissociative disorder for us to examine in relation to possession is conversion hysteria. It was hysteria in general, and conversion hysteria in particular, that launched Freud into his theory of psychoanalysis.

Charcot was actually the first to begin to observe the similarity between the cases of hysteria with which he had been working and the historical accounts of possession. As Charcot looked more closely at this similarity he came to understand that what had been seen as possession historically was in actuality a form of hysterical neurosis.

Freud became intrigued by Charcot's conclusions regarding the hysterical nature of possession and began to expand upon this concept with his own speculations. He agreed with Charcot that possession was a neurosis in "demonological trappings."[1] But Freud was to expand upon this by examining the etiology of this neurosis in the child's relationship to its father. Freud believed that this form of hysterical neurosis arose from the child's ambivalent feelings toward its father. These ambivalent feelings would result in the child tending to split apart its internal representation of the father, so that the father would be viewed as either all-good or all-bad. Though Freud had not conceptualized it in this way, the result is very similar to what we today view as the splitting defense, which we saw to be common in the borderline disorders.[2] But Freud believed that the child was unable to relate these representations with its actual father, and so the representations of a good and an evil father were generalized and then projected onto other individuals or groups within the society, or even formed into the metaphysi-

1. Freud, *A Seventeenth Century Demonological Neurosis*.

2. Wikstrom, *Possession as a Clinical Phenomenon: A Critique of the Medical Model*, 96.

cal constructions of a God and a Devil. Yet Freud believed that in actuality these constructions were merely the projected psychic representations of repressed wishes, impulses and drives.[3]

Freud illustrated this in his study of the Christoph Haizmann story. Christoph Haizmann was a seventeenth-century artist who was believed to have been possessed by the Devil due to his making two separate pacts with the Devil, in which he had sold his soul to Satan. Freud concluded that Haizmann made these pacts in an attempt to gain a father substitute for the actual father he had lost at a young age. The possession that ensued was then the internalization of the negative representation of the father, which Haizmann mistook for the Devil.[4]

This theory does have some clinical support. There are some research studies that show that individuals complaining of possession have also experienced a loss in their immediate family—whether due to divorce or to death—and usually this is their father.[5]

Even so, Freud has been criticized for his father-oriented psychology. The neo-analytic theorists of object-relations theory have made an about-face to deal primarily with the mother as the object of concern for the infant. For Winnicott it is the child's mothering that will determine the deficit in his or her ability to integrate the introjected good and bad object representations of the mother. If there is not this good-enough mothering then the integration of a whole person may not occur and a similar process of the projection of these part-object representations may happen, as we also saw in Freud's earlier theory.

Object relations theory has progressed; it now speaks of the infant's mothering in reference to the primary caretaker, whatever gender that person may be. By so doing Henderson believes that object relations theory may be able to redeem our understanding of possession,[6] for he, like Freud, believes that these representations are what possess a person and not a true devil or god.

The object relations theory of possession does fit more precisely with the research into the internal representations of God. Research using the Semantic Differential Parental Scale—a form of the Semantic Differential Scale molded to measure perceptions of parental figures—has found that individual's representations of God are actually integrations of their

3. Ibid., 97.

4. Freud, *A Seventeenth Century Demonological Neurosis*, 85–86.

5. Schendel, *Cacodemonomania and Exorcism in Children*.

6. Henderson, *Exorcism, Possession, and the Dracula Cult: A Synopsis of Object-relations Psychology*, 132,

symbolic representations of both parental dimensions on the scale. That is, the individual's representation of God is a complex unity of his or her symbolic representation of mother and father.[7]

If we strictly parallel Freud's speculation using this present research we may come to the conclusion that a possession is the result of the individual's attempt to gain a parental substitute, and that in some cases a splitting occurs where the positive maternal aspects of this symbolic representation constellate into the merciful and loving God and the negative paternal aspects constellate into the image of the Devil. Yet to move logically from the symbolic parental figure representation to the representation of God—or the Devil—is a biased procedure. "The representation of God apparently results from a complex interaction between the individual and his milieu, and it cannot be assumed that the idea of God merely reproduces, by some well-determined psychological mechanism, the content of a parental figure."[8]

Even though the conclusions presented by the object-relations theorists seem to be a plausible extension of Freud's speculation, in reality the situation is more complex as we encounter the necessity of considering the cultural determinates of an individual's representation of God and the Devil. And not only the present culture in which a person may be living but also the entire archetypal basis for the concept of a God and a Devil must be considered.

As these different levels of complexity are considered we begin to find that Jung's theory—which we will consider in more detail shortly—accounts better for these research findings. Jung's theory speaks to the archetypal basis of our representations of God and the Devil. Likewise, rather than being a father-oriented psychology, Jung has seen the psychic need to equally stress the maternal aspects of the psyche and the maternal representations within the individual. He has placed the Virgin Mary into the present theological Trinity to form the symbolic whole of a quaternity, thus indicating his conception of a representation of God which is a complex unity of the feminine and masculine aspects, much as Vergote's research indicated the complex unity of the God-image.

Thus, both the psychanalytic and the object relations conceptions of the origin of the God and Devil image, and the subsequent possession of individuals by these images, may be limited due to the lack of

7. Vergote, *The Parental Figures and the Representation of God: A Psychological and Cross-Cultural Study*, 206–7; cf. Rizzuto, *The Birth of the Living God: A Psychological Study*.

8. Vergote, *The Parental Figures and the Representation of God: A Psychological and Cross-Cultural Study*, 205.

consideration of the cultural and archetypal determinates involved. To confidently state that possession is the individual's attempt to gain a lost parental figure has little basis.

Before we leave our discussion of the psychoanalytic view of possession we need to look more closely at hysterical dissociation itself, for it was this process that led us into this discussion. Hysteria has been one of the major diagnostic labels attached to the possessed. One reason is that hypnosis seemed to cure hysteria, and as we saw earlier, hypnosis and possession have been allied in theory. Also many of the dramatic actions of the possessed resemble those of a hysterical neurosis.

Yap's studies have diagnosed many supposedly possessed persons as hysterics.[9] Yet these persons were usually more functional than typical hysterics and the possessed did not exhibit true hysterical personalities, even though they may have had a few of their characteristics.[10] The overt behavior of the possessed may mimic hysteria, yet the basis of this behavior has not been found to be attributable to an underlying hysterical personality. Similarly, Yap diagnosed many of those he studied to be schizophrenic, yet further studies have shown that even though the person may be exhibiting seemingly psychotic behavior, still this is without a concomitant weakening of ego boundaries as we observed in the cultural explanations for possession. Therefore Pattison feels that rather than a disease model being used to understand possession a culturally-minded model is needed.

Pattison has found that when such a culturally-minded model is employed the return of the afflicted person to healthy functioning is usually more easily facilitated than if the culture of the person is ignored. For instance, in the example of the Native American girl who was possessed by her grandfather as he was attempting to pass his shamanic power to her, Pattison gained little ground in the therapeutic process until the cultural form of exorcism was employed.

Henderson also warns of attempting to merely fit possession into one of our current diagnostic categories. As he says, "a well-known pitfall of scholarly endeavor is our propensity to dogmatize those theoretical postulates which are currently in vogue. It is accordingly fashionable at least in professional circles to dismiss the notions of possession and exorcism as outmoded medieval superstitions of, at best, historical interest. Such a dismissal would be decidedly premature."[11]

9. Yap, *The Possession Syndrome: A Comparison of Hong Kong and French Findings.*

10. Pattison, *Possession and Exorcism in Contemporary America.*

11. Henderson, *Exorcism and Possession in Psychotherapy Practice,* 131.

When the model we use to view the universe and the individual is limited to our present rationalistic, digital, or mechanistic model that denies the spirit-world any reality, then we are at a loss to explain and cure possession, except by using our known diagnostic categories and the subsequent methods. But when a worldview that admits the spirit-world is entertained, then possession is better understood and handled. To adequately approach the phenomenon of possession we need to move away from the digital models of human functioning that we so far have been considering. These models tend to be reductionistic and disease-oriented. We now need to turn to the wholistic, analogic models; to models that either explicitly or implicitly encompass an understanding of the human spirit. We shall now turn to the understanding of possession in the psychologies of Rollo May and Carl Gustav Jung.

17

Possession and the Human Spirit: An Existentialist Perspective

N ow we move on to considering two psychological theories that encompass the concept of the human spirit. To speak of the spirit is, for many, to reintroduce a concept that psychologists have for decades been trying to eradicate. For them the spirit harkens back to a time when the church ruled a person's thinking to the detriment of any advancement in science or human knowledge. The thought of a spirit brings to mind ephemeral beings that inhabit a mystic realm that is untouched and untouchable by the science of today. In part this is true, but this concern is unfounded and, as we will see in a moment, it can even be dangerous.

In today's psychological parlance, we would rather refer to the unconscious than speak in the classical language of religion and philosophy by referring to souls and spirits. Yet to merely change the models and metaphors from which we view the universe is not to eliminate the phenomena that in a previous model were explained differently. But this is what many today attempt to do, especially those who ascribe to the psychodynamic and behavior models of human functioning.

When we look closer at what is meant by the "unconscious" we find that it does not in actuality preclude a concept of a soul and a spirit, but rather can easily include such. Too many theorists today tend to reify the concept of the unconscious much as the religious community of the past tended to reify the concept of the soul and the spirit.[1] Yet the unconscious is not a *thing* as such. It is not really even a process. It is actually a description of something that is not something else. The unconscious is merely that which is not conscious. This can mean different things in different theories, but in general what is meant is that those processes that are not

1. Cf. Kuhn, *The Structure of Scientific Revolutions*.

directly associated with, or produced by the portions of the ego with which we are aware comprise the unconscious. We can see that to speak of the unconscious is to actually speak of a generality; a generality that can only be helped by more specificity. This is what both Rollo May and C. G. Jung did with their respective discussions of the daimonic and the spirit.

Though originally trained in the psychoanalytic and neo-Freudian models of psychology, Rollo May attempted to move out of the limitations of these models by embracing existentialism and a human anthropology that includes the human spirit. When May speaks of the human spirit, he does not do so directly but does so in classical terms referring to the ancient Greek concept of the inner *daimon*. For the Greek, the *daimon* was both a subjective inner experience and an objective outer experience.[2] May concurs with this, yet even though acknowledging this, he primarily discusses the daimonic as if it were only an inner subjective phenomenon.[3] But May sees that, in its existential sense, the daimonic is more than a psychic process, for it retains the qualities of being not only personal but also impersonal and even transpersonal.[4]

For May the daimonic is a fundamental human experience.[5] It cannot be said to be a part of the self, but rather it interacts with the psyche and the person-as-self. The daimonic does not arise out of the ego, the self, or any other portion of the psyche, but instead arises out of one's ground of being. This places the daimonic beyond an individual's ability to describe it in any more than partial terms. "The daimonic belongs to that dimension of experience where discursive, rational language can never tell more than part of the story."[6]

It is with this description of the daimonic that we can begin to see its correspondence with the Judeo-Christian concept of the human spirit, for in the thought of Søren Kierkegaard the spirit also arises out of one's ground of being and is the source of one's power and meaning.[7]

It is not surprising that the Greek conception of the daimonic and the Christian conception of the human spirit should be very similar. Much of early Christian theology was a reworking of Greek and Hebrew thought into a creative new formulation. In the thought of St. Paul the then-seldom-used Greek word *agape* was turned into the Christian concept of unconditional

2. May, *Love and Will*, 136.

3. Ibid., 125.

4. Ibid., 177.

5. Ibid., 123.

6. Ibid., 137.

7. Come, *Human Spirit and Holy Spirit*.

love as it stood beside the more commonly used expressions of love seen in
eros and *philos*.

Likewise, the Greek use of *daimon* and *pneuma* were taken by Christian thinkers and used to create a Christian anthropology and a biblical
theology of the human spirit. For this reason, May's theory and biblical
Christianity are quite similar.

The human spirit and the daimon are also similar for both are seen
to have a dual potential: a potential either for good or for evil, for being
creative or for being destructive.[8] When the daimonic is creative it is working in its symbolic mode, "throwing together" the individual, integrating
the individual into a whole. But when the daimonic is destructive it is in
its diabolic mode, tearing apart the individual, isolating the individual, not
only from others and society, but even from the various parts of him- or
herself.[9] It is when the daimonic is in this latter mode of functioning that we
can speak of the spirit as demonic as opposed to daimonic.

In both May's theory and in Christian theology the daimonic and the
spirit when creative leads us into growth and greater potentials.[10] Also, as
in Christianity, May describes the inner daimon or spirit as a guide to the
person as well as being the vital principal within the individual. Likewise,
happiness is found to be living in accord with one's inner daimon or spirit in
both May's thinking and in biblical theology. Yet the most obvious parallel
can be drawn between the Greek concept of the daimon and the biblical
spirit when we see that both are understood to be the part of the person
which relates to the divine.[11]

We can see that May's use of the "daimon concept" and the theological
concept of a human spirit are very similar. But we need to understand that
when May describes the inner daimon that resides in our unconsciousness
he is not returning to an outmoded image of the human being but is rather
updating the archetypal image of the spirit, an image which we may attempt
to avoid but which we cannot expel.

With this view of the human being, May might be able to understand
possession to be something other than a mere psychic disturbance or a state
of psychopathology, and in a manner he does. Yet it is here that we begin
to run into confusion in his theory. May says both that possession is a state
intimately related to the daimonic (which we have seen to be distinct from

8. May, *Love and Will*, 123, 137; Hendry, *The Holy Spirit in Christian Theology*.

9. May, *Love and Will*, 138.

10. May, *Love and Will*, 164; cf. Beck, *Outline of Biblical Psychology*; Come, *Human
Spirit and Holy Spirit*; Pederson, *Israel: Its Life and Culture*.

11. May, *Love and Will*, 137.

the psychic), yet he also says that "'daimon' possession [is] the traditional name . . . for psychosis."[12] It is here that May appears unable to reconcile his understanding of the classical concepts and his psychoanalytic background.

May describes possession as one element of the person taking control of the whole person.[13] He does not expand on this idea, but we can guess that this can happen in at least two manners. The daimonic can take over the individual as a whole thus usurping some of the psychic functions, as when an artist is possessed by a "fit of creativity" and totally against reason goes without food or other personal needs to complete his or her work. Or when a destructive urge overcomes an individual or a group and then—against all reason—a people can destroy others, as seen in the blood-lust of certain societies, or the Holocaust during World War II. The other manner by which one element of the person can take control of the whole may be seen in the onesidedness of a personality, such as in an obsessive or hysterical personality disorder.

Why possession occurs is due to repression and denial of the daimonic. The ego's repression of the daimonic, though, does not cause a possession in the same manner that the repression of sexual conflicts might result in a hysterical reaction. Rather, possession is the *daimonic's* response to the repressive action of the ego. The difference is one of a psychic content's reaction to the ego's attempt at repression and the *daimonic's* action in the face of repression.

Denial of the daimonic is also a precursor to possession, for to deny the daimonic is to make us "accomplices on the side of the destructive possession."[14] While repressed the daimonic is not under any conscious mediation and so it can go astray and this can result in aggression, violence, and a breakdown in the unity of the self. This results in the person feeling alienated both from society and self, making loneliness and alienation concomitants of possession by the daimonic.[15]

It is in the handling of possession that May begins to drift sharply away from the classical conception of possession and healing (or exorcism). For where the classical understanding of healing the destructive aspect of the spirit (or daimon) was to *cast it out* by the power of the gods, May sees the need for the daimonic to be *integrated* into the whole person.

The closest May comes to the idea of casting out the demons is in the concept of confronting the destructive aspect of the daimonic. "Personal

12. Ibid., 123.
13. Ibid.
14. Ibid., 131.
15. Ibid., 146.

autonomy occurs not by avoiding evil, but by directly confronting it."[16] It should not be understood that May accepts the presence of evil as benign and that evil should be accepted without reservation. As a matter of fact, it is on this point that May diverges from many of his colleagues in the Humanistic Psychology movement. May has even said that "the issue of evil—or rather, the issue of not confronting evil—has profound, and to my mind adverse, effects on humanistic psychology. I believe it is the most important error in the humanistic movement."[17] Yet confronting evil is only partially the classical manner of dealing with evil. Evil was to be brought to light only in order that it might be eradicated or cast away. The confrontation was in the service of the final step of removing from oneself that which was evil, or of removing oneself and one's family from an evil situation or place.

However, for May, a person's task is to integrate the daimonic as a whole, the daimonic being both good and evil. May believes that it is by such integration that the destructive side of the daimonic can be made constructive.[18] But the task of integrating the daimonic is not easy, but one that hurts, and he sees this as one reason that people do not accomplish this integration without very hard work.[19]

To explain how to achieve such an integration of the daimonic, May returns to the classical healing methods and extracts another important aspect from them: the naming of the powers. He sees the key to the overcoming of a possessing daimonic as the *naming* of it, much as the exorcist demanded the name of the demon with which he was dealing.

In the psychology of the primitive, the name of a person or object held the power of that one. Thus, to have the name of the demon was to have power over the demon. Likewise, May saw this psychology at work today in our psychotherapy and medical practice.[20] The naming of a disorder gives it a personal meaning and alleviates some of the afflicted person's anxiety. But even though naming is extremely important in overcoming the possession, it holds another danger in the psychotherapy encounter: the danger that the name will lead not to a confrontation with the daimonic but to mere intellectualization.[21]

Rollo May's attempt to bridge the gap between the digital and analogical models of human functioning is important. It provides us with a vision

---

16. May, *The Problem of Evil: An Open Letter to Carl Rodgers.*

17. Ibid.

18. May, *Love and Will*, 130, 134, 163, 167.

19. Ibid., 176..

20. Ibid., 173.

21. Ibid., 174.

of the human being which is more complex in its existential situation than the mechanistic models of psychoanalytically-based theories would have us believe. Yet May has still left us with a sense of confusion in regard to possession. On the one hand, it seems as if he is advocating the modernization of classical thought, but then he turns around and either ignores, or consciously changes, one of the major elements of that thought. The reason for this may be that May was still working too much within the psychoanalytic framework which understands the human being in a dualistic manner: as comprised of conscious and unconscious functioning. But we have seen—while reviewing the cultural determinates of possession—that the phenomena of possession are best understood and handled with a worldview that is tripartite rather than dualistic. With this tripartite viewing of human functioning we are better able to sort out the confusion that we are left with from May's explanation. C. G. Jung was one theorist who approached the human being from this model, and it is to his theory that we turn next.

18

Jungian Psychology and Possession

Jung was one of the few theorists to take the phenomena of possession seriously. In his theory, and in the subsequent speculations of Jungian theorists, possession plays a major role in the occurrence of psychological maladies. Yet, when Jung, or one of these theorists, speak of possession they do not always mean the type to possession described by the exorcist, or found in classical thought. Possession in Jungian thought can mean anything from experiencing and reacting to the world in a one-sided manner, to symbolically being in the clutches of what throughout history has been known as the demonic.

Because possession is used in such a loose manner it is both confusing and at times a seemingly meaningless term in the Jungian literature. But when we come to understand how Jung viewed the human spirit, we can begin to differentiate the different forms of possession that can be understood to exist in the Jungian model of human functioning. Once this is understood we can see that Jung and his followers can speak of possession as both a psychological phenomenon that results in psychopathology, and as a spiritual phenomenon that can result in a classical experience of "demonosis." Therefore, before we enter into a discussion of the Jungian consideration of possession we will need to look at how the human spirit is viewed in Jungian theory.

Jungian psychology has been at times referred to as mystical, esoteric, and spiritual. Surprisingly, though, the concept of the spirit in Jung's thought has not been well defined. In Jung's writings, as well and the writings of Jungian-oriented authors, the spirit is alluded to and described extensively. Yet these descriptions are quite often confusing if not downright contradictory. The answers to such a question as, "What is the spirit?" are many. From one point in Jung's writings we can answer, that the spirit is an archetype of the collective unconscious, or objective psyche.[1] From another vantage point we can answer that the spirit is not an archetype as such, but is actually transcendent to the psyche and so transcendent to the objective psyche.[2] Yet another answer is that the spirit is a projection of a complex into the environment.[3]

What then is the spirit? It is this question that we need to address before we can understand what can go wrong with it and result in a form of possession. We will look at the spirit as it is manifested in Jung's thought: the spirit as the immaterial aspect of the human being, the spirit as an archetype, and the spirit as an incorporeal being. With these distinctions we will be better able to grasp Jung's usage of this concept.

Before launching into the question of the spirit we will first need to understand how it fits into Jung's general understanding of the human being. We need to view Jung's anthropology from two perspectives, that of being and that of knowing.

When viewing the human being from the perspective of being, we are acting as if we could be an objective viewer of reality, as if we are standing on the mountain-top with God looking down on the world untouched by that world and not necessarily touching it. From this perspective we see the human being as a totality, a continuous system, which Jung saw as the primal state of the human person. Then out of the "chaos" of this continuous and undifferentiated totality arises an ego as a center of consciousness. With the emergence of the ego comes the beginnings of a differentiation of human experience into that which is conscious and that which is unconscious. With the ego, the way of being ceases and the way of knowing take ascendancy.

From the standpoint of the ego the human being can be differentiated into three aspects: the body, the psyche, and the spirit (from the Greek words: *soma*, *psyche*, and *pneuma* respectively). From the ego's point of knowing, these aspects seem as independent, discrete parts that constitute the total human being. This agrees with the ancient Greek notion of the tripartite human being, then seen as being body, soul, and mind (from the Greek words: *soma*, *psyche* and *nous*). Yet, from the standpoint of being, there is no such distinction, so Jung here falls closer to the Pauline concept of a continuous entity known as the human being (*anthropos*). Jung described the functioning of the person as being on a spectrum from the body at one end—the infrared—to the spirit at the other—the ultraviolet. Found between these polar opposites is the psyche. The body and

1. Jung, *The Archetypes and the Collective Unconscious*, par. 396.
2. Jung, *The Structure and Dynamics of the Psyche*, par. 420.
3. Ibid., par. 628.

the spirit thus meet at the level of the psyche and are mediated through the psyche. This may sound similar to Freud's id, ego, superego—or more precisely *es, ich,* and *uberich*—configuration, both illustrating a base impulse and higher impulse mediated by an intermediary construct, but this is where the similarity ends.

For Freud the superego arises out of the individual's encounter with parental wishes and the wishes of society. This is not the case with the spirit, which—as we will see—at times may actually lead a person contrary to the desires of the society. Freud also conceived of the ego and the superego arising out of the id. This in no way corresponds to Jung's thought, for the psyche does not arise out of layers of the primal body. Rather, for Jung, the psyche (which does not equate with Freud's ego, but incorporates much more) arises out of the meeting of matter and spirit, out of the coming together of body and spirit. This corresponds to the biblical idea of the conception of the psyche, for it was when the spirit (*ruah* in Hebrew) entered the body that the living being (*nephesh* in Hebrew and *psyche* in Greek) was born.

We must be careful when reading and interpreting Jung to understand the metapsychological frame of reference he is using when he writes. If his reference is ultimate being, then we see that no clear distinction can be made between parts of the person, for the person is actually a total self. If the reference point is the ego, then seemingly clear distinctions among the parts can be made, and we begin to speak of body, psyche, and spirit. But it is imperative to understand that these concepts are only ways of knowing for the ego, and have no reified reality of their own.

With this in mind, let us examine the human being from the perspective of the ego. On the grossest level, there are three parts to the person: the body, the psyche, and the spirit.

The body here corresponds to the Greek word *soma.* This word is distinct from the word *sarx,* which primarily means the flesh or the physiological functioning of the person. Jung speaks of the body in a more encompassing manner than this. The body is that part of the person closer to the earth, the part more tied to our biological heritage, more in the sense of the Greek word *zoe.* Nathan Schwartz-Salant refers to the body as the Self's "outer manifestation."[4] Jung viewed the "living body with its special characteristics [as] a system of functions for adapting to environmental conditions."[5] Thus the body does have its characteristic of sarx. It does carry the functions of physiological life and is the carrier of the organs of sense. Yet the body is more

4. Schwartz-Salant, *Narcissism and Character Transformation.*, 120.
5. Jung, *The Structure and Dynamics of the Psyche*, par. 326.

than this for there is also an unconscious element to it. At times Jung refers to this as the subtle body or as the somatic unconscious.

From the level of being the unconscious is continuous throughout the person. It is those areas of the person not in the sphere of conscious awareness. Yet the ego experiences the unconscious differently depending upon where the experience is occurring in the body-psyche-spirit scheme. "When the unconscious is approached from the framework of the ego, its psychic and somatic manifestations are a source of very different experiences."[6] Whereas the sarx aspect of the body allows the person to experience the environment in a reactive manner (the environment impinging upon the senses), the somatic unconscious allows the person to experience the environment in a more active manner by "seeing through the body."[7] Schwartz-Salant describes the functioning of the somatic unconscious in his book, *Narcissism and Character Transformation*:

> By being close to our body, with psychic awareness relatively low, we are like a measuring instrument in flowing water or a magnetic field; we can use our own reactions to know when the other person's energy is fading and when it is present. But just as in science, where one must know the characteristics of the measuring instrument, whose own nature distorts the results, so too we must be able to filter out our own personal reactions. In fact, this is a much easier process working near the somatic unconscious than the psychic unconscious. By not having to know we are much less involved in the power-motivated countertransference reactions.
>
> The tightening up of our own body, perturbations of sensations in head, chest, belly, sexual organs, throat and so forth, all help track the parts of the patient that attempt to split-off, and reveal the fact that the patient is temporarily leaving the here and now. Just as it is possible to walk into a room of people and "pick up" that something is out of order, perhaps dangerous, or that someone is in a complex, so too body consciousness can operate in the here and now, in a more or less continuous way. It is difficult to explain this process causally, except in the unscientific sense that something going on in another person "causes" something to happen in us. In this way, by listening and organizing according to our body consciousness and physical babblings, a new order can appear. It comes up from below, like the resurrection of the dead god Osiris. The new order is the

6. Schwartz-Salant, *Narcissism and Character Transformation*, 120.

7. Ibid., 125.

resurrected Osiris. And it can be a new dimension of vision, an imaginal seeing, as much as an awareness that suddenly puts order into the previous day's events. Here I must stress that this imaginal seeing is a vague, shadowy vision, not a clear one of solar nature. Trusting it now becomes the cardinal issue. In this state one is often discovering, along with the patient, their split-off parts that begin to feel seen.[8]

At this level of the somatic unconscious will also be found the concept of the "instinct." Jung has described an instinct to be any action that is not under conscious control.[9] Yet this definition was written early in his thinking. He later writes:

> If . . . we survey the unconscious processes as a whole, we find it impossible to class them all as instinctive, even though no differentiation is made between them in ordinary speech. If you suddenly meet a snake and get a violent fright, you can legitimately call this impulse instinctive because it is not different from the instinctive fear of snakes in monkeys. It is just the uniformity of the phenomenon and the regularity of its recurrence which are the most characteristic qualities of the instinctive action. As Lloyd Morgan aptly remarks, it would be as uninteresting to bet on an instinctive reaction as on the rising of the sun tomorrow. On the other hand, it may also happen that someone is regularly seized with fright whenever he meets a perfectly harmless hen. Although the mechanism of fright in this case is just as much an unconscious impulse as the instinct, we must nevertheless distinguish between the two processes. In the former case the fear of snakes is a purposive process of general occurrence; the latter when habitual, is a phobia and not an instinct, since it occurs only in isolation and is not a general peculiarity.[10]

Here he concludes that "only those unconscious processes which are inherited, and occur uniformly and regularly, can be called instinctive."[11] This definition includes both the biological instinct, such as those for self-preservation, as well as the archetypes of the objective psyche. But Jung finally even makes a distinction between these inherited processes later in

8. Ibid., 125–26.
9. Jung, *Psychological Types*, par. 765.
10. Jung, *The Structure and Dynamics of the Psyche*, par. 266.
11. Ibid., par. 267.

his life when he comes to the conclusion that "archetype and instinct are the most polar opposites imaginable."[12]

The development of the concept of the instinct is illustrative of our need to read and interpret the meaning in Jung's thought in the context of when he was writing. His thought that the instinct is anything unconscious, and then that the instinct is anything unconscious that is inherited, uniform, and regular arise from his writings around 1920. But his final distinction between the archetype and the instinct was developed in his writings of around 1948. We can see that in his more developed formulations, the instincts are clearly associated with those unconscious processes which are inherited, occur uniformly and regularly, and are associated with the body. We shall see that this formulation places the archetype as distinct from the instincts by its being an unconscious process which is inherited; it occurs uniformly among people but is associated with the human spirit, rather than with the body.

As we move along the spectrum of human functioning, we cross through the grey area where body and psyche mesh and move into the realm of the psyche proper. The psyche is the area of functioning on which Jung concentrated most of his efforts. Thus, the psyche is the best known of these areas in Jung's work.

As stated earlier, Jung has postulated a tripartite human being along the lines of the ancient Greek philosophers. Yet Jung elaborates on these philosophers in two ways. First, Jung moves toward a more biblical understanding of the psychic level by expanding the body-mind-spirit compendium to see it more as a body-soul-spirit compendium. The soul here is not equal with the mind but rather is supraordinate to the mind, the mind being but one function of the soul. But Jung even expands on this basic biblical conception of the human being: for even though *psyche* is the Greek word for soul, Jung sees the soul as only one part of what he calls the psyche. For Jung, the psyche itself is tripartite, comprising consciousness (with the ego as its center), the personal unconscious, and the collective unconscious or the objective psyche. In this schema the contents of the personal unconscious are equivalent with the more ancient concept of the soul. Thus, in Jung's thought a person could have many souls, depending upon the multiplicity of contents of the personal unconscious. Jung found validation for his view in his study of primitive societies, where the concept of an individual having multiple souls is common.[13]

---

12. Ibid., par. 406.
13. Ibid., par. 217.

Distinguishing the three levels of the psyche, we first see that consciousness is defined by those psychic contents with which the ego is in relationship. As with all levels of the psyche, consciousness is dynamic and so shifting. "The whole essence of consciousness is discrimination, distinguishing ego from non-ego, subject from object, positive from negative and so forth."[14]

The personal unconscious is that area of the unconscious most closely associated with the ego. Jung described it as such:

> The personal unconscious . . . includes all those psychic contents which have been forgotten during the course of the individual's life. Traces of them are still preserved in the unconscious, even if all conscious memory of them has been lost. In addition, it contains all subliminal impressions or perceptions which have too little energy to reach consciousness. To these we must add unconscious combinations of ideas that are still too feeble and too indistinct to cross over the threshold. Finally, the personal unconscious contains all psychic contents that are incompatible with the conscious attitude.[15]

The personal unconscious is made up of complexes, and it is the complex that most resembles the primitive's idea of the soul. The complex is made of the person's associations and experiences as they relate to the central element of the complex: the archetype.

The archetypes are the contents of the collective unconscious. Unlike the personal unconscious, the collective unconscious (or objective psyche) does not owe its existence to personal experience. Rather the objective psyche is "a second psychic system of a collective, universal, and impersonal nature which is identical in all individuals. This collective unconscious does not develop individually but is inherited. It consists of pre-existent forms, the archetypes, which can only become conscious secondarily and which give definite form to certain psychic contents."[16]

Our consideration of the objective psyche now brings us to the far end of the spectrum of human functioning, and to the deepest level of the human being. As we encounter the archetypal realm within the person we begin to touch the spirit. Spirit is not a part of the psyche, but is truly beyond, or transcendent to the psyche. It is quite the opposite of the base part

---

14. Jung, *Psychological Types*, par. 179.

15. Jung, *The Structure and Dynamics of the Psyche*, par. 588.

16. Jung, *The Archetypes and the Collective Unconscious*, par. 90.

of the human being encountered in the body.[17] While the body represents the material aspect of the person, the spirit is the immaterial.[18]

> Just as the "psychic infra-red," the biological instinctual psyche, gradually passes over into the physiology of the organism and thus merges with its chemical and physical conditions, so the "psychic ultra-violet," the archetype, describes a field which exhibits none of the peculiarities of the physiological and yet, in the last analysis, can no longer be regarded as psychic, although it manifests itself psychically. But physiological processes behave in the same way, without on that account being declared psychic. Although there is no form of existence that is not mediated to us psychically and only psychically, it would hardly do to say that everything is merely psychic. We must apply this argument logically to the archetypes as well. Since their essential being is unconscious to us, and still they are experienced as spontaneous agencies, there is probably no alternative now but to describe their nature, in accordance with their chiefest effect, as "spirit," in the sense which I attempted to make plain in my paper "The Phenomenology of the Spirit in Fairytales." If so, the position of the archetype would be located beyond the psychic sphere, analogous to the position of physiological instinct, which is immediately rooted in the stuff of the organism and, with its psychoid nature, forms the bridge to matter in general. In archetypal conceptions and instinctual perceptions, spirit and matter confront one another on the psychic plane. Matter and spirit both appear in the psychic realm as distinctive qualities of conscious contents. The ultimate nature of both is transcendental, that is, irrepresentable, since the psyche and its contents are the only reality which is given to us without a medium.[19]

The human spirit is that which empowers the psyche—it is the dynamic principle within the individual.[20] It is the spirit that is the mover, the energizer of the person. One of the hallmarks of the spirit is that of spontaneous movement and activity.[21] Another manner by which we can visualize

---

17. Jung, *The Structure and Dynamics of the Psyche*, pars. 380, 392, 406, 748; *Two Essays on Analytical Psychology*, par. 172.

18. Jung, *The Archetypes and the Collective Unconscious*, par. 392.

19. Jung, *The Structure and Dynamics of the Psyche*, par. 420.

20. Jung, *The Archetypes and the Collective Unconscious*, par. 389.

21. Ibid., par. 393.

this dynamic activity of the spirit is by seeing the spirit as the guide of the mind and as the guide of the person.[22]

The spirit guides in three principle fashions. First, the spirit is the seat of wisdom and counsel.[23] It is in spirit that we gain the discernment of which way to move, what to do and when to do it. For wisdom is different from intellect in that both may have access to knowledge, but wisdom "knows" the direction a person needs to go to reach a certain goal. Wisdom need not be considered "good" though. "Wisdom seeks the middle path and pays for this audacity by a dubious affinity with daemon and beast, and so is open to moral misinterpretation."[24] Wisdom directs the person toward the goal of a completed self, and whether that self is one which is morally good or morally evil is of no consequence to Jung's concept of wisdom. Thus, the spirit gives the person counsel which the mind and the will then determine whether or not to follow.

A second manner in which the spirit acts as a guide is that the spirit is the source of meaning within and for the person.[25] As we know from our reading of the existentialist literature and from other sources, a life without meaning is one of futility, one of colorlessness, one resembling a living death. The spirit provides meaning in a person's life and by so doing gives a person a direction, a goal. It adds color; it actually gives life.

A third, related, aspect of spirit as guide is the spirit as the creative impulse in us.[26] It is the person that can see meaning where others do not that can bring new life, who can be creative.

One aspect of this creative function of the spirit is that the spirit is the source of the archetypes. Another of the spirit's hallmarks is that it independently produces images, while yet another is the spirit's ability to autonomously and sovereignly manipulate these images.[27] Thus, the spirit not only guides by influencing the mind with the wisdom of its counsel, but also guides by providing the images that inhabit the objective psyche of the individual. This is why, as we saw earlier, the archetypes cannot actually be considered psychic. Though they inhabit the objective process of the unconscious, their origin is transcendent to the psyche. And the spirit as the guide of both the conscious and the unconscious shows itself as a wholistic guide, as the guide of the whole person. This guidance, once again, need not

---

22. Jung, *The Structure and Dynamics of the Psyche*, par. 629.

23. Jung, *The Archetypes and the Collective Unconscious*, par. 398.

24. Ibid., par. 420.

25. Ibid., par. 682; Jung, *The Spirit in Man, Art, and Literature*, pars. 15, 89, 90.

26. Jung, *The Archetypes and the Collective Unconscious*, par. 393.

27. Ibid.

necessarily be seen as good, for the spirit is actually neither good nor evil, but should be seen as morally neutral.

> As can readily be seen, the common modern idea of spirit ill accords with the Christian view, which regards it as the *summum bonum*, as God himself. To be sure, there is also the idea of an evil spirit. But the modern idea cannot be equated with that either, since for us spirit is not necessarily evil; we would have to call it morally indifferent or neutral. When the Bible says "God is spirit," it sounds more like a definition of a substance, or like a qualification. But the devil too, it seems, is endowed with the same peculiar spiritual substance, albeit an evil and corrupt one.[28]

The spirit then can be destructive as well as creative. Thus, the spirit is not what some theologians or philosophers would refer to as the essence of the person, the unchangeable, base quality of the individual determined from the beginning and fatalistically determining the person. Rather, the spirit is full of possibilities, possibilities for growth as well as for the denial of such growth.[29] The spirit is not absolute but is relative to the life lived by the person, relative to the will of the person and so is itself in need of completion.

So far, we have been looking at the spirit in its aspect as the immaterial part of the person. We also encounter the spirit in the psyche. When Jung speaks of the spirit as a part of the psyche, what he is referring to are actually the archetypes, or autonomous complexes not associated with the ego and not to be associated with the ego. Jung differentiates between complexes that the ego may associate with and other complexes. The former are complexes of the personal unconscious and so are part of what Jung sees as the realm of the soul, and so he speaks of these as soul-complexes. The complexes or archetypes of the objective psyche are then referred to as spirit-complexes.

> The plurality of souls indicates a plurality of relatively autonomous complexes that can behave like spirits. The soul-complexes seem to belong to the ego and the loss of them appears pathological. The opposite is true of the spirit-complexes: their association with the ego causes illness, and their dissociation from it brings recovery. Accordingly, primitive pathology recognizes two causes of illness: loss of soul, and possession by spirit. The two theories keep one another more of less balanced. We therefore have to postulate the existence of unconscious

28. Ibid., par. 394.
29. Jung, *The Structure and Dynamics of the Psyche*, pars. 644–45.

complexes that normally belong to the ego, and of those that normally should not become associated with it. The former are the soul-complexes, the latter the spirit-complexes.[30]

The spirit-complexes thus should not be integrated to the ego, for this will result in psychic-inflation or possession by the spirit-complex.[31]

As with the spirit of the person, the archetype of the spirit is morally neutral. Whether the spirit as archetype will work for good or for evil depends upon the person's free will.[32] The spirit-complex can store up the richest experiences of life and the deepest of reflections,[33] but it can also point towards the chthonic.[34]

The archetype of the spirit, as with the human spirit, can bring insight, understanding, good advice, determination of problems and a sense of planning that cannot be mustered by one's own conscious resources.[35] This form of guidance is usually encountered in dreams and visions where the spirit-complex is encountered.

The spirit-complex can take many forms in the unconscious, though it usually manifests itself as a personal being. One of the most common forms of this is the encounter with the wise old man. In alchemy, the *senex et juvenis*, or the old man and youth at once, is a symbol for the archetype of the spirit. It is also encountered in mythology and literature, as in the ghost of Christmas past in Charles Dicken's *A Christmas Carol*. Other common forms are wisdom-giving animals met in many fairy tales. Water is at times a symbol of the spirit, but usually of a spirit to which one is not attending.[36] When spirits themselves are encountered in dreams, this does not necessarily mean one has encountered the human spirit, but rather an encounter with an archetype has occurred, for in dreams the archetypes are often seen as spirits.

As we look at the functions of the human spirit—or the spirit as the immaterial part of the person—and the spirit-complex, we begin to see many similarities between these and Jung's concept of the Self. As with the spirit, the Self is a dynamic force within the person. Jung stated that "the

---

30. Ibid., par. 587

31. Jung, *The Archetypes and the Collective Unconscious*, par. 393; *The Structure and Dynamics of the Psyche*, par. 587.

32. Jung, *The Archetypes and the Collective Unconscious*, par. 454.

33. Jung, *The Structure and Dynamics of the Psyche*, par. 633.

34. Jung, *The Archetypes and the Collective Unconscious*, par. 413.

35. Ibid., par. 398.

36. Ibid., par. 40.

ego stands to the Self as the moved to the mover."[37] The Self also holds the guiding function we associated with the spirit. We see that it is directive and the central planner.[38]

There are many other ways in which the Self and the spirit are similar. Both the Self and the human spirit are given credit as giving birth to the ego or the soul.[39] Both the Self and the spirit are described as being higher, or wider, forms of consciousness supraordinate to the consciousness of the ego.[40]

Jung discriminated between the Self and the ego saying that "the ego is only the subject of my consciousness, while the Self is the subject of my totality."[41] The Self is the totality of the body and psyche together and thus the Self is transcendent to either and both.[42] Likewise the spirit is transcendent to both the body and the psyche, and though Jung does not directly speak to the spirit as the totality of body and psyche, still this seems to be where he was leading. Kierkegaard, in his writings on the human spirit, drew the same conclusion regarding the spirit as Jung has done regarding the Self, that the spirit is the totality of the human being, the transcendent property of the body and soul union.

> The spirit . . . for Kierkegaard was neither a third entity from some other world, seeking release to that other world, nor a synthesis that swallows up and blurs all distinctions. Rather, human spirit is a realized unity of the whole man that preserves, indeed is even posited on the grounds of, a continuing presence and operation of the bodily and soulish dimensions of the human self. That such was Kierkegaard's view was eminently clear when he said that, before achieving selfhood, man "is not an animal, but neither is he properly a man. The instant he becomes a man he becomes such only by being at the same time an animal." Man qua man, then is a realized indissolvable unity of body and soul, denoted by the term "spirit," or, in contemporary language, "self" or "person."[43]

37. Jung, *Psychology and Religion: West and East*, par. 391.

38. Whitmont, *The Symbolic Quest: Basic Concepts in Analytical Psychology*, 219.

39. Cf. spirit gives birth to the soul: Jung, *The Archetypes and the Collective Unconscious*, par. 32; *The Structure and Dynamics of the Psyche*, par. 667; self gives birth to the ego: Whitmont, *The Symbolic Quest: Basic Concepts in Analytical Psychology*, 217.

40. Jung, *The Structure and Dynamics of the Psyche*, pars. 643, 645; Whitmont, *The Symbolic Quest: Basic Concepts in Analytical Psychology*, 217.

41. Jung, *Psychology and Religion: West and East*, par. 391.

42. Schwartz-Salant, *Narcissism and Character Transformation*, 120.

43. Come, *Human Spirit and Holy Spirit*, 37.

The Self has also the aspect of future orientation. It is the mover toward the goal of truly being a person, or the completion of the individual. It is not only the mover but it is also the goal of this growth process. Thus, it has the quality of being the future of the individual, a future that is present in the individual now. But the goal is not one that a person should ever actually expect to attain, but only to which to draw close. Thus, the Self has the quality of becoming and not of being.[44] It expresses a predestined wholeness of each person.[45] The Self, as with the spirit, is morally neutral. Not only can the Self be seen as constructive, but it also has a dark, destructive aspect.[46] The Self at times will confront the ego with a direction which the ego will find morally distasteful. So the Self can direct the individual in a direction counter to the cultural or societal demands. But Jung believed this was in the interests of individuation.

We can see from this cursory review of the Self that it and the spirit have much in common. Actually, it seems as if Jung has combined two levels of being into this concept of the Self, and so this concept has been one of the most difficult to comprehend. The Self seems to be on the two levels of being transcendent to the psyche and of being intrapsychic. Whether he developed the Self out of the Hindu tradition of Atman-atman, or out of the Christian tradition is difficult to determine.

From the Hindu tradition we can see that there is an atman, or spirit, in every person that is a reflection or part of the cosmic Atman or spirit. This more closely resembles the gnostic concept of each person containing a spark of the divine within them. Jung was fascinated by the gnostic view of the human being and researched the gnostics extensively. Therefore, it is plausible that the Self may be a construct closely resembling the theology of the gnostics. Yet, Jung's Self still seems to be more easily compared to the traditional Christian anthropology of the spirit and the heart. The transpsychic aspects of the Self correspond to what we have been discussing as the spirit as an immaterial part of the person, while the intrapsychic aspects of the Self correspond to the spirit as an archetype and the Christian idea of the heart.

The Self as an intrapsychic archetype is the image of the human spirit within the psyche. Much as the human being was to be God's proxy, God's representative in the creation, so too, the Self as the heart is the spirit's representative in the psychic order. It is through the Self, or the heart, that the spirit lets its directions be known, its will be experienced. Whether it is

---

44. Whitmont, *The Symbolic Quest: Basic Concepts in Analytical Psychology,* 222.

45. Ibid., 219.

46. Ibid., 225.

through the image of the wise old man in a dream, or a talking animal in a fairy tale, or a numinous intuition that seems to "come from the heart," the Self mediates the desires of the spirit. Being the mediator of the spirit, being the representative of the spirit, the Self of course will seem similar to the spirit: it will reflect the spirit, or the totality of the person. When we see the Self as the heart of the person and as the agency of spirit—or Self-totality— representation, then the saying in Proverbs makes clear sense: "As in water face reflects face, so the heart of man reflects the man."[47]

Finally we approach the question of the spirit as an incorporeal being. Are there such things as spirits—independent, incorporeal beings—in the universe? In essence there are two ways of approaching this question: asking whether there really are spirits and asking whether what many people see in dreams, visions, and hallucinations are actually independent beings. To the former question Jung has little to say, though what little he does say is potent. But he elucidates the latter question quite a bit more.

In most of Jung's writings—and in the writings of his followers—the spirits seen by the primitive and by the modern in dreams, visions, and hallucinations are actually the projections of autonomous complexes. They are complexes split-off from consciousness and then experienced by the ego as foreign, independent beings.[48] These apparitions appear when one loses one's adaptation to reality.[49] When a person begins to accept the projection as a part of the unconscious and regains their adaptation to life, then the apparition recedes as the complex is no longer in ascendancy but is inte- grated into consciousness—if it is a soul-complex—or removed from the ego-complex—if it is a spirit-complex.

Seemingly then, what throughout history have been seen as indepen- dent, incorporeal, spirit-beings are actually parts of our own selves pro- jected into—and so encountered in—the environment. This means that the gods, demons, and angels of the mythologies of the world find their bases in the complexes and archetypes of the unconscious. Yet Jung was not willing to accept this as an absolute explanation, or description, for the phenomena of "spirits." Thus, when Jung made the statement, "spirits, therefore, viewed from the psychological angle, are unconscious autonomous complexes which appear as projections because they have no direct associations with the ego,"[50] he felt the need to footnote it by saying:

47. Proverbs 27:19.

48. Jung, *The Structure and Dynamics of the Psyche*, pars. 585, 628; *Two Essays on Analytical Psychology*, pars. 293, 294, 296.

49. Jung, *The Structure and Dynamics of the Psyche*, par. 597.

50. Ibid., par. 585.

This should not be misconstrued as a metaphysical statement.
The question of whether spirits exist in themselves is far from
having been settled. Psychology is not concerned with things
as they are "in themselves," but only with what people think
about them.[51]

Jung, as he wrote his professional papers, felt the need to stay close to
concrete data and not lose himself in mystical, metaphysical speculation.
Though he may have personally believed that a spirit-world existed, still
as far as the psyche was concerned this did not matter. Early in his career
Jung attempted to control his speculation by psychologizing the spirit. This
can be seen in his early attempts to see spirit as the psyche until by his later
thought the spirit had taken on an autonomous reality within the total person. So too with the concept of incorporeal spirits. In 1919 he wrote:

These parapsychic phenomena seem to be connected as a rule
with the presence of a medium. They are, so far as my experience goes, the exteriorized effects of unconscious complexes. I
for one am certainly convinced that they are exteriorizations. I
have repeatedly observed the telepathic effects of unconscious
complexes, and also a number of parapsychic phenomena. But
in all this I see no proof whatever of the existence of real spirits,
and until such proof is forthcoming I must regard this whole
territory as an appendix of psychology.[52]

It is this statement that most people follow today and see as the defini-
tive explanation of the spiritual: the spiritual is the psychic exteriorized. Yet
Jung was not to remain content with his own early thoughts and in 1948 he
wrote the following footnote to the above statement:

After collecting psychological experiences from many people
and many countries for fifty years, I no longer feel as certain as I
did in 1919, when I wrote this sentence. To put it bluntly, I doubt
whether an exclusively psychological approach can do justice to
the phenomena in question. Not only the findings of parapsychology, but my own theoretical reflections, outlined in "On the
Nature of the Psyche," have led me to certain postulates which
touch on the realm of nuclear physics and the conception of the
space-time continuum. This opens up the whole question of the
transpsychic reality immediately underlying the psyche.[53]

51. Ibid., par. 585n.
52. Ibid., par. 600
53. Ibid., par. 600n.

For Jung the idea of the independent reality of spirits was not a closed subject, but rather was an area of opening interest for him even as he drew close to the end of his life. For the ego to experience the split-off complex of the psyche as a "spirit" was a reality. But this need not preclude the actuality of spirits that were not complexes. The validity of the former statement has been accepted easily by the psychological community. The fact that the world of the spirit, and the actuality of spirits might also be true, has virtually been ignored.

A Jungian View of Possession

As we have seen, Jung differentiated among three aspects of the spirit in his writings. But when it comes to his explanation of spirit-possession only one of these becomes important to us: the spirit as archetype. Though we have seen that Jung did not completely deny the existence of incorporeal spirits, still most of his writings on the phenomena of spirit-possession were in regard to the ego's assimilation by an archetype.

Possession in analytical psychology is actually a very broad phenomenon, covering the occurrence of the most obscure mood to the most florid of psychoses. For the Jungian all forms of psychopathology are the result of some form of possession, either due to a soul-complex or a spirit-complex. That is, possession is related either to the ego and the personal field of the individual, or it is related to the Self and that area of functioning general to the whole human species.

Possession by a soul-complex occurs when a part of the personal psyche which is split-off, and so autonomous from the ego, returns to usurp the central role of the ego and so subjugate it.[54] By so doing, the complex substitutes its qualities for those of the ego and one will objectively observe the substitution of inferior abilities for those of the ego's more well developed abilities. Normally the ego is to encounter and integrate these split-off aspects of the personal unconscious, but in a possession the ego does not integrate the complex but rather is assimilated by it.

> As a rule there is a marked unconsciousness of any complexes, and this naturally guarantees them all the more freedom of action. In such cases their powers of assimilation become especially pronounced, since unconsciousness helps the complex to assimilate even the ego, the result being a momentary and unconscious alteration of personality known as identification

---

54. Jung, *The Archetypes and the Collective Unconscious*, par. 277.

with the complex. In the Middle Ages it went by another name: it was called possession.[55]

This is the origin of many of the moods into which we fall, and to the neurotic psychopathologies. The psychotic and character disorders are more commonly attributed to a possession by the archetypes.

In normal functioning, the ego is to relate to the Self, neither attempting to integrate it nor to ignore it. Thus, in healthy functioning we are to maintain what is called the ego—Self axis by which the ego is able to encounter the archetypes of the collective unconscious, but not be overcome by them. Yet, if the ego does attempt to either ignore the Self and the contents of the collective unconscious; or, if it begins to identify with the aspects which rightly belong to the Self, then the Self or the archetype will overcome the ego, resulting in an inflated attitude in the ego, or possession. The person will then act and perceive as would the archetype. No longer is the person able to function as one with a will or a choice, but he or she must act as the archetypal pattern demands. Thus a person may become like a wise old man, or like a witch, or any other possible archetypal form. It is to this phenomenon that Jung attributes the classical phenomena of demonic possessions and ancestor possessions.[56] One becomes the Devil or a specific demon according to the manifestation of one of the darker aspects of the Self. And it is that darker aspect that rules the person's life. The individual as ego actually is possessed by the Devil as an archetype, and as such the person truly has no control over his or her actions.

In both, the possessions by a personal complex and by an archetype the individual has lost a large amount of control to an unconscious aspect of his or her self. By so doing he or she has been consumed by an one-sided attitude toward both his or her outer and inner worlds.

The etiology of possession is just as broad as are the types of psychopathologies that can be described. The precursors to a true spirit-possession, though, have more limited parameters. An obvious precursor is an ego weakened by developmental traumas. This results in an incomplete formation of the ego—Self axis and so lends power to the possibility of some aspect of the Self assimilating this infirm ego. It is one of Jung's most influential followers, Marie Louise von Franz, who gives us a compelling insight into three major roads to possession as seen in the world's fairy tales.

Throughout her investigation of fairy tales von Franz has distilled three consistent roads to a possession. These are the use of alcohol and drugs, being alone in nature, and a naive approach to evil. Drinking and the

55. Jung, *The Structure and Dynamics of the Psyche*, par. 204.
56. Jung, *The Practice of Psychotherapy*.

use of drugs can be seen to lead to possession due to their effect on altering consciousness and so weakening the ego's boundaries with the unconscious. "So drinking is for the primitive one of the simplest and easiest ways by which he opens the door to being possessed by evil."[57]

Loneliness was also a very common fairy tale motif in association with possession. This form of loneliness was being separated from the group or village to which one belonged, or "being among people with whom you have no emotional feeling ties."[58] This being alone could either be in the form of being left by others as in the following story, or venturing out into nature on one's own or with a sole companion as in the story we will hear in a moment. In the following South American Indian story of "The Outwitted Wood Spirit" von Franz illustrates the first type of aloneness.

> A whole family was invited to a drinking feast and all went except the daughter who stayed at home alone. In the late afternoon a girlfriend came to visit her whom she had not seen for a long time. At least she thought it was her girlfriend Dai-adalla, but actually it was a wood spirit who had taken on her friend's form in order to carry out his evil intentions more easily. As the girls were very good friends, the wood spirit, in the form of Dai-adalla, asked her what she was doing alone at home. When the girl explained that she had not wanted to go to the party, the spirit said that it would stay the night with her and keep her company. When evening came and they could hear the frogs croaking, the girl suggested that, as they liked eating frogs, they might go and catch some.
>
> So they went out into the dark and after a time began to call out to each other to ask how many frogs the other had caught. The wood spirit when asked answered that he had caught a lot, but that he always ate them directly he caught them. This strange answer, that he ate the animals raw, frightened the girl and she realized the real nature of her supposed girlfriend. So when the wood spirit called out again asking how many she had caught, she answered that she had caught a lot, but that she had put them in her calabash. All the time she was wondering how she could get away safely. She told the wood spirit to be quiet and not talk, saying that he frightened away the frogs, because she knew that from her voice he could tell where she was standing. Then she crept quietly home and turned over all the pots in the house without making any noise, threw away the frogs, and climbed up onto the roof and waited to see what would happen.

57. von Franz, *The Shadow and Evil in Fairytales*, 142.
58. Ibid.

So afterwards, the wood spirit, not getting any answer to his questions, realized that he had been outwitted and hurried back to the house. In the dark he stumbled around among the pots trying to find his prey. At last he cried out, loud enough for the girl to hear, that if he had only known she was going to try to get away he would have eaten her with the frogs.

He hunted fruitlessly, looking in all the pots, until dawn came and then he had to leave. The girl then came down and waited for her parents and when they came she told them that the wood spirit had visited her in the form of her friend. Then her father said that next time they told her to come with them, she would obey.[59]

Besides the seemingly obvious moral in the story—there is danger in not obeying one's parents—there is an even more profound point; remaining alone in nature—being isolated from others—places one in danger of being devoured by the spirits; that is, being possessed.

The Icelandic fairy tale of "Trunt, Trunt, and the Trolls in the Mountain" illustrates von Franz's second type of being alone in nature. In this instance it is not that one is abandoned to nature by others, as in the previous story, but that one may willingly venture out into it.

Two men once went to the mountains to collect herbs. One night they both lay in their tent, but one slept and the other lay awake. The one who was awake saw how the one who slept went out. He followed him but could hardly walk fast enough and the distance between them always grew greater. The man was going towards the glaciers. On the top of a glacier the other saw an enormous giantess. She gestured by holding out her hand and then drawing it back toward her breast, and like that she bewitches the man, drawing him to her. The man ran straight into her arms and she ran away with him . . .

A year later the people of that district went to collect herbs again at the same place and the man who had been bewitched came to them, but he was so quiet and reserved and incommunicative that one could hardly get a word out of him. The people asked him who he believed in, and he said that he believed in God.

The second year he again came to the herb people, but this time he had become so hobgoblinish that they were afraid of him. And when they asked him who he believed in, he did not answer. And this time he stayed with them a shorter time. The

59. Ibid., 138.

third year he came again, but had become a real troll and he looked awful. But one of the people ventured to ask him what he believed in and he said that he believed in Trunt, Trunt and the Trolls in the Mountains, and he disappeared. Since then he has never been seen again and for many years nobody ventured to collect herbs at that place.[60]

These two stories illustrate the dangers of being alone in nature. They differ only in the manner that one became so alone. In the first story there was a passive aloneness, the girl was left there by her parents. In the second story it was an active aloneness, the men went out into nature to collect herbs. Either way, whether one consciously enters it alone or is left there, the dangers are the same: the arcane powers that dwell there will attempt to possess the lonely one.

If we begin to see how nature in these stories is also a metaphor for our personal form of nature, the collective unconscious, then we can better understand how such a possession might happen. The ego that ventures into or explores the unconscious on its own—without the safety of the ego—Self axis—places itself at the power of the contents of the unconscious. Likewise, the ego that is left vulnerable to the unconscious—because of traumas and the like—is also susceptible to the powers held within the unconscious, and so in danger of a possible possession by a content of the unconscious.

Closely allied with this theme is the next manner of a person being open to possession. This involves an individual's naive approach to evil or to the arcane powers that surround us. The following Swiss story illustrates this point:

> Two men [an older cattle herder and a young boy] were herd-ing the cattle high up on the mountains. . . . In order to protect himself and his herds the Senn (herdsman) as one calls him, has to go out in the evening and recite the evening benediction over the cattle and the Alp in the four directions of the horizon. The custom is practiced so that God may protect the cattle, the Alp, and the men on it. One evening the cattle herder came out of the hut and looked around, and a voice up in the mountains called out, "Shall I let it go?" And he, instead of getting unduly frightened said, "Oh, you can hold it still longer!" And nothing happened. The next day passed and the next evening the voice said, "Shall I let it go?" The herder called out, "Oh, you can hold it longer!" But the boy got nervous and thought that was not the right way to behave and that it was getting very dangerous so he started running away. Then he suddenly heard a cry from

60. Ibid., 140–41.

the top of the mountain, "I can't hold it any longer!" And with
an awful roar the whole mountain collapsed, burying cattle and
huts and the older herdsman, but the boy just escaped at the
edge of the valley.[61]

We can see from this that the younger man had a realistic respect
for the nature power while the older man had a naive lack of concern. The
results of these attitudes were dramatic, for the one with respect was able
to escape intact while the naive attitude led to the older man being overwhelmed by the power. This also tells us that we need to maintain a realistic
concern for the powers of nature, of the unconscious, and of evil, for it we
turn our backs on these in a naive fashion, then a possession by these powers is almost assuredly to follow.

Not only does showing a lack of concern for the power of evil leave
one vulnerable, the opposite does so as well. To show an infantile or naive
curiosity in regard to these powers can also lead one into trouble as the
Grimm fairy tale of "Mrs. Trude" shows.

There was once a little girl who was obstinate and prying and
rather impertinent, and she didn't always do what her parents
told her. One day she said to her parents that she had heard
so much about Mrs. Trude she would go to see what she was
like. People said that she looked so funny and that everything
she had looked so wonderful, and that there were such strange
things in her house, and the girl was very curious and wanted
to see it. Her parents forbade her to do this and said that Mrs.
Trude was a very bad woman who did evil things and that she
would not be their child any longer if she went there. But the
girl paid no attention to what her parents said and went all the
same. When she got there Mrs. Trude asked her why she was
so white. "Oh," said the child, trembling all over, "What I saw
frightened me so!" "What did you see?" "I saw a black man
on your staircase." "That was the charcoal burner, who burns
charcoal in the forest." "And then I saw a green man!" "Oh, that
was the hunter!" "And afterwards I saw a blood-red man!" "That
was the butcher!" "Oh, Mrs. Trude, I am shivering with fear! I
looked through the window and I didn't see you, but the devil
with a fiery head!" "Ah-ha," she said, "you saw the witch in her
true make-up! I've waited for you for long and now you shall
give me light!" And then she turned the girl into a block of wood

61. Ibid., 143–44.

which she threw onto the fire and when it was glowing red she warmed herself by it and said, "That gives a good light!"[62]

It is this naive curiosity that agrees quite closely with what much of the religious literature on possession sees as a cause of possession or an opening to evil: dabbling in the occult. The occult made a resurgence in the modern world and with it has come a growing wave of possession with which the religious community has had to deal. The attempts at discerning the future, reading other's thoughts, controlling objects and people, channeling (mediumship), and gaining paranormal powers, has left the realm of the serious psychic researcher, witch, and sorcerer, and has now become a parlor game. Unbeknownst to these people is the fact that to gain such archetypal power one must fall into the grips of an archetype; that is, one has to become possessed. By being possessed by an archetype, one gains the life-energy connected with it as well as the paranormal gifts attached to it.[63]

To so approach evil, or the arcane powers of nature, with an infantile curiosity, or, with a naive attitude that these can be encountered and used without any adverse effects, is not merely dangerous but is a road to a true loss of oneself in possession. "If one looks at something evil, Plato once said, something evil falls into one's own soul. One cannot look at evil without something in oneself being aroused in response to it, because evil is an archetype and every archetype has an infectious impact upon people."[64] I must agree with von Franz when she says, "the most terrible evil I know, I would say [is] the phenomenon of possession. The worst thing one can meet, or which I have met in my life, is people who have been assimilated by these archetypes of evil power."[65]

To conclude von Franz's analysis, we see that even though she expresses three major roads to possession, there is also a fourth manner of being possessed. Giving in to the experience of being excessively driven to action is the final road to possession: to be caught in a mood of haste.

> There is a famous alchemical saying which was a favorite quotation of Dr. Jung: "All haste is of the devil." The wonderful thing about that is that the devil himself easily gets into a hasty attitude. He is hasty by nature and that's why all haste is of the devil. If we get hasty we are in the devil; if we are in a hurry-up mood we say "things must be decided today," "this evening I have to post the letter," "I must come out in a taxi so that you can sign

62. Ibid.
63. Ibid., 129.
64. Ibid., 270.
65. Ibid., 142.

it, because tomorrow morning will be too late," etc. If you get a phone call like that you know who is behind it. Dr. Jung had a wonderful way of losing such a document on his writing desk, not even consciously putting the thing off, but just losing it on his desk. The devil is personified haste.[66]

It may seem odd that in a discussion of the Jungian view of how one becomes possessed that the story of Faust does not arise since this story so influenced Jung's thinking. Goethe's *Faust* was a seminal work for Jung, and it does deal with how Faust sells his soul to the devil, Mephistopheles, and by so doing gains gifts and powers. In regard to the discussion so far it is not difficult to see how this can be a metaphor for the ego purposefully giving in to the darker aspects of the Self and by doing so being possessed by these aspects of the collective unconscious. Yet the story of Faust is not truly appropriate to the study at hand. Faust is not a story of involuntary possession, but rather it fits more in a study of witchcraft, sorcery, and the like, for Faust is an illustration of a truly voluntary possession, the selling of one's soul in order to gain the arcane gifts of the Devil.

So, by way of summary, we have seen that a person may be possessed by either a complex of the personal sphere, or by an archetype. The person may be possessed because he or she in some manner or attitude opened up or weakened the ego to the onslaughts of the unconscious; to the powers of evil and nature. If the person is possessed by an autonomous complex, then the complex first needs to be removed from its controlling aspect and then integrated into the ego-complex, thus enhancing the ego rather than overpowering it.[67]

If it is an archetype that is the possessor, then it must be removed and kept from the ego. The archetype must be taken back by the Self and only related to by the ego through the safe distance and mediation of the ego—Self axis. Thus, what is needed is a true psychic exorcism, the true casting out from the ego of the possessing archetype, and the need for a command that that spirit-complex not return to once again assimilate the ego. This cannot be accomplished merely by intellectual means. The ego has no power to save itself. It is the reformation of the ego–Self axis that will lead to the accomplishing of the exorcism. Only the person as a total unity can save the ego.

> Freud's "psychological formula" is only an apparent substitute for the daemonically vital thing that causes a neurosis. In reality only the spirit can cast out the "spirit"—not the intellect, which

66. Ibid., 270.

67. Jung, *The Archetypes and the Collective Unconscious*, par. 387.

at best is a mere assistant, like Faust's Wagner, and scarcely fitted to play the role of an exorcist.[68]

The difficulty in the process of psychic exorcism is not so much with the archetype's resistance at being cast out, but with the ego's enjoyment of its condition. For to once again be free of the archetype also means to be separate from those powers that were gained during the possession. "As soon as you fall into an archetype, or identify with the powers of the unconscious, you get those supernatural gifts and that is one reason why people do not like to be exorcised or re-humanized again. The loss of those gifts accounts for one of the resistances against therapy."[69]

We have seen that analytical psychology can be quite helpful in providing us with an understanding of the dynamics of the possessed state. It is useful in comprehending the manner by which a person can fall into such a state, as well as describing what may be occurring within the individual's psyche. That this is so is understandable, since much of this theory's perspective on psychopathology is drawn from the historical accounts of possession, as well as from the fairy tales and myths surrounding the subject. Yet, even though the theory is drawn from these data, still it does little to assist us in diagnosing such a possession, or to differentiate it from any other pathological state. This is actually a criticism of Jungian theory in general; it is good metapsychology, but difficult to apply in practice.

Though a complex or archetype may possess a person, in themselves neither can be directly observed. It is only by means of the effects that these psychic contents have upon the person—and the subsequent reactions, actions and perceptions of that person—that allows us to discern these contents' activity. These behaviors and perceptions manifest themselves as the schizophrenic syndrome, the hysterical reaction and the like, but nowhere does the Jungian literature adequately indicate to us how to practically recognize the difference between the action of a psychic content resulting in schizophrenia, and such an action that may be seen as spirit-possession. This may be because these theorists assume that we already have methods to diagnose such cases and only need to understand the underlying dynamics. Yet such is not the case. Jung and his followers have placed before us the possibility of a type of possession that calls for a form of psychic exorcism, yet they do not tell us how to recognize this very form of possession. The Jungian may be able to do so using such assessment techniques as dream analysis and the observation of interpersonal dynamics, yet this confines the ability to make such a diagnosis only

68. Jung, *The Spirit in Man, Art, and Literature*, par. 73.
69. von Franz, *The Shadow and Evil in Fairytales*, 129.

to those who hold to Jungian beliefs. This, obviously, is not adequate for the general public. What Jung and analytical psychology does provide us is a useful model for understanding the dynamics of the possession state within the psyche, whatever the cause of that state may be. What is still needed is an objective, usable form of descriptive diagnosis. It is to just such a description that we now turn our attention.

19

Three Cases of Possession

The first step in any study is locating the phenomena to be observed. If a meteorologist wishes to investigate the after-effects of a tornado he must first locate a tornado. If an ornithologist desires to study the feeding patterns of the red-tailed hawk first she must find the hawk. Performing these tasks requires knowledge of the criteria for classification. The meteorologist must know the characteristic wind patterns, air pressure and visual cues which indicate the presence of a tornado. The ornithologist must observe the feather coloration, flight pattern and size of the red-tailed hawk to distinguish it from a robin, a turkey vulture or any other type of hawk. Likewise, in the study of psychopathology, criteria must be met before a study of a disorder can commence.

To study the schizophrenic's reaction to certain medications a patient must first meet the diagnostic criteria for schizophrenia before the drug is administered and measurements taken. To observe the effect of psychoanalytic psychotherapy on endogenous depression a patient necessarily must exhibit the characteristic signs of depression for the study to be valid. So, to study possession we must first note the characteristics of possession in order to determine what cases to include. But here is precisely the problem, for we have no such commonly agreed upon set of characteristics. Not only this, but the purpose of this study is to discover just such a set of characteristics. How then does one study a phenomenon without first being able to identify it?

This could be an impossible obstacle to overcome, for finding cases to examine required some preliminary criteria for determining the presence of a possession state. The criteria utilized were simple and straightforward: persons were selected who were believed, by experienced and competent exorcists, to be possessed and whose symptoms were alleviated by an exorcism.

As I searched for those who were possessed I encountered the extremes of Christian exorcism practices. At one point I was taken to a secluded and secret ceremony that resembled an ancient pagan rite, complete with food offerings and other gifts presented on a sacrificial pyre. Late one evening I went with a small religious group to a secluded beach. Once there they began to build the ritualistic bonfire. On top of this each person placed an offering, which was usually food. The fire was then lit. The group sat in a semi-circle around the blaze and began to clap two sticks together in studied rhythm. After a certain number of claps, each person would toss some small object into the fire and then continue the stick clapping. This went on for about a half hour, with the dampness of the ocean breeze becoming less noticeable as the fire grew larger and hotter. Suddenly the clapping stopped and the rite as complete. The clapping of the sticks and the sacrifices were all part of the exorcism of the inner demons, however to these practitioners the devils and demons exorcised in this ceremony were understood more as unconscious contents than as bodiless spirits. It was thus difficult to determine how they differentiated a possessed person from a person with a common mental disorder.

I also found myself experiencing the other extreme of possession belief and practice when I attended a conference on exorcism at a Four-Square Gospel Fellowship. The speaker at this gathering seemed to perceive most misfortunes as forms of possession or demonic oppression calling for exorcism. He told a story of how a friend fell, twisted an ankle and immediately cast a demon out of the ankle and was healed. Exorcisms were also performed with repeated dramatic encounters such as when, in a loud frantic voice, the husband of a young woman continued to command a Jezebel spirit to come out of her while constantly pushing on her forehead with the heel of his palm. For minutes he did this waiting for the expected cough, vomit, or sneeze, which would indicate that the demon had left. Yet no such event came about. Vehemently he continued to push on her forehead until her whole head was bouncing back and forth and she was sobbing, filled with the guilt that she did not have enough faith, or enough love for God, that the demon would leave her. This was the other extreme, a view of the demonic that makes no room for mental or emotional disorders, and even little respect for the truly physical disorders of the body.

In order to gather cases to study, I needed to find persons who approached the matter of possession in a more sober and broad-minded manner. I found four such persons. Two of these were priests of the Episcopal Church and two were laypersons of this denomination who were involved in the deliverance ministry—a form of exorcism ministry most often practiced in neo-Pentecostal circles. In discussions with these four people I came to find that they distinguished between ailments which were physical in origin, those which were psychological in origin, and those which were caused by some demonic influence. This was the type of person I determined most appropriate due to their balanced view of illness. By utilizing the judgments of these people I was able to screen out the obviously physical diseases and the commonly understood mental disorders. Common forms of depression and even schizophrenia were recognized by these religious workers for what they were. But they also made the distinction of cases which they would say were obvious possessions. These cases were the ones which interested me.

From these four exorcists I collected fourteen cases, which they could recall in depth. From these fourteen I developed a general description of the occurrences, the signs, and the symptoms experienced in a possession. But the question arises as to whether these cases were not actually forms of psychopathology that persons untrained in psychological diagnosis might not recognize. In order to answer this question I asked five independent and experienced psychodiagnosticians (psychiatrists and psychologists) to evaluate the cases. We shall review the results of their findings later.

In order that we might have a common basis from which to discuss the phenomena of possession, let us look at three representative cases out of the fourteen. These cases are true, yet significant descriptive data and certain life events have been changed to protect their individual identities. The primary signs and symptoms, though, have been left unaltered.

Vivian

Vivian was a rather attractive woman in her early thirties. Life for her had never been easy. She was raised by a mother who was jealous of the attention she believed her husband to be giving the child and who constantly competed with Vivian for his company. Vivian's father, a prominent professional man, paid little attention to this competition; he was more interested in his growing professional reputation and practice. This competition with her mother, and lack of true emotional contact with her father, left the child emotionally isolated.

Even though Vivian's mother gave her little nurturance or positive attention, she still feared the time when Vivian would leave home. Her mother attempted to keep Vivian a child in order to hold on to her. To finally make the break from home, Vivian married a man whom she did not really love, but rather saw as a means of escape from a confining and confusing situation.

This marriage lasted only a short while, and was filled with physical and emotional abuse. When this abuse finally became unbearable Vivian left her husband and began to work as a legal secretary in order to support herself. In her office she met a man who took an interest in her and showed sincere concern for her needs. After a period of dating they were married and began to live what they hoped to be a happy married life.

During her teenage years Vivian had developed a very seductive and manipulative attitude, and this attitude increased as the years went on. This was first evident in her early teens when she discovered that she could manipulate her father into siding with her against her mother. Later she became fascinated by the way she could draw the attention of men. She found that she was attractive to men of all types and that she could use this power to get herself what she wanted. She had been able to manipulate her first husband into marriage only to find out that this relationship became abusive and unsatisfying. She eventually left this marriage and entered the other which would seem to meet her needs. At first the realization of how her seductiveness could work for her was exciting, but soon after the end of her first marriage she realized that she was beginning to lose control of it. She found that she would unintentionally act provocatively with men. Even when she became aware of what she was doing she could find no manner of controlling it. When an episode of manipulation and seduction was over, and she had regained control, Vivian would experience intense feelings of guilt and worthlessness.

An underlying sense of depression, which had always been present in a small degree, now pervaded much of her life. She began to sleep less and experienced a subsequent loss of energy. She lost interest in her usual activities and began to take a dark and gloomy perspective on life. Soon she even developed thoughts of suicide.

Interspersed with the periods of depression were periods of intense activity and elation. Yet it was an elation with which Vivian found it difficult to identify. When she found herself entertaining seductive and manipulative thoughts and then began acting these out, she experienced it as if she were looking out from the body of somebody else and observing the actions of another person.

During these periods of intense activity and dissociation she would become a charming, sharp-witted, and sexy woman who believed herself able to manipulate the world to meet her needs. At other times she would take on the demeanor of a dependent, helpless girl who needed the protection of a man, and then turn around and become vindictive and shrewd. After one of these periods of uncontrolled manipulations, however, she would experience herself as being quite empty, as if she had in some way been depleted of her life-energy.

This alone may not have been enough to prompt Vivian to seek help, but soon other people began to see through her charms. Even though she initially appeared warm and sensitive to those around her they soon began to experience her as self-centered and superficial. She ended up having few friends, and was even beginning to estrange her new husband. Because of this she knew she needed to make a change in her life. But how?

It was sometime during this period that she began to see dark figures appearing in her presence. In the room where she was sitting, an apparition appeared, standing quietly as if watching her. She became understandably terrified. So it was that she came to consider and start taking seriously the possibility that she was possessed.

Vivian went to her priest for help. He recommended someone with whom she might speak: an exorcist who lived in a nearby town. As she was speaking with the exorcist he began to pray silently, making no indication of this to Vivian. As he did so Vivian momentarily fainted, and almost immediately came to. But it was not the same Vivian who revived as the one with whom he was previously speaking. Her tone of voice had changed dramatically, becoming lower and at times difficult to comprehend. And when he could comprehend her words she would lapse into a language unknown to the minister and—up until this point—to Vivian herself.

The temperature in the room dropped noticeably, to the point where the minister felt quite chilled, and an acrid stench became quite apparent. Suddenly he had the feeling that an alien presence had entered the room. It was a feeling like those one experiences when alone in a dark place and is sure some unseen person is there as well.

Looking into Vivian's eyes he could sense that she was mocking him, belittling him and his efforts to help her. This was all that the minister needed to hear and see. Waiting no longer to determine whether this was a case of schizophrenia, depression, or possession—for the latter now seemed obvious to him—he began to pray aloud in the name of Jesus Christ that the spirit should leave Vivian. As he began his prayer the curtain nearby ripped sharply down the middle, but he did not stop praying. In the midst of his prayer a feeling of suffocating pressure overcame him to the point where he thought he might actually die if he did not stop or leave the room. At this point he did stop, but first commanded that the demon be bound in the name of Jesus.

Soon after this meeting the minister gathered together a team to pray with Vivian. During these prayers Vivian would dissociate into the other personality, and soon it was seen that there were three personalities. A personality of rebellion was first identified and as cast out. Identified next was a personality of manipulation, and finally a mocking personality. Vivian did not remember what happened when the other personalities were engaged and to this extent was not aware that she had such well-defined other personalities residing within her. She was aware, though, that it was "as if" another had been working through her much of the time.

After these sessions of exorcism, Vivian was able to begin living a healthier life. The uncontrollable seductive and manipulative behaviors were gone and, though she might occasionally be tempted to act in such a manner again, she now had control of it. Her depression also began to lift. No longer did she have a sense of inner emptiness or depletion. It was for her as if an inner parasite had been removed. She now could begin to learn appropriate and adaptive ways of relating to others, a thing she had found impossible to do before.

A cursory review of this case could easily draw a therapist to the conclusion that Vivian is suffering from some sort of major depressed state with dissociative and psychotic features. She certainly exhibited many of the classic symptoms of depression: the sad affect, the feelings of guilt and worthlessness, even thoughts of suicide. If we were to concentrate solely on these symptoms, and on the others that comprise the depressive syndromes, then we could easily diagnose her as depressed, or in more technical terms, as experiencing some form of mood disorder.

The diagnosticians that reviewed this case also came to this conclusion. Some saw her as exhibiting a mixed bipolar disorder, the more specific description of what is commonly known as manic-depressive, which indicates a person who exhibits periods of both elation and sadness. Others gave her a diagnosis of major depression. With this diagnosis Vivian's experience of dark apparitions could be understood, because some psychotic manifestations are encountered in severe cases of major depression. However, the diagnosticians were not excessively pleased with these diagnoses, for they seemed to ignore a significant amount of what was happening to Vivian. Even when they considered that she might be suffering from a borderline personality disorder—a character abnormality that shows signs of manipulating others and carries with it the same sense of emptiness that Vivian experienced—still they were not satisfied that this was the most helpful description of her case. Yet, they could find none better and so were forced to fall back on these diagnostic descriptions.

Much, though, had been left out. Many of Vivian's most troublesome experiences are not accounted for by these descriptions, as well as the very odd experiences of those attempting to help her. It is these unaccounted for experiences that indicate that something significantly different from a mood disorder was occurring in Vivian's life.

Henry

Henry was a rather plain looking man in his late thirties. He was a hard-working professional whose dedication to his job had already cost him his first marriage and was about to cost him a second.

Raised by upper middle-class parents who treated him well, Henry was provided with a good home and education. His home life, though, was not without its problems. Henry's parents fought a great deal and would accuse each other of infidelity. This concerned him, as well as confused him regarding the meaning of marriage, although it did not prevent him from falling in love and getting married. Yet the charming, seemingly understanding and assertive man whom his first wife married soon changed into an aggressive, arrogant, quarrelsome, and vindictive person. He had exhibited some of these qualities throughout much of his life, but now they were becoming even more prominent.

Henry had for a long time been quite a womanizer and heavy drinker, but now he found that he was beginning to lose control of the times that his feelings of lust and the need for a drink would arise. It soon became apparent that Henry was an alcoholic. His alcoholism and affairs with women, together with an abusive sexual attitude toward his wife, spelled disaster for his marriage.

After the divorce he began to withdraw socially. He became more involved in his work, to the point of being a workaholic. He had few close friends; instead of relationships, he substituted fantasies of success and power.

Then, into this narrowing tunnel of self-preoccupation entered a rather quiet and caring woman whom he met at an office gathering. She seemed to be drawn to him as a man in need of reassurance and caring, and this caregiving attitude touched a responsive chord in Henry. After a few months they were married. Still Henry could not seem to control his drinking or his desire to be sexually involved with other women. The thought of women and drinking created in him a very elated mood. His mind seemed to race with excitement as he pondered the possibilities of an evening of drinking and picking up women. His thoughts would inevitably lead to action. After the excitement and elation wore off, Henry would realize that he actually did not enjoy what he was doing, and knew that he had gone too far. He was totally out of control. Whenever these thoughts arose in his mind he could not avoid them, however diligently he might try. Finally he would tire of resisting and would give in to them and the actions that resulted.

As Henry realized his helplessness he became increasingly depressed. Thoughts of suicide and death seemed to him the only response to his feelings of worthlessness and emptiness. His sleep was erratic and he began to appear constantly fatigued. And so he would fluctuate between a period of inflation and excitation and a period of severe emptiness and despair.

He also began to develop a paranoid style of relating to the world. He experienced undue social anxiety as well as an apprehensive expectation of some undefinable harm coming to him. He exhibited an increasing need to keep track of what was happening around him and was quite touchy. He would fly off the handle at the slightest provocation exploding into angry tirades over which he had no conscious control. After these episodes his feelings of worthlessness only seemed to increase. He also became very jealous regarding his wife. He was constantly suspicious that she was having extramarital affairs, even though he knew this was a ridiculous possibility.

Then one day Henry's fear that he had lost control of himself became actualized: he began to hear voices. The voices that he heard were varied. Some were barely audible while those that were clear tended to vary in tone. The voices would speak about matters of religion or morality in a very coherent manner. Because of this Henry was sure that he was going crazy. He became convinced of this when he saw standing in front of him what seemed to be the dark figure of a cloaked man. Henry became so frightened that he shared his experiences with his wife. She became concerned, but not because she thought he was mentally ill. She believed that he was possessed. Henry latched onto this explanation and began to blame his problems on demons. He continued to see dark figures from time to time, and the voices continued to attempt to convince him that his drinking and sexual behavior were all that could be expected of him and that it was wrong to deny these because of some moldy moral proscriptions.

Henry finally decided he needed help and went to an exorcist. After hearing this story the exorcist agreed that Henry was probably either oppressed by demons or possessed and that an exorcism would be attempted. When Henry met with the team of persons who would perform the exorcism he was rather apprehensive and unsure that he was doing the right thing. He finally decided to go through with it and sat down allowing the group to begin to pray for him.

They had hardly begun when Henry became aware of another personality within him. It was almost a parody of lust and abuse and Henry seemed unable to control the thought or desire to escape this situation, a desire that the voice forcibly impressed upon him. Henry jumped up and began to run out of the room. Some of the group attempted to stop him but he threw them aside as if they were small children. Likewise, when he finally settled down and some of the group attempted to bring him back, they could not move him. It was as if he had become as heavy and large as a rock, and it was not for some time that they could get him back into the room.

Throughout the whole episode those in the room felt that they were in the presence of something inhuman. As they prayed an acrid stench filled their nostrils and the temperature in the room dropped, giving the sense that a door had been left open on a winter day.

At least three personalities were exorcised from Henry, each providing its own voice in Henry's mind and own style of relating to the group. At one point, while praying for the personality to leave Henry, the group experienced a sensation of being choked, as if all the oxygen in the room was gone and they needed air. After the personality left Henry this sensation ceased for the group.

After the exorcism, which took several meetings, Henry's obsessions left him. His depression began to lift and his paranoid style changed as he became more caring and open. Additional counseling was needed to help him deal with some of his conceptions of marriage and how his own parents related with each other and with him, but on the whole Henry's life was changed dramatically by his exorcism.

Even more so than in Vivian's case, Henry's can be diagnosed in several differing ways, depending on which signs and symptoms are focused upon. If you are impressed by his experience of hearing voices and seeing apparitions you may be led to a diagnosis of psychosis as were two of the diagnosticians who reviewed the case. One saw him as exhibiting an atypical psychosis. This is a description that essentially says that the individual has psychotic type symptoms, but does not adequately fit any of the schizophrenic syndromes. Another diagnostician thought it was clearer than that, and gave Henry a diagnosis of undifferentiated schizophrenia.

If you concentrate on Henry's mood you may diagnose him as being depressed, or as exhibiting the same mixed bipolar disorder as we encountered with Vivian. This is how one diagnostician viewed Henry.

Finally, if you focus on his interpersonal relationships you may encounter the character distortions Henry exhibits, and so diagnose him as a mixed personality disorder. Yet, all of these diagnoses ignore extremely important aspects of Henry's case. Because of that, these diagnosticians were generally dissatisfied with the descriptions available to them. If they had had a diagnostic description which took in more of the significant experiences in Henry's life, they indicated that they gladly would have used it.

Maggie

For most of her life Maggie had been happy. Her childhood was one of relative peace and security. Her parents were financially secure and maintained a stable and happy home for both themselves and their children. In high school Maggie had many friends, being an attractive and energetic young girl. She was also a serious student and subsequently did well academically. After graduation she went off to college where, like most students of the early seventies, she became nominally involved in the use of drugs. Her drug use never became more than a social activity, however. While in college she met a fellow psychology major whom a few years later she married. After graduation he went into business and she took up the role of housewife.

Being an adventurous and intelligent woman, Maggie continued to find things to interest her. She would read constantly and investigated new areas in which to broaden her horizons of knowledge. One of these areas was religion.

Maggie's family had never been exceptionally devout. They attended church on Christmas and Easter, and occasionally on a few other Sundays of the year, but they never became active members of any church. Maggie herself had never shown much of an interest in religion during childhood. Yet now in her late twenties, she had begun to look into religion. She was fascinated by the philosophical tenets of the various world religions. Her interest in psychology seemed to be enhanced by this new study of the world's religions and myths.

Because of this new interest, Maggie also became intrigued by certain religious practices, especially meditation. The more she read about it, the more fascinated she was by the stories. Finally she decided to try it out herself. Remembering what the many gurus and swamis had done and taught, she sat down, closed her eyes and began to recite a mantra. Not long into this meditation she found herself experiencing a feeling she had never encountered before. It was as if she were no longer a part of her body. This was similar to feelings she had when she had used certain perception altering drugs, but this time she seemed to have more control over the matter and a feeling of clarity which she did not have with the drugs.

Then, while concentrating on this feeling and still reciting her mantra, she experienced a darkness approaching her, an enveloping darkness coming like a quickly moving storm behind her closed eyes. Before she was aware of it the darkness had come upon her and had enveloped her. Fear struck her as she struggled to free herself from this darkness. Finally, after what appeared to be an eternity she opened her eyes, and the familiarity of her living room comforted her. Still trembling, but with the intensity of the fear subsiding, Maggie vowed never to do that again.

Maggie continued to read about the various religions and their philosophies, but she now noticed that she was feeling more and more depressed during the days. When she was with other people she would forget this as she could laugh and enjoy her friends, but more and more a feeling of despair was creeping into her daily existence. After a few months the despair was becoming pervasive. She was aware of an emptiness growing within her that threatened to suck the life out of her.

As the emptiness grew so did the fluctuations in her emotional reactions. Her times of happiness now seemed strained and superficial. She laughed harder with less genuineness, and at times she broke out in purposeless laughter. Her reactions to the negative were also exaggerated. She would perceive a delay in her husband's arrival home to mean that he had certainly been in an accident and had died. Her times of despair were deep and seemingly inescapable. One day, all this seemed to come together in a coherent vision, a vision of a void coming to engulf her; a void reminiscent of what she encountered in her meditation.

From then on her despair would come to her joined with an inner vision of this engulfing void. Maggie could not figure out what was wrong with her, but knew that she needed help. Not being religious, she thought about finding a psychiatrist, but knew of none. A friend of hers knew of a priest in the area who did counseling and recommended that Maggie see him. Not feeling particularly comfortable about seeing a priest, but feeling less comfortable with her situation she relented and set up an appointment.

The day she was to see the priest was fair and bright. Though feeling the despair heavy upon her, she was still able to drag herself to her car and make the drive to the church. Once in his office she began to relate her story to him; how she felt and the depression that was enveloping her. As she spoke the priest began to pray silently for her even as he continued to listen and speak. But even as he began this silent prayer Maggie became more restless. Her eyes became widened and glazed. Suddenly, with no warning, she jumped up and screamed. Her feet swept upward from the floor, her head now touching the carpet. The priest looked on in astonishment for she had made no move to flip herself, but had been swept off the floor by another force. Just as suddenly her feet, pointing toward the ceiling, swirled downward and she was standing again. In astonishment the priest took a step back, and now speechless began to pray more intensely. Maggie then assumed a lotus position on the floor, mimicking other Eastern meditation practices as well.

Knowing now that he was dealing with a possession, the priest began to command the demons in the name of Christ to come out of Maggie. As he did so her face contorted into a hideous form and she continued to scream. The priest persisted in his commands and grabbed a bowl to prepare for what he knew would come next. As he continued to command the demon to leave, Maggie let loose a screech and gagged. The priest shoved the bowl in front of her and she spit up phlegm into it. She grew quiet for a while. Still he persisted and soon she yelled again, once more gagging uncontrollably and spitting up phlegm. Though she had eaten before she came to the session, she did not vomit any food matter, only phlegm.

This continued for about an hour after which they both decided they needed to stop; exhaustion setting in on each of them. After this session, things began to settle down for Maggie. Her sense of despair lifted. A joy in life began to return, and a new sense of life came upon her; joy and excitement that she had previously experienced up until the day she had first encountered the void.

Maggie's case presented problems for the diagnosticians. Her history was normal enough and gave few if any hints of a potential problem. The only precipitant to her problem seemed to be one instance of meditation. Whether this event triggered some memory of an earlier drug experience or some other repressed or dissociated event is unknown. Diagnostically, a form of mood disorder, such as major depression, seems in order, yet none of the diagnosticians felt that her case exhibited enough evidence to so classify her. In the end they felt that no clear diagnosis was fitting.

The lack of diagnosis for Maggie, along with the inadequacy of diagnosis in the cases of Vivian and Henry, indicate that something different from a depression or psychosis was occurring in these cases. This "something different" has similarities across the cases.

The first similarity is a sense of being out-of-control of oneself. Vivian experienced a loss of control of her seductive and manipulative thoughts and behaviors; Henry lost control of his sexual behavior and alcoholic desires; Maggie had the sense of being overcome by a void against which she was powerless. All three also experienced a fluctuating sense of self, with periods of elation—or in Maggie's case, a sense of escape into superficiality—and a sense of emptiness or depletion.

The experience of losing control would later develop into a sense that someone or something else was producing these thoughts. This sense of loss of control, as well as the fluctuating sense of self-inflation and self-depletion, was joined by other, even more startling manifestations. We saw in Vivian's and Henry's cases the startling effects on those around them; the drop in temperature, the stench as well as Vivian's and Henry's experience of seeing apparitions and hearing voices. There are other commonalities as well, and these were seen not only in these three cases but in all fourteen that were studied.

These commonalities are what make up the possessive states disorder: a new description, which—as we will see—the diagnosticians found much more useful a tool for understanding these cases.

20

The Diagnosis of Possession

I n this chapter we will set forth the characteristics that distinguish possession from other forms of pathology. To do this requires a detailed
analysis of the possessive state and an in depth comparison of it to the other
diagnostic categories. If your only desire is to know the characteristics of
possession, then this analysis may become too detailed and technical, and
you may wish to go directly to the end of the chapter where a summary of
the possessive states disorder is listed. However, if you are interested in how
possession is different from the commonly encountered forms of psychopathology then you will want to read the complete chapter.

Before we can begin to understand the uniqueness of the possession
diagnosis, it is necessary to have a cursory understanding of the diagnostic categories commonly is use today. These are set forth in the American
Psychiatric Association's *Diagnostic and Statistical Manual*, the standard for
psychiatric and psychological diagnosis. The criteria in this manual tends to
change every ten years or so. Even so, there are some consistent aspects that
we can observe over the decades.

The first category of interest with regard to possession is the psychotic disorders. Over time, within this category we find the various diagnoses
of schizophrenia, brief reactive psychosis, schizophreniform disorder,
schizoaffective disorder, and atypical psychotic disorder. The appearance
of all of these disorders is similar, leaving the major criteria for a differentiation the duration of the symptoms involved. For example, the brief
reactive psychosis resembled schizophrenia except that the symptoms
had been present for less than two weeks. Likewise the schizophreniform
disorder was similar to schizophrenia, but the person has only been exhibiting the psychotic phenomena for a period between two weeks and
six months. Since all, except for the schizoaffective and atypical psychotic

disorder, resemble schizophrenia we will concentrate on understanding the characteristics of this malady.

The schizophrenic's thoughts and perceptions are different from those around him or her. This person may have delusions of almost any nature. He or she may also perceive things that are not present. Thus, the schizophrenic "may hear, see, feel, smell, and taste things that are not there."[1] The most common form of hallucination is auditory, while most visual hallucinations are correlates of a physical abnormality in the brain. The emotions of the schizophrenic are also impaired. In certain cases the emotional expression will be blunted, at other times it may merely be inappropriate or vary greatly from moment to moment. His or her emotions may be so impaired that "the person generates an uncanny or eerie impact on the observer."[2]

The schizophrenic is almost always socially withdrawn, and his or her normal life functioning impaired. So there will be a noticeable deterioration in work performance, communications with others, and appearance.

The research into schizophrenia has indicated that if a person is to exhibit the disorder he or she will usually do so before the age of forty-five. It is extremely rare for a person to experience their initial schizophrenic episode after this age.

There have been five commonly agreed upon types of schizophrenia that further distinguish persons with the former set of symptoms. These are the disorganized, catatonic, paranoid, undifferentiated, and residual types.

The disorganized type has incoherence as its main characteristic. The catatonic types can exhibit a broad spectrum of physical reactions, ranging from little response to stimulation to gross excitement; from acting in the opposite manner than requested to assuming odd physical postures and rigidity. Persecutory and grandiose delusions are the primary features of the paranoid type. Grandiose or persecutory hallucinations, as well as delusional jealousy, may also be indicative of this type. Though the undifferentiated type is "not meant to allow for evasion of a distinct diagnosis, nor . . . be used as a wastebasket term,"[3] still it has been used when the criteria for the other types is either not met or they overlap. Finally there is the residual type. "This diagnosis is used when there are no prominent [hallucinations, delusions, incoherence, illogical thinking, or the like] present when the person is seen, but these symptoms have been present at least one time in the past."[4]

1. Webb, *DSM-III Training Guide*, 72.
2. Ibid.
3. Ibid., 76.
4. Ibid.

If a person who seems to be psychotic exhibits some of these symptoms, but fails to meet the criteria for schizophrenia then the atypical psychosis diagnosis is usually employed. Likewise, if a therapist cannot make the distinction between schizophrenia and a mood disorder then the schizoaffective diagnosis was used.

Closely allied to these psychotic disorders are the paranoid disorders. The major distinction among these is that paranoid disorders have no hallucinations or bizarre delusions. Rather the paranoid disorders feature "an organized delusional system in an otherwise more or less intact individual."[5] The delusions must be plausible and of a persecutory or jealous nature.

The next category is the mood disorders, which are distinguished by a disturbance of mood. "Mood is a pervasive emotion and there can eventually be distortions in thinking and behavior as a result of the disturbance."[6] What concerns us most in this discussion are the major mood disorders, which include major depression and the bipolar syndromes.

A major depression is distinguished by a full depressive syndrome with no fluctuation to elation. The depressive syndrome exhibits a mood characterized by sadness, a loss of enthusiasm, a loss of old interests, boredom, and feelings of worthlessness. The depressed person also shows a loss of appetite, low energy, sleep disturbances, and self-destructive acts.

A bipolar disorder is diagnosed when a person exhibits a full manic episode, usually in connection with the individual experiencing a depressed episode at one point in time. There are four subclassifications of this disorder: manic, hypomanic, depressed, and mixed.

The manic subclassification is used when the individual meets the criteria for a manic episode. The manic episode is distinguished by an elated, expansive mood. The person with a manic syndrome will seem tireless and show little need for sleep. He or she may be restless, aggressive, indiscrete, and even promiscuous. Hypomanic is when a person exhibits the elation but does not meet the criteria for a full manic episode.

When a person has had a manic episode but is presently exhibiting major depressive symptoms, then the depressed subclass is utilized. If there is a full manic and depressive syndrome present, but depression is prominent then the mixed diagnosis is employed. However, all bipolar disorders show a fluctuation in mood at some time.

Another class of disorders are those which have anxiety as the major characteristic. These anxiety disorders include general anxiety, phobias, panic attacks, obsessions, compulsions, and traumatic reactions. Of these,

5. Ibid., 79.
6. Ibid., 24.

the obsessions, compulsions, and general anxiety are of primary interest for our consideration. According to Webb, the obsessive compulsive disorder is characterized by:

> recurrent obsessions and/or compulsions. Obsessions are recurrent, persistent ideas, thoughts, images, or impulses that are experienced as being senseless, repugnant, and involuntarily produced. Compulsions are repetitive and seemingly purposeful behaviors that are performed according to certain rules or in stereotyped fashion. They are designed to produce or prevent some future event or situation. Obsessive Compulsive Disorder may feature either obsessions or compulsions or both. The disorder is a source of distress and interferes with an individual's role and function.[7]

The generalized anxiety disorder features generalized, persistent anxiety, with an anxious mood present for at least one month. Also none of the symptoms of phobic or obsessive compulsive disorders are present. The somatoform disorders are those which result in certain physical manifestations such as illness, pain, or paralysis all of which have no physical basis, but are psychological in origin.

The dissociative disorders are a class of disorders which include such syndromes as amnesia, fugue states, depersonalization and multiple personalities. Most important for our consideration is the multiple personality disorder. The predominant presenting symptom in the diagnosis of dissociative identity disorder, or the multiple personality, is the existence of two or more distinct personalities in one individual. Each personality is an integrated unit with its own memories, behaviors, and relationships, and becomes the dominant and controlling force in the individual's life at a particular time. Subpersonalities are often not aware of each other and the shift from one to another generally occurs under stress and quite suddenly.

Delirium is a disorder directly related to organic abnormalities of the brain. This is a pathological condition in which an individual experiences a disturbance in attention, psychomotor activity, perception, memory, and the ability to know where he or she may be, the time of day, or day of the month. Webb reports that "vivid dreams, nightmares, misperceptions, illusions, and hallucinations are common," and that "there is a variable subjective state ranging from terror to apathy to rage."[8]

So far we have been considering what are referred to as clinical syndromes, conditions associated with a general state of being, many times

7. Ibid., 95.
8. Ibid., 66.

assumed to be transitory or situationally induced. Now we turn our attention to another group of disorders associated with the character structure of the individual, the personality disorders.

The first is the paranoid personality. These people are characterized by an all-encompassing, inappropriate mistrust of others, excessive vigilance and sensitivity to what is happening around him or her, and little emotional expression.

The schizotypal personality disorder is often diagnosed when an individual seems to be schizophrenic but is not so severe as to warrant this latter diagnosis. The schizotypal personality exhibits many of the signs and symptoms of the schizophrenic, the social withdrawal, perceptual distortions and the distortions of the thinking process. However, in this disorder the content of thought is not quite delusional, with the individual being aware that his or her thoughts are odd.

The paranoid and schizotypal personalities can be generally characterized by the impression that the person is odd or eccentric. However, another group of disorders are characterized by dramatic, emotional or erratic behavior. These are the histrionic, borderline, narcissistic, and antisocial personality disorders.

The histrionic personality is the newer name for what was once known as the hysterical personality. The common features of this disorder are dramatic behaviors such as drawing attention to oneself, emotional outbursts, and overly dramatic gestures. These persons are experienced by others as superficial, vain and manipulative.

The borderline personality is indicative of a greater disturbance in the individual's identity. This person is usually impulsive, self-destructive, has pervasive feelings of inner emptiness as well as having intense, but short-lived relationships. He or she may also be insecure with regard to who he or she is, what sexual identity to acquire, and what to do in life. A person with a narcissistic personality disorder, on the other hand, exhibits "a grandiose sense of self-importance or uniqueness; fantasies of unlimited success or ideal love; a constant need for attention and admiration; overreaction or indifference to criticism or defeat; feelings of entitlement; exploitiveness; and lack of empathy."[9] The antisocial personality disorder differs from these because this person will display a chronic and continuous behavior of violating others' rights in an overt manner.

The final category of character disorder we shall look at is the diagnosis of a mixed personality disorder. This is essentially a diagnosis applicable to a person who exhibits the symptomology of one or more of the various

9. Ibid., 127.

personality disorders. This is only utilized, though, when the criteria are not clearly met for any singular disorder. If the full criteria for a disorder were present, then that diagnosis is the appropriate one to be given.

With this background in diagnostic categorization and the phenomenology of possession, we can now approach answers to the primary questions posed at the outset. Are the present categories of psychopathology adequate to account for cases of demonic possession? and, Do the phenomena found in cases of demonic possession warrant their own diagnostic category? Answers to these questions can partially be seen in the cases of possession enumerated earlier. The most telling evidence, though, comes from the review of all fourteen cases of possession gathered.

The five experienced psychiatrists and psychologists were given these case descriptions for their examination and asked to provide a diagnosis compatible with the *Diagnostic and Statistical Manual of Mental Disorders*. Additionally, each then examined these cases using the newly synthesized criteria for the possessive states disorder. After examination and diagnosis these raters indicated their level of satisfaction with both the new description and the standard categories in depicting these proposed cases of possession. This led to the conclusion that the present diagnostic categories did not adequately describe the cases of demonic possession which were studied.

The reasons for coming to this conclusion were three-fold. First, there was no consistent diagnosis provided for the cases of demonic possession examined. Second, even for those diagnoses used, the overall satisfaction of the diagnosticians with these categories was moderate to low. Finally, the present diagnostic categories could not account for certain highly significant abnormalities happening in the lives of the individuals studied.

Also, confidence in the use of the present categories of psychopathology was eroded by the fact that for any given case, one diagnostician would provide a diagnosis quite different from another, the same case being seen by the first as exhibiting schizophrenic processes and by the other, delirium. With such confusion it is not surprising that these raters were not completely satisfied with the usual diagnostic descriptions with which they were provided. Each case exhibited aspects of many of the typical psychopathological conditions; aspects of psychoses, depression and various personality disorders. To choose one diagnosis over any other meant that certain of these aspects necessarily had to be ignored.

For example: in more than half the cases the patients experienced inappropriate guilt, or feelings of worthlessness, yet over a third of the proposed diagnoses of the cases could not account for this experience. Likewise, six other major areas of affliction were left unaccounted for by the proposed diagnoses. The patient's experience of losing self-control, or being

controlled by something or someone else, is not addressed by the majority
of the diagnoses utilized. Few of the diagnostic categories could account
for the bizarre religious revulsions experienced by the patient, such as a
patient's destruction of religious objects, and the feelings of suffocation and
struggle during prayer.

Because of the other major symptoms in each case, the diagnosticians
were forced to leave untouched the patient's experience of having more than
one personality present within him or herself. None of the diagnosticians
found the multiple personality, or dissociative identity disorder to be a viable
alternative, and yet in many cases were unable to account for the patient's
experience of other personalities. In some instances these were accounted
for by a diagnosis of either undifferentiated or paranoid schizophrenia, but
for the most part it was ignored. Many of the patients we encountered in this
study experienced the hearing of voices, the seeing of dark figures and the
envisioning of apparitions. In some instances this was considered a part of a
schizophrenic syndrome or a major depression with psychotic features, but
in other cases neither of these applied. This left the diagnostician unable to
account for these visions and voices experienced by the patient, an oversight
which was inappropriate and of glaring significance.

Two sets of phenomena were totally ignored by the present diagnostic
categories: those phenomena which dealt with transpersonal occurrences
and those of a parapsychological nature. Transpersonal psychology and
parapsychology are both fields of study that are exceptionally young and
still filled with faulty research, which leads more to speculation than to fact-
finding. The existent body of research that is informative is still small and
not widely read. For this reason, reports of transpersonal and parapsychological phenomena are viewed with skepticism by the majority of researchers and clinicians. Because of this, the inclusion of such data here is, at first,
questionable. Yet transpersonal or parapsychological factors were reported
in twelve of the fourteen cases. We are therefore faced with the dilemma of
including these findings and facing the scrutiny of the skeptical or rejecting these data and so ignoring an observance which is both common and
unique to these cases. It is because of this commonality across the cases, and
because these phenomena are indicators unique to the possessive state that
I have chosen to include them.

The parapsychological, or paranormal, phenomena that were encountered were such things as levitation, objects flying seemingly under their
own power, the hearing of unaccounted for footsteps, and the like. None of
these could be explained by the present diagnostic categories. Transpersonal
events were reported in nine cases and included those phenomena directly
experienced by persons in the vicinity of the patient. Others in the vicinity

felt a lowering of the room temperature in which the patient was found, or they perceived an acrid, sulfurous odor around the patient. When praying for the person, others may have felt the same sense of suffocating pressure that the patient experienced. These types of phenomena are not commonly experienced in most psychopathological disorders, and so are not found in any of the present diagnostic categories. These happenings are startling and significant when encountered. The oversight of these phenomena—which occurs when using any of the present diagnostic categories—is wholly unsatisfactory and needs rectification.

It is not surprising to find the present diagnostic categories inadequate in cases like these. The history of possession bears out this conclusion. We have seen how many civilizations and cultures of the past maintained a separation between the phenomena involved in spirit-possessions and those involved in "madnessess," or what corresponds closely to what we describe today in our present diagnostic system for psychopathology.

This conclusion would not surprise the student of various forms of possession, either. For, throughout the occurrences of possession world-wide, spirit-possession has been seen as essentially non-pathological and distinct from the forms of madness or mental disorder which were exhibited in the society. Where its presence did indicate pathology to the society, it was still viewed as a spiritual concern and not one which was mental.

Finally, this result should come as no surprise to many psychological researchers. Pattison for several years stated a preference for describing possession by means of a culturally-minded model and not a disease-oriented model. Henderson has warned us not to attempt to fit possession into any of our current diagnostic categories, and Peck researched the independence of demonic possessions from others forms of psychopathology.

This present work is, therefore, not the unfolding of some new finding, but rather an extension of what has been known for centuries, and only recently lost or subsumed by the wave of positivism and rationalism that swept across psychology during the last one hundred years. The diagnostic raters of this study have encountered the difficulty of working on one task while using the tools appropriate to another.

Merely because we have found these present diagnostic categories inadequate in regard to cases of demonic possession, we need not be left in the dark, nor need we feel lost in our understanding of the phenomena. We merely need to set aside our restricting preconceptions, and develop a description that is consistent and descriptive of the phenomena we are encountering in these fourteen cases—in other words, a new diagnostic description.

The construction of this new diagnostic category was accomplished by
a review of the fourteen cases gathered from the religious workers, as well
as a consideration of the relative importance of each phenomenon involved.
What was produced was a seven-feature description: the possessive states
disorder. These seven features included the most prominent as well as the
most unique factors found in the cases, thus giving the possessive states
disorder a distinguishing characteristic when compared with the present
diagnostic categories. These seven features were an (1) experienced loss of
self-control; (2) a sense of self that fluctuated between periods of emptiness
and periods of inflation, or grandiosity; (3) the hearing of voices and seeing
of visions; and (4) the presence of other personalities within the person. Also
seen were phenomena seemingly unique to possessive states. These were (5)
behaviors that exhibit a patient's extreme revulsion to religious items or matters; (6) paranormal or parapsychological occurrences; and (7) phenomena
that seem to affect persons in the vicinity of the patient.

We can supplement these criteria with what we know of how to
distinguish the origin of an experience. Transpersonal phenomena affecting the psyche are distinguished from intrapsychic productions by five
characteristics:

The first and most obvious is this: a person experiences a vision, voice,
or feeling as coming from outside of him- or herself, from a wholly other.
The important aspect here is that the event is a spontaneous, immediate
experience, rather than a subsequent interpretation of an event as having
come from the wholly other. Secondarily, the experience is numinous. Associated with this is the third factor, the presence of numinous fear or awe.
Fourth, there is an unusual clarity to the experience; a clarity marked by
the gaining of a cognizance that is instantaneous rather than gradual (like
the awareness gained when listening to another person speaking rather
than the knowledge gained by means of reasoning through a personal
thought). Clarity is also exhibited in the establishment of the experience
in long-lasting memory. Finally, when a visual image is involved there is
usually some form of luminosity involved, whether of beautiful light or of
shadowy darkness.

These five qualities of experiencing the *wholly other* hold true whether
the experience is perceived as an inner event or outer encounter. Each may
be present to a different degree in various situations, and if there is no visual
image the factor of luminosity may not be present. However, these are the
factors we may use in our differentiating of the spiritual experience from the
primarily intrapsychic.

These five characteristics of an encounter with a transpersonal event combined with the seven diagnostic criteria mentioned above, lend a level of confidence to the validity of diagnosing a true possession.

The essential feature of a possession, though, was the experience of being controlled by someone, or something, alien to oneself. This experience was usually manifested in a subsequent loss of control in one or more of four areas of functioning: thinking; anger; impulsive behaviors; and uncontrollable physical reactions.

The loss of thought control was seen in the form of ruminations, obsession, temptations, and expectations of disaster, harm, or death. Uncontrollable anger was seen in the sudden outbursts of fury, or excessive anger, that were frequently encountered among those possessed. Along with the fury experienced by the patient, he or she may have had the overwhelming temptation to utter a stream of profanities, and would then do so, deluging those around with disparaging epithets. Impulsivity could be seen in almost any area of life, but the most commonly observed areas were sex, excessive alcohol or drug use, gambling, and overeating.

Finally, the uncontrolled physical reactions were seen as some unintentional distortions of the body. The body might have become contorted, the facial features distort, or certain physical functions cease for no apparent reason.

Some form of a loss of self-control was seen in all of the fourteen cases reviewed in this study, and has a historical and cross-cultural basis. Throughout history, and in the various forms of possession which we earlier reviewed, losing of control of some aspect of functioning was central to the spirit-possession.

The truly unique aspects to the possessive states disorder lie in three areas: revulsive religious behavior, paranormal or parapsychological occurrences, and the impact on others in the vicinity of the patient. The revulsive religious behaviors were especially seen in relation to religious objects and ceremonies, as well as to prayer. The patient may have had an extremely negative reaction to prayer. There were cases where the person came to a religious worker asking for prayer in order to gain help for his or her problems, but instead of feeling comforted, the patient fell into a trance, exhibited an outburst of fury, or experienced an inner agitation during the other's prayer. If the patient attempted to pray it was possible that he or she would begin to experience the sensation of being choked or suffocated.

Prayer was not the only catalyst in provoking the revulsive religious behaviors. The presence of religious symbols and objects could do so as well. The individual might suddenly rip a Bible to shreds, or pull a religious picture off the wall. Likewise, a Bible, a cross, or even the mentioning of the name of Jesus could cause this person to be violently agitated. For many who experienced being possessed, it was nearly impossible for them to articulate the name of Jesus. One person in this study also had difficulty in saying the Lord's Prayer, even though desiring to do so.

Probably the most startling aspects to this disorder—and for many the most questionable—were the paranormal, or parapsychological, phenomena which were frequently encountered. These included poltergeist-type phenomena of moving objects, footsteps, rapping and the like. One of the more spectacular poltergeist-type exhibitions was the destruction of religious objects by an unknown force.

Poltergeist-type phenomena were not the only paranormal occurrences met during a possession. Certain patients also exhibited some form of telepathy, or clairvoyance. One of the most startling forms of these was seen when someone brought a hidden religious object into the patient's presence, or began to pray silently for the person. Even though the patient was given no clue that this had occurred, still he or she flew into a fury or fell into a trance.

Also encountered—though infrequently—were occurrences of levitation, or the patient becoming so heavy that many persons could not move him. Similarly, some patients exhibited a strength far beyond that which would be considered normal to a given situation. There are times when, in extreme situations, normal people have been known to develop excessive strength. There have been instances when a frail woman has lifted a car to get it off her trapped husband. Whether these are instances of some form of possession or not, we cannot say. But the possessed individual in this study did not have this external stimulus to inspire her, but rather exhibited the strength in what might otherwise be considered an average situation.

Equally as surprising as the encountering of paranormal phenomena was that they occurred in over seventy percent of the cases studied. Rather than being rare, some form of parapsychological occurrence may be the norm in cases of possession.

Unlike most disorders, there is not only an effect on the behavior and experience of the patient, but also on others in the vicinity. A person living with the patient, or someone attempting to help, may experience some of the above-mentioned poltergeist-type phenomena. A helper, praying with or for the patient, may experience the same suffocating or choking feeling that the patient experienced. Some persons also mentioned having the feeling that there was an alien presence near while they were with the patient. Also common in many cases was the experience of a lowered temperature around the possessed person and that there was an especially acrid, or sulfurous odor present.

Though all of these experiences are rare within standard mental disorders, they appear common in the history of possession, and to the forms of possession known throughout the world. Paranormal phenomena have been experienced in all forms of possession. Likewise, some effect— whether internal or external—on others in the vicinity is well known in the literature on demonic possessions. To smell a sulfurous odor, feel a lowered temperature, or have objects fly across the room are commonly expected phenomena in demonic possessions. Malachi Martin in his book, *Hostage to the Devil*, describes how, before an exorcism was to take place in a private home, the exorcist had all movable objects either nailed down or removed in order to prevent such poltergeist-type activity from happening. Smelling a sulfurous odor was also experienced by those present in a shamanic séance, while the lowering of temperatures combined with cold breezes was commonly reported in Spiritualist séances.

Another feature of the possessive state is the fluctuating experience of the self. This is an important aspect as it occurs in nearly all of the cases reviewed in this study. The person's sense of self was seen to fluctuate between a feeling of despair, depletion or an experience of inner emptiness, and the feeling of inflation and grandiosity. How long each mood remained was variable. Some persons seemed to exhibit one or the other mood predominately, shifting only briefly to the other pole. Other persons would shift back and forth, exhibiting both aspects to a relatively equal degree.

These periods were determined by the person's sense of self-control, with the feelings of emptiness and depletion usually occurring during periods when the person felt in relative control of him- or herself, and the inflated mood being associated with periods when the person experienced another as being in control. On the surface this shift in mood is reminiscent of the narcissist's mode of functioning, yet there is a basic difference between the two. The narcissist's mood tends to fluctuate in response to external cues, depending on whether his or her narcissistic needs are being supplied, or if a narcissistic injury has been delivered by another in the environment. The mood fluctuation of the person in a possessive state is due to internal cues rather than environmental ones. It is the internal sense of control and independence that seems to trigger the response.

Behaviorally, the emptiness or depletion phase was observed as a sad affect, inappropriate feelings of guilt and worthlessness. It was also seen in the patient's perceived loss of energy and his or her loss of interest in usual activities. Not uncommon—and needing to be watched—was the suicidal ideation and attempts of the patient, which also marked the emptiness phase of this fluctuating sense of self. Some patients expressed the feeling of emptiness as a feeling of inner darkness, or as being depleted or drained by the one controlling him or her. It was also experienced as a deep void within.

The periods of inflation were marked by egocentric, self-indulgent behaviors and attitudes. The person seemed vain and demanding, and had a grandiose sense of self-importance. During this phase the patient might have been occupied with fantasies of power, brilliance, beauty or ideal love. A lack of empathy, or true caring for others, also marked the inflated mood of the person.

Though not spoken of in the above manner, these periods of emptiness and inflation were also encountered in many other forms of possession. We find these mood swings in the Voodoo possessions of Haiti and in shamanic possessions across the world. In these the mood is attributed to the possessing deity. In Voodoo it may be a capricious deity that possessed a person and compels him or her to exhibit the inflated mood. Or it may be a somber deity creating an atmosphere of solemnness and sadness. The Spiritualists or the Voodooists—or any others who utilize mediumistic trances as the primary form of possession—may find themselves feeling depleted or drained after the spirit has left, and ecstatic or inflated during the period of possession. All of this indicates the connection among the various other forms of possession which are practiced and the demonic possessions on which the possessive states diagnosis is based.

Another aspect to this disorder is the seemingly hallucinatory experiences of the patient. In nine of the fourteen cases studied the individual either heard audible voices, saw a vision of dark figures or perceived an apparition. This alone might draw one to conclude that the individual was in some manner psychotic. Yet these visions and voices more closely resembled the form found in mystical phenomena than in psychosis. It is generally recognized that certain forms of visions and voices have a non-pathological character, especially when these occur during the individual's practice of religion. Similarly these visions and voices found in the possessive state also have a different flavor to them than those found in the psychotic state, for these experiences have a greater sense of integrity than the hallucinatory experiences of the schizophrenic.

In the possessed condition the individual experiences these voices and visions as completely alien and separate from him or herself. They are not experienced as dream-like, nor does the person feel as if he or she has lost touch with reality. Rather, the vision or voice has such an integrity that the person can maintain an adequate processing of external reality. The vision or voice itself also seems to retain a constant quality over time and is recognized as being distinct in itself. This is unlike the experience of the schizophrenic. The psychotic voice or vision may in the extreme have the quality of independence and distinction from the individual, but, as the patient begins to reintegrate the weak, psychotic ego into a stronger functioning ego, the hallucination begins to lose its integrity. As the patient's processing of external reality improves the hallucination loses its independent quality and slowly becomes more internalized and accepted as a part of the self.

Not so with the visions and voices of the possessed. Here, even after normal life is resumed, the one-time patient still accepts the independence of these phenomena, and does not accept them as a projected part of the self. The dynamics underlying this acceptance or rejection of the phenomena's source was not studied in this research, and would lend a greater understanding of this aspect of the possessive state if known. But for our present purpose, which is to outline the phenomenological parameters which distinguish the possessive state from any other, this difference in the perceived quality of the vision and voice is sufficient to assist us.

Visions and voices were a common occurrence in the history and phenomenology of spirit-possessions. These were possibly as essential to the possessions of the past as was the perceived loss of control. To the shaman, the seeing of a spirit and the hearing of the spirit voice was imperative; even when not in a shamanic trance these continued to be an important part of daily life. A vision or a voice was also imperative to the spiritualistic séance. And so it is for most forms of possession. The possessive states disorder does not differ in this regard, but once again follows an age-old pattern.

The final features of the possessive state, elucidated in this study, are the dissociative aspects. These are such states as trances and the presence of more than one personality.

For many, such as Kenny,[10] possession and multiple personalities are essentially synonymous. Yet in this study only half of the fourteen cases exhibited the presence of more than one personality within the patient. This is a difference between this present study and the research into other forms of possession. The exhibiting of other personalities is a common occurrence to most forms of possession. The occurrence of a spirit-personality speaking through the possessed happened in almost all forms. Yet, most of the forms in which this occurred were voluntary, or ceremonial, possessions. In the demonic or involuntary possession this was not always the case. As we saw in our review of the Christian perspective of demonic possession, the absence of observable multiple personalities is common, at least until the spirit is commanded to make itself present during the exorcism.

It was not determined why other personalities were not encountered in the remaining seven cases. Whether it was because they were not actually

---

10. Kenny, *Multiple Personality and Spirit Possession.*

present, or if it was only that these other personalities had not come to conscious awareness is a question for further study.

When more than one personality is exhibited in a patient it may seem difficult to distinguish this from a case of multiple personality, or dissociative identity disorder. Much of what occurs in a multiple personality is also seen in the possessive state. In both we may see the person enter a trance-like transitional condition which will introduce the presence of an alternate personality. In each the alternate personality may either completely usurp the identity personality of the individual, or the ego-identity personality may be able to relate to the alternates by means of an internal conversation that is experienced as quite real by the patient.

A startling similarity is in the voice fluctuation of the possessed and the multiple personality. The voice of the possessed person was one of the most affected areas while the patient was exhibiting the presence of another personality. His or her voice would alter to match that of the "other". The patient's voice might reach a falsetto, as is commonly seen in both shamanic and spiritualistic practices, or it may become so low that it is difficult to distinguish the words.

The final aspects of these dissociative features of the possessive state actually overlap with the paranormal phenomena. These aspects are the possessed's abilities to either speak a previously unknown language, understand a previously unknown language, or both. The reason for subsuming these under the dissociative features is that they indicate the presence of another personality speaking through the individual, or inspiring the speech or understanding of the patient's own personality. But this is also where the differentiation between a possession state and a multiple personality becomes clearer.

The similarities between the possession phenomena and the multiple personality phenomena might lead one to assume that they are the same thing, or at least sisters in some manner. Authors and researchers in the area of multiple personality disorders have even alluded to the possibility of what they call demonic alternate personalities within the person which will appear as possessing spirits.[11] However, as we once again look at the diagnostician's assessments of these cases, multiple personality did not figure highly, even where alternate personalities appeared. Thus it is more likely that multiple personality is a symptom of possession than possession being a form of multiple personality. It is a matter of which subsumes which, and it is this that assists us with the differentiation between the two, for the possessive states disorder appears to have multiple personality as one of its

11. Putnam, *Diagnosis and Treatment of Multiple Personality Disorder*.

possible phenomena. The differentiation is completed when the other phenomena associated with a possession are present; phenomena not usually in the dissociative identity disorder, or the multiple personality.

Again, looking at the paranormal phenomena associated with speech, the ability to speak a previously unknown language was present in three of the fourteen cases studied, while the ability to understand a previously unknown language was seen in only one of them. Yet this is one of the primary criteria used by the Roman Catholic Church to distinguish a "true" possession from one which is "false," or a psychological manifestation.

The ability to speak the unknown language was spontaneous, with the person just blurting out the words. This was similar with the understanding of the language. In the Roman Catholic Church extensive research into the patient's past is done in order to determine that this is not the releasing of some previously repressed memory. This was not necessary here, for the church did this to determine if the language was a repressed memory or the voice of an independent, incorporeal spirit. This is actually an intriguing question—and one worthy of more research—but for our purpose, which is, once again, to determine the phenomenology of possession, all that is of concern is that the patient does speak or understand this language. Whether or not this is due to the unconscious, or to an independent spirit, makes no difference at this point. Obviously, if the patient is consciously multi-lingual this becomes a moot point, and not a diagnostic indicator; what we are referring to is a language that is not consciously accessible to the patient.

As with the other features of this disorder, so here as well we can see that to speak or understand a previously unknown language occurs in almost every other form of possession. It may take the form of the shaman's gaining a spirit or animal language, or the spirit-medium speaking in a foreign tongue during a séance. Whatever the form, the commonality of the phenomena once again indicates the heritage into which this possessive states description falls.

As all of the above phenomena have been attributed to possession before, it might be asked what need is there of this description we are calling the possessive states disorder? The answer is quite simple. The uniqueness of this description is that it collects these phenomena and places them according to priority, to provide a systematic manner for diagnosing the case of possession. Even the Roman Catholic Church, which is possibly the most esteemed student of possession—having the history and experience behind it—has no systematized manner to determine valid possessions and only takes into account the most gross forms of phenomena.

> Especially, [the priest] should not believe too readily that a
> person is possessed by an evil spirit; but he ought to ascertain
> the signs by which a person possessed can be distinguished
> from one who is suffering from some illness, especially one
> of a psychological nature. Signs of possession may be the fol-
> lowing: ability to speak with some facility in a strange tongue
> or to understand it when spoken by another; the faculty of
> divulging future and hidden events; display of powers which
> are beyond the subject's age and natural condition; and various
> other indications which, when taken together as a whole, build
> up the evidence.[12]

These remarks were taken from the general rules concerning exorcism
in the Roman Catholic Church's *Roman Ritual*, the manual which priests
are to follow. Thus, the possessive states disorder is a new step toward a
description that both refines the diagnosis of possession and illustrates its
uniqueness within the family of non-physical illnesses.

As we review each of the features of the possessive state we are able
to see that many of these features are characteristic of other diagnostic
categories. Taken independently of the other phenomena occurring in the
possession syndrome, each feature could be mistaken as an indicator of
another disorder. On closer examination one can see that there are subtle
distinctions between the way these features are manifested in the possession
state and the manner in which they occur in other disorders. It is actually
only when the phenomena are considered *as a whole* that the systematic
uniqueness of the possessive states disorder stands forth.

Up to this point in the study of psychopathology, paranormal phenomena, and their significant effects upon others in the environment have
not existed as criteria for diagnosis. We can assume that this is primarily
true because such phenomena are not readily accepted by most researchers as truly existing, possibly because they are not largely present in other
psychopathological syndromes. Because of this—and because these are seen
as common occurrences in the possessive state—when these phenomena
are experienced in conjunction with the perceived loss of control to another
and with the mood fluctuations, we can assume that this is indicative of a
possessive states disorder. In no other disorder has this pattern of phenomena been recorded, but at least one of these two features occurred in twelve
of the fourteen cases of demonic possession which were studied. When one
of these two are not present the job of making the diagnosis falls to the
understanding of the subtle differences in the features otherwise common

12. Weller, *The Roman Ritual*, 641.

to many disorders. This would, obviously, make the task of distinguishing the possessive states disorder from any other more difficult, and this was reflected in the diagnostic raters' assessment of the two cases which exhibited no paranormal features, or effects on others in the vicinity. When examining these two cases the diagnosticians were unable to make a determination whether these were best described by the possessive states disorder, or one of the usual diagnostic categories.

It is important, then, to gain an understanding of the subtle differences in the other features of this disorder. If the patient was only experiencing a loss of self-control, then certain other disorders come to mind, such as certain anxiety disorders. The experienced loss of thought control may raise the possibility of an obsessive compulsive disorder. The loss of bodily control brings forth the possibilities of generalized anxiety disorder or one of the somatoform disorders. The fury and streams of profanity lead us to consider the possible applicability of a Tourette's disorder diagnosis. This may be why some of the diagnosticians used a few of these diagnoses to describe the cases in this study.

Interestingly, though, the obsessive compulsive disorder was never seen as applicable to the cases. Generalized anxiety was seen to apply to one case, while a diagnosis of some form of somatoform disorder was used for four cases. But, when looking at a case of possession in a systematic manner none of these diagnoses then seem applicable.

In neither of these anxiety disorders, obsessive compulsive or generalized, are there the fluctuations to the inflated mood which is an important aspect of the possessive state. Likewise, hallucinatory experiences as well as dissociative features are not seen in these anxiety disorders. Finally, while the possessed experiences the uncontrolled thoughts or actions as being due to the influence of another, the obsessive compulsive will attribute them to his or her own lack of will power.

The diagnosis of a somatoform disorder, especially conversion disorder, can explain the loss of certain aspects of bodily control, when these occur. But this family of disorders is incapable of explaining the various other phenomena happening in the possession: the visions and voices, the paranormal occurrences, the impact on others in the vicinity, the presence of other personalities or the revulsive religious behaviors. Likewise, Tourette's disorder can be used to explain the flow of profanities and the unaccounted-for rage, yet the other features of the possessive states disorder are foreign to its normal pattern.

As it stands alone, the mood fluctuation, imperative to the diagnosis of the possessive state, leads us to another group of disorders: the mood disorders. One or the other forms of the bipolar disorders was seen in five of the fourteen cases, while a major depression was diagnosed in two of these as well. Yet in these disorders there is usually no perceived loss of self-control to another. Neither are the dissociative aspects or the features affecting others seen in these. At times, a major depression may exhibit psychotic features, and so account for the voices heard by some who are possessed, but visual hallucinations are rare—if actually non-existent—in the mood disorders. Also a diagnosis of major depression only accounts for the empty phase of the mood fluctuation, ignoring the period of inflation.

Paranoia, as well as the narcissistic, borderline, histrionic, and paranoid personality disorders can account for the inflated phase of the mood flux. The diagnosticians seemed to think so, for they attributed a diagnosis of border-line or histrionic each to five cases. Yet, dissociative features such as more than one personality or trances, as well as hallucinations, are not consistent in the narcissistic, paranoid, histrionic or borderline personality disorders. Also loss of self-control is inconsistent with the narcissistic or paranoid disorders. Though a diagnosis of a mixed personality disorder is seemingly valid in most of these cases—if only because the phenomena are present—it is not descriptive of the whole disorder for precisely these same reasons.

If the person's belief that someone else is controlling him or her was not enough, then the occurrence of hallucinatory-type experiences surely inclined the diagnosticians to reach for a diagnosis of psychosis. The raters used three psychotic disorder diagnoses: undifferentiated schizophrenia, paranoid schizophrenia, and atypical psychosis. The problems with these diagnoses lay mostly in their inability to account for the mood swings the patient experienced. They also could not account for the presence of other personalities in the individual. In certain forms of schizophrenia a person may be delusional and believe that there is someone else inside him or her, but this other is not usually made manifest, as occurs in the possession state.

When the schizophrenia assumption was based solely on the occurrence of the patient hearing a voice or seeing a vision, this assumption needed to be tested against the subtle difference between the hallucinations of the possessive—and for that matter the mystical—state, and those occurring commonly in psychotic episodes. This distinction was elucidated earlier in this discussion. One of the grab-bag categories used to describe these cases was the schizoaffective disorder. This diagnosis was used in half of the fourteen cases. However, it is merely a category used to catch cases that do not quite fit either one of the mood disorders or one of the schizophrenic disorders. It was essentially used to describe a disorder with both psychotic features and affective features, but gives us no other specifics upon which to build an understanding of a case. A more appropriate diagnosis may be a major depression with psychotic features. But as we have already observed, the major depression diagnosis is not adequate to describe the possession state as a whole.

Another diagnosis which occurred among four of the studied cases was delirium. The essential feature of delirium is a clouding of consciousness. Hallucinations, disturbances of sleep, and increased or decreased psychomotor activity are also characteristic of this disorder. This fits the features of the possessive state quite closely. Yet the duration of delirium is usually brief and rarely lasts a full month. The phenomena of the possessions existed in some instances for many years. Thus, even though on first examination, the person in the possessive state may seem to be manifesting a delirium syndrome, after sufficient observation the differentiation should be simple to provide.

Paranoia was used for only one of the fourteen cases. Paranoia would not usually fit, due to the common occurrence of seemingly psychotic phenomena. Thus, a paranoid schizophrenic assessment would be more commonly made than that of a true paranoid disorder. But even where the hallucinations did not exist, the paranoid disorder could not account for the presence of other personalities within the individual or the fluctuations from the empty to inflated mood.

It is interesting that even though half of the cases studied included the presence of other personalities, none of the diagnosticians saw any of these cases as a dissociative identity, or multiple personality disorder. This may be because the psychotic features of these cases overrode the significance of the other personality, the rater seeing this as merely another psychotic symptom. Five of these seven cases which exhibited alternate personalities were seen as either undifferentiated or paranoid schizophrenics; the other two cases were seen as either atypical psychoses or major depressions with psychotic features. But it may also be due to the fact that the multiple personality, as it is defined from the research literature, just does not account for the full manifestation of the cases as we discussed earlier.

Taken alone, any sub-group of phenomena found in these cases can easily lead to many of the presently accepted diagnoses. Yet, when these diagnoses are held up to the light of the complete case, none is found to be accurate in regard to its description. It is true that no category can ever describe any individual case with absolute accuracy. But for most cases, the diagnostic descriptions found in the presently accepted diagnostic manual are very close. There may be minor variations in certain aspects of a description when dealing with the actual individual, yet on the whole one can get a good picture of the individual when reading the description of the related disorder. This is not true for these cases of possession. This does not point to any errors in the diagnostic manual, it only points to the fact that the manual does not contain a description that fits the phenomena found in these cases. It does not have a category that describes cases of possession.

From the above discussion, we can see that the possessive states disorder appears to describe occurrences of possession more adequately than do any of the present diagnostic categories. Even though this may seem to be the fact on paper, does this also apply to the clinical judgment of diagnosticians? This was the final question asked of the diagnostic raters in this study.

When we look at the results of these ratings we find that the possessive states disorder fares well in the diagnosticians' judgment. For only two of the fourteen cases are the diagnosticians unsure whether the new diagnosis is an adequate description. For eight of the fourteen they felt sure that the possessive states disorder accurately described the cases. For the remaining four cases, these diagnosticians held some doubts as to the new diagnosis' applicability, yet it was still on the whole better than any of the present diagnostic descriptions available to them.

These results still leave us with a sense of ambiguity in regard to whether the raters were on the whole satisfied with this new description. Statistically we can state that in over half of the cases studied the raters did find this possessive states disorder description fitting the phenomena in the cases to at least some degree. But there were other cases with which the raters would not be as confident in using the possessive states disorder as the diagnosis. This ambiguity fades, though, as we move from looking at cases in a general manner and begin to review the satisfaction with the diagnoses on a case-by-case basis. When we do this we begin to gain a more positive outlook on the use of the possessive states disorder as a diagnostic tool, for we find that this diagnostic description was chosen more consistently as the best description of the cases studied than any other possible category.

The results of these independent diagnosticians' assessments enable us to give credibility to the possessive states disorder. We saw that it could account for phenomena where other categories were inadequate. We also saw that the possessive states disorder was consistent with the known possession states of the past and present, with the phenomena in these being in accord. Likewise, we have just seen that this diagnostic category was believed to be useful in certain cases of demonic possessions used in this study.

We have now come to see that the present categories of psychopathology have not been sufficient to describe cases of possession. These categories were not able to account for much of what occurred during a possession, neither could these present diagnostic descriptions inspire the diagnosticians to use them with significant confidence or consistency.

Thus, we encountered the need to find a more descriptive category which could be used to distinguish the possessive state from any other with confidence and consistency. We have seen the need to develop a description which would encompass the significant phenomena found across the cases of possession which we studied; a description which would include such things as (1) the individual's perceived loss of self-control to another; (2) the fluctuations in the sense of self between emptiness and inflation; (3) the visions and voices which were experienced; (4) the dissociative qualities; (5) the revulsive religious behaviors; (6) the paranormal events and (7) the experiences which affect persons in the vicinity of the patient. The possessive states disorder is an attempt at such a description. It is a description which provides diagnosticians with a category to use with more confidence and consistency when attempting to diagnose the case of possession; a description which will more efficiently guide in distinguishing a possession state from any other.

The Possessive States Diagnostic Description

The essential feature of this disorder is an experience of being controlled by someone, or something, alien to oneself, with a subsequent loss of control in any of four areas: thinking; anger and profanity; impulsive behaviors; and physical reactions. A person may experience his or her actions, speech, thoughts, and body as being under the authority of another to such an extent that he or she may speak, think, or act and yet not understand how this transpired, having the experience of being out-of-control. The loss of control of thought can be in the form of ruminations, obsessions, temptations, expectations of disaster, harm, or death, and the like. In the extreme these may seem to take the form of delusions, yet the thinking is not truly delusional since the person does not accept these as his or her own beliefs, but experiences these thoughts as those of the controlling entity.

The uncontrollable anger can be seen in sudden outbursts of fury, excessive anger, or the tendency to counterattack any perceived threat. The person may also begin to have uncontrollable outbursts of profanity, at times expressly related to religion or those who are religious.

Impulsivity may be seen in almost any area of life, but especially in such areas as sex, gambling, substance abuse, overeating, and the like. The uncontrollable physical reactions can be seen in such things as uncontrolled contortions of the body, facial distortions, and the loss of certain physical functions for no apparent reason.

The person's sense of self fluctuates between feelings of despair, depletion, or an experience of inner emptiness, and the feeling of inflation and
grandiosity. These fluctuations may vary in duration, with some persons
exhibiting one or the other period predominantly. The fluctuations differ
from those seen in narcissistic persons where the fluctuations in mood are
dependent on external circumstances. The person in a possessive state fluctuates in mood due to internal cues. The feelings of emptiness and depletion usually occur during periods when the person feels in relative control
of him- or herself. The inflated periods are usually associated with periods
when the person experiences him- or herself as not in control.

The emptiness and depression can be seen in periods of sad affect,
inappropriate feelings of guilt and worthlessness, a perceived loss of energy,
loss of interest in usual activities, suicidal ideation, threats and even suicide
attempts. The person may also express these feelings of emptiness as a feeling of inner darkness, as a feeling of being depleted or drained by the one
controlling them, or as a void within.

The periods of inflation are marked by an egocentric, self-indulgent
behavior and attitude. The person may seem vain and demanding, have a
grandiose sense of self-importance, and be preoccupied with fantasies of
power, brilliance, beauty or ideal love. The person may expect special favors
from others without assuming reciprocal responsibilities, and show little
caring or empathy for others.

Also characteristic of this disorder are certain visions and voices seen
and heard by the person; dissociative aspects; a revulsive reaction to religious behaviors or objects; paranormal, or parapsychological, occurrences,
as well as certain phenomena experienced by others around the person.

Often a person in this state will experience seeing dark figures and apparitions. The individual may also hear audible and coherent voices. These
experiences have a greater sense of integrity than the hallucinatory experiences of the schizophrenic, and are not the result of a known organic condition. The individual experiences these voices and visions as completely alien
and separate from him- or herself. They are not experienced as dream-like,
nor does the person feel as if he or she has lost touch with reality. Rather
the vision or voice has such an integrity that the person can maintain an
adequate processing of external reality while the vision or voice retains a
constant quality over time and is recognized as being distinct in itself. This
is unlike schizophrenic hallucinations which begin to lose their independent quality and slowly become more internalized as the person's processing
of external reality improves.

The presence of such dissociative states as trances and more than
one personality are also frequently encountered. When more than one

personality is encountered the person may be in a trance state and so is unaware of its presence. In rare instances the person may experience these other personalities during normal consciousness, and may then be in communication with these other personalities. When more than one personality is present the distinction between the possessive state and dissociative identity disorder is made more difficult. Each has the symptom of more than one personality present in the same individual, however in DID this is the predominate symptom, while it is a secondary symptom of the possessive state. Also, in DID the behavior of the alternate personalities can take any general form, while in the possessive states disorder the sense of being controlled by others, the affective fluctuations, and the other behaviors are specific.

Along with the presence of the alternate personalities come extreme variations and alterations in the person's voice. Infrequent, but startling when seen, is the person's ability to speak, and possibly even comprehend, a previously unknown language.

Frequently the person may exhibit revulsive behavior in relationship to religion, or religious objects. The person may have an extremely negative reaction to prayer. Even when the person desires to have someone pray for him or her—asking a person to pray—he or she may fall into a trance, have an outburst of fury, or experience an inner agitation during the prayer. If the patient attempts to pray, he or she may feel as if being suffocated or choked. This feeling of suffocation or being choked may be experienced by others as well, while praying for the person. Other revulsive reactions to religion include the destruction of religious objects, a deep fear and disgust for certain religious objects and a difficulty in articulating the name of Jesus, or the Lord's Prayer, even when desiring to do so.

Probably the most startling aspects to this disorder are the paranormal, or parapsychological, phenomena that are frequently encountered. Some form of poltergeist-type phenomena may be experienced either by the patient, or by those present with the patient. Poltergeist phenomena are things such as the hearing of footsteps or noises that have no physical source; objects flying or moving on their own; religious objects being destroyed by an unknown force.

Some form of telepathy may also be exhibited by the person. The person may be able to read another's thoughts as well as relate aspects of another's life that the patient had no way of knowing. A startling form of telepathy is seen if someone, without the knowledge of the patient, attempts to pray for the patient, or has a holy object hidden but present: in such an instance the patient may fly into a fury or fall into a trance.

Other paranormal occurrences include the person exhibiting a strength out-of-proportion to age or situation. Rarely seen, but significant when present, is the occurrence of the person levitating, or becoming so heavy that many persons are unable to move the patient.

Unlike most disorders, there may be an obvious impact on others in the vicinity of the patient; they may experience odd phenomena as well. Already mentioned are the poltergeist-type phenomena and the feeling of suffocation while praying. Likewise, others may have the feeling that the person has lost a human quality, or is empty. Other phenomena include a feeling of an alien presence in the vicinity of the person; the smelling of a stench, especially an acrid stench, around the person; a feeling of lowered temperature, possibly even freezing temperatures, in the area of the patient.

Associated Features: Associated with the anxiety and depressed affect during the emptiness phase are various physical manifestations such as a great deal of sweating, increased heart pounding and respiration, clammy hands, dry mouth, upset stomach, diarrhea, facial flushing and the like. Some persons also experience extreme tension and shakiness and an inability to relax. There may also be a deterioration in functioning: socially, at work and cognitively.

Predisposing Factors: Involvement in some form of occult practices, or participation in certain cults and mind-control activities may predispose a person to this condition.

Differential Diagnosis: This disorder has features of many other disorders, but when paranormal phenomena, or the phenomena experienced by others is encountered, this diagnostic category should be seriously considered.

The experience of emptiness or inflation may be the symptom of other disorders such as paranoia, major depression, and bipolar disorders, as well as the narcissistic, borderline, histrionic and paranoid personality disorders. Dissociative features and hallucinations are not found in narcissistic, paranoid or borderline personalities. There is also usually no loss of self-control in the narcissistic or paranoid disorder.

In major depression and bipolar disorders there is usually no loss of self-control, dissociative features, or visual hallucinations. In major depression there are no fluctuations from feelings of emptiness to feelings of inflation or grandiosity. Likewise, in the obsessive-compulsive disorder there are no fluctuations to the inflated mood, no dissociative features, and no hallucinations. The obsessive-compulsives also experience their behavior as their own, and do not attribute it to another usurping their volition.

In the dissociative identity disorder there are usually no fluctuations in mood from emptiness to inflation nor are there visual hallucinations.

In Schizophrenia the hallucinations are more dream-like and the person's sense of self-reality is impaired, where in the possessive state the hallucinatory experiences have more integrity and do not impair the person's sense of identity or the processing of reality. Likewise, the person in a possessive state does not have true delusions since these are experienced as the thoughts of the controlling entity while the person maintains an independent reality. Even the thought that they are being controlled is not truly delusional since, to the degree that they are out-of-control, this is true.

The histrionic personality can be distinguished from this disorder by the presence of other personalities and/or the revulsive religious behaviors of the person.

Diagnostic Criteria for the Possessive States Disorder

A, B, and C must be present

A. The experience of being controlled by someone, or something, other than oneself, with a subsequent loss of self-control in one of four areas: thinking, anger or profanity; impulsivity; or physical functioning.

B. A sense of self that fluctuates between periods of emptiness and periods of inflation, though one period may predominate. This fluctuation is not due to external circumstances, but corresponds to whether the person is feeling in control of him- or herself, or is feeling out-of-control.

C. At least one of the following is present:

   1. The person experiences visions of dark figures or apparitions and/or the person hears coherent voices that have a real, and not a dream-like, quality.

   2. Trances, or the presence of more than one personality. Also there may be variations in voice or the ability to speak or understand a previously unknown language.

   3. Revulsive religious reactions, such as extreme negative reactions to prayer, or to religious objects. The inability to articulate the name Jesus, or the destruction of religious objects.

4. Some form of paranormal phenomena, such as poltergeist-type phenomena, telepathy, levitation, or strength out of proportion to age or situation.

5. There is an impact on others: Paranormal phenomena, stench, coldness or the feeling of an alien presence or that the patient has lost a human quality, is experienced by someone other than the patient.

Additional Characteristics When Present Increasing Validity

1. The patient experiences a vision, voice, or feeling as coming from outside of him- or herself, attributed to a wholly other. The important aspect here is that the event is a spontaneous, immediate experience, rather than a subsequent interpretation of an event as having come from the wholly other.

2. The experience is numinous.

3. The presence of numinous fear or awe.

4. There is an unusual clarity to the experience; a clarity marked by the gaining of a cognizance that is instantaneous rather than gradual (like the awareness gained when listening to another person speaking rather than the knowledge gained by means of reasoning through a personal thought). Clarity is also exhibited in the establishment of the experience in long-lasting memory.

5. When a visual image is involved there is some form of luminosity involved, whether of beautiful light or of shadowy darkness.

21

The Fall of Satan: The Intrapsychic Dynamics of the Possession State

A voiding the pitfall of a circular argument, the possession state was first defined as a condition healed by exorcism. In the process of examining the history of each case, it turned out that many had also experienced failed courses of psychiatric and psychotherapeutic interventions, leaving successful exorcism not only the criteria by which a possession was defined, but by implication assigning to exorcism the label of treatment of choice for an involuntary possession state.

In the introduction we met a man whose son had committed suicide and who subsequently was possessed by the same obsessive, murderous thoughts and compulsive desires that had plagued his son. This man had originally taken his concern to his priest, who then addressed it to his bishop. They—not believing in possession—referred him to multiple psychiatrists; none with whom he found any relief. He had numerous courses of various medications and forms of psychotherapy. Nothing diminished the obsessive thoughts or compulsions. Fortunately, another priest—believing that possession was possible—referred him to an exorcist. After a week of prayer, psychotherapy, and exorcism he finally found relief.

Exorcism has always been associated with the belief that illness is not merely due to something going on within an individual, but is also due to the effect of *an outer force*. That outer force was commonly imaged as a demon or a god, but whichever it was, it was an independent entity that was instigating the affliction. This concept has been rejected by modern thinkers as primitive, but even C. G. Jung—whose initial understanding of spirit-possession was dominated by the idea that the possessing agent was of archetypal origin, and as such a content of the objective psyche—at the end of his career essentially accepted that the rejection of spirits was naïve and premature.

Certainly, exorcism has played a part in every significant culture and major religion up to this day. It is integral to shamanism, which has held a foundational role in the development of many forms of religion. The exorcist shaman, allied with his or her totem spirit, will go in search of the spirit that is afflicting the patient and then—with the assistance and power of the totem spirit—do battle to defeat the offending spirit. If the spirit associated with the shaman is stronger than the spirit possessing the patient the exorcism will work. If not, the patient will remain afflicted and the exorcist may either be injured, sickened, or themselves be possessed if they do not retreat in time.

This concept is still active even in seemingly progressive societies. Recently, in a San Francisco suburb, a man believed that he was being cursed by a local witch. His multiple illnesses and misfortunes lent credibility to this belief, so he contacted a local Wiccan coven. They sent one of their more experienced practitioners to combat the curse, but she found herself outmatched and soon told the patient that he would have to find a more powerful spirit to combat the curse sent against him, for the spirit with her was not as powerful as the one by which he was cursed.

The shamanic understanding is at the basis of most beliefs in possession and exorcism. Even Buddhism, which in the West is embraced in a mostly intellectual and philosophical manner, addresses possession and exorcism by viewing it as spirits influencing the body and soul of an afflicted person; the role of the Buddhist exorcist is to drive away the offending spirit. It is said that a large number of Buddhist exorcists still function in Japan. A Buddhist exorcism is performed by a temple's chief priest and his assistant, reading appropriate scriptures and burning special incense. Carrying a wooden staff with metal rings threaded onto it the priest is able to create an unearthly sound to scare evil spirits away. In some Buddhist traditions, spirits are driven out of a person's body by causing physical discomfort such as fasting, bathing in extremely cold water, or slapping the skin of the possessed person.

The reading of scriptures, the burning of incense, the production of irritating sounds—the banging of drums, pans, cymbals, the ringing of bells, and firecrackers—are common in Taoism, Hinduism, Islam, and Christianity. Also common to all is that the success of an exorcism is believed to be related to the strength of the spirit associated with the exorcist relative to the possessing spirit. The lesser spirits give way to the stronger spirits.

The various religions assert cosmologies that describe a hierarchy of spirits. Buddhism has multiple levels of heavens and hells, populated by souls reincarnating or assigned to them. Each level also implies a varying degree of spiritual power.

Likewise, early Christian cosmologies assign degrees of power to the angelic spirits. The early author known as (Pseudo-)Dionysus the Areopagite developed a celestial hierarchy, with good angels and bad belonging to one choir or another. Citizenship in a certain choir also meant a specific degree of power. These citizens of the heavenly realms were species, much as there are species on the earthly realm. In the material realm a rabbit would never think of contending with a tiger, and likewise one of the dominions or thrones may not find a mere angel a major obstacle.

We see this theme throughout cultures and religions. In Native American societies, for example, a hawk, wolf, or bear spirit far outstrip a deer spirit in the shamanic spirit world. In Buddhism, a Buddha or Bodhisattva will certainly be more powerful and therefore more effective in contending against a mere "hungry" spirit or a demon spirit.

This common concept has been an effective Christian evangelistic technique, for in Christianity the Holy Spirit is known to be the Spirit of the creator God. It would seem obvious that the creator of a spirit is more powerful than the spirit created, and so the Holy Spirit of Jesus would be the most effective exorcising agent possible. If a person is convinced that all things were created through Jesus, then it is because of Jesus that the wolf, bear, hungry spirit, or Satan himself even exists. To address a society that is worshiping one of these lesser, created spirits and offer them the opportunity to join with the highest spirit would be an attractive choice. This was certainly known in Native American Lakota society, for it was understood that these nature spirits were created by—and submitted to—the one creator God, *Wakan Taka*, the Great Spirit.

So whether it is Spiritualism, Voodoo, Santeria, Taoism, Buddhism, Hinduism, Judaism, Wicca, or Christianity, all agree that possession is by definition dealing with an entity other than the personality of the patient, and exorcism is the act of separating the patient's personality from that other. It is this experience of, and belief in, another entity that clearly differentiates possession and subsequent exorcism from the other psychopathological conditions treated with psychotherapy. Even when C. G. Jung initially saw exorcism as the separation of an archetypal content of the objective psyche from the personal unconscious and ego, by the end he gave a sincere nod to the real possibility that the possessing agent was an independent spirit.

All of these explanations demand the acceptance of an externally possessing entity, but do such things exist and can they affect another person's psyche? The existence of spirits is a matter of metaphysics, theology, and faith. However, that an independent personality can significantly influence the psyche of another person is an accepted fact. Merely observe the phenomenon of projective identification. The manner by which the influence of what we may refer to as a "wholly other" works has been explored and explained in another work, so at this point we will merely accept the possibility as an experienced reality.[1]

This brings us to the necessity of understanding the interplay of the wholly other and the intrapsychic dynamics of the afflicted that may account for the phenomena observed and experienced during a possession. As we observed in an earlier chapter, a mythic understanding is integral to the comprehension of much what occurs within the psyche.

The works of many modern theorists have indicated that the patterns of our lives, our personalities, and our abnormal behaviors can be described by specific *guiding myths*. Rollo May looked extensively at how the Greek myths are descriptive of many intrapsychic processes, as did Jean Shinoda Bolen, who explored how the Greek goddesses and gods are guiding symbols for various forms of feminine and masculine psychology.[2] C. G. Jung concentrated on the workings of medieval alchemy as metaphors for the developmental processes of the psyche. It is not surprising then that the possession state also has a guiding myth that is illustrative of this condition.

Throughout the Judeo-Christian world, the stories that best describe the possessed condition are those linked with the fall of angels. Traditional Christian interpretations of this event follow a common pattern: At one time, before the fall of humanity but after the creation of the universe, God had in the heavenly court a multitude of spirits. These spirits were known as angels, for just as the Greek meaning of their name implies (*angelos* is to be translated messenger), they were the messengers of God. Just as the human beings would undergo a period of probation in the Garden of Eden—a period when they would be free to choose between good and evil—so too the angels underwent a period in which they would be free to choose to do God's will or to rebel against it. It was during this period that one of the supreme angels, Lucifer—possibly the supreme angel in the order of the Cherubim—chose to rebel against God:

> In that period of probation one of the supreme Angels recognized his exceeding power, beauty, and knowledge but failed to give thanks and glory to God. He became envious and intolerant of God's supreme dominion and thereby he constituted himself as the adversary of God: he became Satan. Like a sinister flash of lightning his evil mind was made manifest in the spirit world. Because of his exalted position many Angels

---

1. Isaacs, *Revelations and Possession: Distinguishing Spiritual From Psychological Experiences.*

2. Bolen, *Gods in Everyman*; May, *The Cry for Myth.*

followed him in his mad campaign of hate and rebellion. It was then that a cry and a challenge was heard in the heavens, and a leader was seen to rise from the lowest Hierarchy, from the Choir of the Archangels. His battle cry: "Who is like God?" was his mighty weapon and it became, later, his own name: Michael. "And there was a great battle in heaven, Michael and his Angels fought with the dragon, and the dragon fought and his Angels. And they prevailed not, neither was their place found any more in heaven. And that great dragon was cast out, that old serpent, who is called the devil and Satan, who seduceth the whole world; and he was cast down unto the earth, and his angels were thrown down with him."[3]

It had been Satan's desire to become the ultimate ruler. He was determined to replace God with himself, or at least to create for himself a condition in which God was not supreme; a condition in which there would no longer be a unity in heaven, with God at the center of that unity, but rather a multiplicity in which he, Satan, could have his own dominion. Yet, his effort to do so had failed.

How you are fallen from heaven,
    O Day Star, son of Dawn!
How you are cut down to the ground,
    you who laid the nations low!
You said in your heart,
    "I will ascend to heaven;
    above the stars of God
I will set my throne on high;
    I will sit on the mount of assembly
    in the far reaches of the north;
I will ascend above the heights of the clouds;
    I will make myself like the Most High."
But you are brought down to Sheol,
    to the far reaches of the pit.[4]

It was pride that was Satan's undoing and had led to his being cast out of heaven, and it was pride and hate that continued to drive him to battle with God. Once cast down to earth, Satan still fought to replace God with

3. Parente, *Beyond Space*, 57.
4. Isaiah 14:12–15.

himself. He determined to do this by destroying God's relationship with the creation, and that could be accomplished by destroying God's relationship with the stewards of that creation: the human beings. It was Satan's goal to turn the worship of the human beings away from God and to himself. Satan, and his attendant fallen horde, would accomplish this by using the same means that caused their own downfall: pride.

Thus, Satan would feed on the pride and greed of humans, on the desires of each human to be the center of his or her own private universe. In the Garden of Eden, Satan entices Eve to break her relationship with God by working on her pride, on her desire to be like God. As she looks at the forbidden fruit of the tree of the knowledge of good and evil, the serpent says to her: "God knows that when you eat of it your eyes will be opened, and you will be like God, knowing good and evil."[5] Eve eats, then Adam eats, and the human beings' intimate relationship with God is broken. Likewise, it is the temptation by which Satan attempts to dissuade Jesus from his mission: "Again, the devil took him to a very high mountain and showed him all the kingdoms of the world and their glory. And he said to him, 'All these I will give you, if you will fall down and worship me.'" Then Jesus said to him, "Be gone, Satan! For it is written, 'You shall worship the Lord your God and him only shall you serve.'"[6]

Pride became the ultimate weapon in Satan's war to replace God with himself in the hearts of human beings. Yet even when he could accomplish this in certain individuals, he found that he still despised and hated these humans who worshiped him. He despised them because they were created in the image of the God whom he despised, and they also had the potential to become even greater than he and all his angels, because of the potential deifying of humanity in the incarnation of Jesus Christ. And so Satan would draw humans' worship of God to himself, he would accept the new adherent into his community with pleasure, and in the end destroy this human object of contempt, a story mirrored later in Goethe's *Faust*.

For us to understand how this story relates to our intrapsychic reality, we need to remind ourselves of the picture of healthy intrapsychic development. We all enter this world as a being of potential; a being with the potential to be creative, destructive, passive, active, tender, hard, or any of a vast multitude of manners. In early life all of this is still in a state of undifferentiated potentiality within the psyche. However, as we grow and progress through childhood and adolescence we begin to become more differentiated—taking on more of some aspects of that potential and less

5. Genesis 3:5.
6. Matthew 4:8–10.

of others—and as we grow we begin to develop an identity. Most often we come to think of our whole selves as merely being made up of those parts with which we now identify, and it is for this reason that we call this the *ego*, the Greek and Latin word for *I*.

However, the ego is not the totality of the person, but only a small portion which becomes the nominal center of our conscious lives. There is within each human being a true center which delineates each person as greater and far more intricate than the ego can ever be. At this center is a power which draws each of us toward this higher, or deeper, experience of ourselves, a power which allows us to be our true complete selves, not merely the handful of limited possibilities known as the ego. As we saw earlier in this work, this inner reality of our total self is what Carl Jung called the Self, capitalizing the word to make it distinct from the sense of identity centralized in the ego. Yet Jung was by no means the first to understand and experience this deeper truth, for this centering power has been known for centuries as the *imago dei*: the image of God within us.

The goal of our psychic lives is that the ego would connect in a primary relationship with this inner image of God, that there would be a sort of inner marriage between the ego and the *imago dei*. By doing so, the individual no longer remains limited to the resources of the ego, but can experience his or her total self and live a fuller life. By the ego no longer experiencing itself as the true person, but rather keeping its focus on the higher (or deeper) aspects of the *imago dei*, the individual begins to take on more and more of this image of wholeness. The person no longer is limited only to those few parts of him- or herself with which the ego is identified, but continues to become more and more like the image of God within. So the person actualizes the plea of Jesus that we become perfect (or complete) just as the Father in heaven is already perfect and complete.

In possession, this relationship of the ego to the *imago dei* is broken and usurped. This is the hallmark of possession. The ego no longer relates to the higher self in a primary way, but a "new god" takes the place of the *imago dei*.

The new inner god can take on many forms, for almost any archetypal content may serve in this role. Yet, in the most bizarre cases of possession this usurping central image may actually take the form of an inner archetypal devil. In traditional Jungian psychology the archetype of the Devil, in its varied forms, is seen as an aspect of the dark side of the Self. Such a picture of the Self—or of the image of God within us—contains not only its light aspects of goodness and wholeness, but also its dark aspects of destruction and evil. For Jung the *imago dei* was like the image of Kali, the goddess who on one hand deals out life, and on the other death.

Jung developed his concept of a two-sided image of God not only from his intensive studies of Buddhism and Hinduism, but also from his attraction to the god Abraxas. In his private writings, *Seven Sermons for the Dead*, found in the appendix to *Memories, Dreams, Reflections*, he describes this attractive, yet fear-inspiring god:

> Hard to know is the deity of Abraxas. Its power is the greatest, because man perceiveth it not. From the sun he draweth the *summum bonum*; from the devil the *infinum malum*; but from Abraxas LIFE, altogether indefinite, the mother of good and evil.
>
> Smaller and weaker life seemeth to be than the *summum bonum*; wherefore is it also hard to conceive that Abraxas transcendeth even the sun in power, who is himself the radiant source of all the force of life.
>
> Abraxas is the sun, and at the same time the eternally sucking gorge of the void, the belittling and dismembering devil.
>
> The power of Abraxas is twofold; but ye see it not, because for your eyes the warring opposites of this power are extinguished.
>
> What the god-sun speaketh is life.
>
> What the devil speaketh is death.
>
> But Abraxas speaketh that hallowed and accursed word which is life and death at the same time.
>
> Abraxas begetteth truth and lying, good and evil, light and darkness, in the same word and in the same act. Wherefore is Abraxas terrible.[7]

Abraxas filled a need for Jung. From the time that he was a young child he could not comprehend the intellectualized and sterile God that his father—and the Swiss Reformed Church—then preached. He knew there to be more to the world, more to God than he was being presented: a dark more. Jung's own feelings and drives seem to issue forth in the words of one of Herman Hesse's characters, Demian. In the novel of the same name, Hesse has his character questioning the validity of the then unquestionable Christian catechism:

> "I know," he said in a resigned tone of voice, "it's the same old story: don't take these stories seriously! But I have to tell you something: this is one of the very places that reveals the poverty of this religion most distinctly. The point is that this God of both Old and New Testaments is certainly an extraordinary figure

---

7. Jung, *Memories, Dreams, Reflections*, 383.

but not what he purports to represent. He is all that is good, noble, fatherly, beautiful, elevated, sentimental—true! But the world consists of something else besides. And what is left over is ascribed to the devil, this entire slice of world, this entire half is suppressed and hushed up. In exactly the same way they praise God as the father of all life but simply refuse to say a word about our sexual life on which it's all based, describing it whenever possible as sinful, the work of the devil. I have no objection to worshiping this God Jehovah, far from it. But I mean we ought to consider everything sacred, the entire world, not merely this artificially separated half! Thus alongside the divine service we should also have a service for the devil. I feel that would be right. Otherwise you must create for yourself a God that contains the devil too and in front of which you needn't close your eyes when the most natural things in the world take place."[8]

This god, Abraxas, was one that fit and fulfilled many of the speculations Jung had so long entertained. He culminated his argument for the dark side of God in his paper *Answer to Job*.[9] Here Jung examined the Old Testament story of Job in the light of his understanding of the supreme, transcendent god Abraxas, and used this story to illustrate the darker aspects of God, which he felt the Christianity of his day was ignoring; ignoring to the detriment of our psychological and spiritual growth. At this point in his spiritual development, Jung did not believe that he was attacking the essence of Christianity; rather he thought that adopting such a view would enhance Christianity as a whole. Subsequently, many Christian thinkers have adopted such a view of evil even though Jung himself did not remain completely satisfied with it.

That there are dark aspects to the unconscious is undeniable. That there are dark aspects to the human spirit may also be true. And as far as Jung's conception of the Self is correlated with the human spirit as a whole, then his argument may stand. But to attempt to describe God, and therefore the *imago dei*, as both dark and light, utilizing the story of Job, is questionable. A monist conception of God will necessarily imply such a combination of the dark and light aspects of the deity. However, the story of Job illustrates more a monotheistic view which modifies this view of God, separating evil from him by at least a few paces. This separation will be important in understanding not only the story of Job, but the intrapsychic process of possession.

8. Hesse, *Demain*, 67.
9. Jung, *Psychology and Religion: West and East.*

In the story of Job, much evil befalls this man for seemingly no good reason. Job was a holy man, yet he loses his family, his wealth, and his health. By the end of the story all of these are restored to him in even greater measure by God, yet in the meantime his life is beset by evil. It is the propagator of such evil that is of interest to us here.

Jung argued that because God allows evil to happen to Job that this illustrates the dark, terrible aspects of God: that the Hebrew Yahweh is none other than Abraxas. When analyzing the story with a monistic understanding of God, the idea of Yahweh and Abraxas being comparable can be understood. However, the writer of Job was not monistic but monotheistic, so to maintain the integrity of the Job story, we cannot attribute the evil conceived or done as being directly from God; it was merely allowed by God. God does *permit* it to be done, and this mysterious act of God is at first incomprehensible if we maintain the view of an all-good God who allows only good. Yet if we understand that God also abides evil to allow human beings free will, then we can conceive of how God could permit this evil to be done to Job without being the principle cause of it. We can also see that Job is a figure of the faithful servant of God, one who would not curse God in his affliction because God was not the cause. Job here is a partial illustration of what St. Paul would later recommend as faithful action: "we urge you, brothers, admonish the idle, encourage the fainthearted, help the weak, be patient with them all. See that no one repays anyone evil for evil, but always seek to do good to one another and to everyone. Rejoice always, pray without ceasing, give thanks in all circumstances; for this is the will of God in Christ Jesus for you."[10]

The propagator of evil in the story of Job was not God, it was Satan. Satan, here, is not seen as an explicit aspect of God, as his right or left hand performing his will. Satan is merely one member of the heavenly court; a created being, ultimately subservient to the one God. Yet, as we saw earlier in the story of Satan's fall, he did not remain subservient but was one who followed his own will. Thus, it was Satan, not God, who caused and created the afflictions of Job. And it was Satan, and not God, who carried the aspects of darkness and evil in this story. So if we view the story of Job as a metaphor for intrapsychic functioning, we observe that the evil exemplified by Satan is an image, or archetype, different from the *imago dei*.

Jung himself may not have maintained his view of a God with both dark and light aspects, but rather may have come to understand evil in some rather traditional manners. Morton Kelsey—an Episcopal clergyman, retired university professor, and follower of Jung—has, in his book

---

10. 1 Thessalonians 5:14–18.

Christianity as Psychology, argued that by the end of his life Jung had become more of a traditional Christian than even he, Jung, might have known; he now understood that God was love and that evil was an independent destructive force:

> Jung proposed that just as there is a healing reality that seeks to bring us to wholeness (what Christians call God or the risen Christ or the Holy Spirit), there is also a destructive force that tries to pull us down into its own destructiveness. Jung saw evil as a reality both within and beyond the human psyche, a reality that tries to cripple us. Radical evil needs to be distinguished from our personal human shadow, which may consist of good parts of ourselves that we have repressed and that we need to face and deal with. Essential evil cannot be handled by human beings alone, but only with the intervention of God or, as Christians would say, by the risen Christ who has already defeated evil. The Fathers called evil Death and believed that it affected human beings in four ways: morally in sin, psychologically in demonic possession and mental illness, physically in sickness and disability, and finally in physical death itself.[11]

While many, if not most, modern Jungians may contest Kelsey's interpretation of Jung's view of evil, Kelsey supports this view by drawing from some of the later writings of Jung, especially from his autobiography where he equates God with love.[12] Kelsey goes on to say:

> Jung's writing about evil is ambiguous. At times as in *The Answer to Job* he portrayed evil as a part of God, while in *Aion* . . . he made no reference to this idea. John Sanford has pointed out to me passages in the second volume of his Letters . . . supporting the former idea. However, there is no suggestion of this idea in the passage equating God with love. . . . In *Aion* and other places evil is seen as a radical and destructive force apart from God.[13]

Following this line of thought we can see that possession by evil is the usurpation of the role of the *imago dei* in the psyche by an inner principle of evil autonomous of the true Self. Possession is not the overwhelming of the ego by the dark aspects of the Self, for this would result in a form of psychosis. Rather, it is the creation of a false ego-Self relationship, where the Self is replaced by a dark archetypal form.

---

11. Kelsey, *Christianity as Psychology*, 41.

12. Cf. Jung, *Memories, Dreams, Reflections*, 354.

13. Kelsey, *Christianity as Psychology*, 41n.

The implications of this on a psychic level are many. First, unlike in psychotic states, the possessed state is one where the ego remains intact, but is in the sway of a more powerful archetypal element. Normally, in the healthy ego-Self relationship the Self would enhance the ego's functioning by providing it with its power of creativity and growth. In the possessed state the false Self cannot provide the ego with these abilities, but only with what is in its limited purview. Thus, the individual experiences thoughts, impulses, and actions as ego-alien, as if another was driving him or her to think or do these things. Indeed, this is what is happening, for one other than the ego is controlling these experiences.

Likewise, John Weir Perry[14] has described schizophrenia as a process by which the ego is overwhelmed by the Self, with the person then acting out the inflated attitude of this ruling archetypal image. Not so in possession. During a possession the ego is not initially annihilated, nor is it in connection with the Self, rather the ego remains intact and in connection with the destructive image of the Devil.

This alienation of the ego from the *imago dei* results in the individual becoming separated from his or her own inner resource of creativity and hope. Such a separation will usually result in a severe loss of energy for growth or life and so develop into a form of depression. "The mechanism of depression is loss of libido. The life energy and interest disappear into the unconscious, and the conscious life is left high and dry, sterile, arid, miserable and isolated. One feels oneself to be in a barren place, a wilderness or desert, where nothing grows and no life can flourish."[15] And this is what has actually happened, for the ego has left its oasis of the *imago dei* and gone alone into the desert of the unconscious where it meets the *imago diabolus*: the Devil within.

We encounter such depression with its experience of emptiness and meaninglessness in most cases of possession, but not only depression but also inflation and elation are experienced by the possessed. This fluctuation can be understood if we observe the individual's fluctuation in relation to the inner images.

When the individual is elated he or she is at that moment most likely experiencing the overpowering energy of the archetypal master. The person's sense of power comes from that archetype of the Devil, and the Devil is the image of unbridled power. When this archetype is not being directly experienced, the ego experiences its own state of alienation from the inner image of God and senses its barrenness and meaninglessness.

14. Perry, *The Far Side of Madness.*
15. Harding, *The Value and Meaning of Depression,* 4.

This relationship of the ego to the inner Devil is unlike the relationship of the ego to the image of God. When the ego is directly experiencing this latter image it is placed into a state of ecstasy or beyond ecstasy, yet when not conscious of such intimate contact the ego still experiences a sense of fullness and meaning because it remains energized by its constant relation to the *imago dei*.

Thus we see that the possessed condition is well described by the story of the fall of Satan, and the usurping of the rightful position of the image of God in an individual's life by the archetype of evil. This story provides us with a paradigm by which to understand the major characteristics of the possessed state.

The individual's sense of a loss of control to another occurs when the intact ego is inundated by the archetype of evil and compelled to act or think in a manner consistent with the archetype. The fluctuations in the sense of self can also be envisioned when it is understood that an influx of energy from the archetypal evil occurs and results in a feeling of inflation; when this influx ceases a sense of deprivation follows. This inner emptiness is experienced for two reasons: first, the ego is not being supplied any energy from its source in the archetypal evil, but second, and more importantly, it is due to its estrangement from the image of God within. The experience of visions and voices, the trances and experience of multiple personalities, as well as the revulsive religious behaviors and paranormal activities, can to some extent be seen as the result of the archetype of evil's interaction with the ego. Yet, these latter manifestations are also more difficult to understand using a purely psychological model, and fit more appropriately into a spiritual or transpersonal understanding of the disorder, an understanding which we shall explore momentarily.

Though the fall of Satan may be an appropriate model for the observed intrapsychic functioning, the possessed individual may experience it differently, and may see the story of *Faust* as more descriptive. As Faust gave himself willingly to the Devil—in the form of Mephistopheles—and so willingly rejected God, so too the ego gives itself over to the inner image of evil and so rejects the *imago dei*. Sometimes this is deliberate and conscious as in the case of many possessions resulting from direct, willful bonding to the image of the Devil, and the Devil himself, by participating in Satanic religious activities; however, it can also be subtle and unconscious, as observed from the implications of naive approaches to many cults and occult practices.

Why would people sell their souls? Why is it that, whether deliberately or subtly, the person would opt for a relationship with the archetype of evil rather than the image of God? This question takes us far afield into the realms of morality and motivation, but, as Maria Louise von Franz has observed, there is power in the archetypes. The quest for power—whether it be out of curiosity, greed, or naiveté—contributes to the forming of the false ego-Self relationship.

At this point the student of the psyche usually rests. An intrapsychic explanation does not necessarily have ramifications in metaphysics. So, to have explained the inner workings of possession does not lead to a rejection of a metaphysical belief in God or the Devil, nor need it lead to a repudiation of someone's experience of incorporeal spirits. Actually, the believer in God is led to an even greater acceptance of the existence of demonic entities and the Devil. For the *imago dei* is just that, the image of the true God within the individual. Likewise, the inner image of the Devil, which is so vividly experienced by the possessed, is the intrapsychic counterpart of an independent spiritual entity. Morton Kelsey mentions that it was difficult for Carl Jung to understand why Western Europeans could not grasp the validity of the nonphysical, transpsychic dimension, but preferred to remain enmeshed in an intellectually limiting form of materialism.

> Jung felt that religion was necessary for human development, and he could not imagine why people could not understand that he was speaking of a real, nonphysical dimension of reality when he spoke of the human psyche and the spiritual realm from which it issued. He wrote in a letter: "I did not create the psyche. If we speak of God as an archetype, we say nothing about His real nature, but are letting it be known that God already has a place in that part of the psyche which is pre-existent to consciousness, and that therefore he cannot be considered an invention of consciousness. We neither make Him nor remove or eliminate Him, but bring Him closer to the possibility of being experienced."[16]

Much of the truth of such an assertion rests on matters of faith. To the scientist this can only be alluded to, never proven. But to the person of faith these matters cannot be ignored. However, one need not maintain a faith stance to embrace such a conception of reality. Erich Neumann in his essay, *The Psyche and the Transformation of the Reality Planes: A Metapsychological Essay*,[17] has argued that much of our understanding of reality comes from an ego-centered bias; a bias that impedes our ability to truly comprehend reality, since it comes from such a limited, and limiting, foundation. The ego is but one aspect of our person, not the totality:

---

16. Kelsey, *Christianity as Psychology*, 39.

17. Neumann, *The Place of Creation*.

Ego-consciousness represents a specifically restricted field of knowledge in which the world-continuum is broken up into constituent parts. But we must not say "into its own constituents parts," since this breaking up of the world-continuum by the conscious mind into things, attributes, and forms as separate realities which exist side by side is not even what we as total personalities directly perceive. It is the world of our ego-consciousness, artificial in a sense, that makes the world appear thus to our rationally cognizing ego. As experiencing totalities, in heightened or lowered states of consciousness, we experience the world as something altogether different. We are only just beginning to recognize that different psychic constellations are associated with different experiences of the world, and that the world experience associated with our ego-consciousness is only one form, and not necessarily the one that is most comprehensive and closest to reality. But since we habitually identify ourselves with ego-consciousness, we assume its corresponding experience of the world to be "the" correct world experience per se.[18]

This throws open that whole discussion of what it means to say that something is a part of us, or not a part; what is inside and what is outside. It depends entirely upon the point of reference at which one begins. We need not explore this too greatly at this juncture, since we have done so extensively in earlier chapters, and Neumann has done such a grand job in the above-mentioned essay. However it becomes much clearer that for an ego-consciousness to say that there is not a spiritual or psychic reality independent of itself is the height of neurotic inflation. That there are such independent aspects of reality are quite obvious. What these are is much more the question to be asked rather than do they or do they not exist.

From the perspective of holistic religion, the development of the total person arises not from the forming of a linear relationship between the ego and the Self (the image of God within), but through a triangulation of the ego to the Self to the Trinitarian God.

18. Ibid., 9–10.

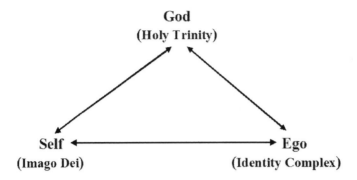

If the relationship remains linear in any of its possible aspects then total development will be inhibited. If the ego relates only to the individual Self, the individual will neglect the transpersonal aspects of the reality by which he or she is surrounded. These transpersonal aspects are inherent in this inner image, but they may be ignored if the individual is not also acknowledging the external reality as well. This may lead to the faulty and limited thinking encountered in the fourth level of consciousness.[19] Likewise, if the ego only relates to the external transpersonal reality, and ignores the inner development established in the Self-ego relationship, then a true, whole relationship to God cannot be attained. If the Self-God relationship is the only one developed the person is unable to function in this world and once again cannot develop holistically. This may contribute to the faulty and limited thinking of the third level of consciousness, as well as to a detachment from external, consensual, reality. A person with Zen madness has such an orientation, Zen madness being "a sickness . . . which frequently causes people to become detached from this world, yet never to pass through the prison of deluding images to satori."[20] The healthy development of the whole individual is the triangulated relationship where the ego–Self relationship is both enhanced by and enhances the ego–God relationship, and where the God–Self relationship continues to energize this inner image of wholeness.

Possession is a usurpation of healthy ego relationships on various different levels. On the psychic level the ego relates to the inner image of evil and so the healthy relationship of ego to Self is broken and holistic psychic development is inhibited. On a spiritual, or transpsychic, level the ego relates not to God, but to a transpersonal aspect of evil, commonly referred to as either the Devil or demons. Thus, in possession, a different form of triangulation is encountered.

---

19. Cf. Isaacs, *Revelations and Possession*.
20. Kelsey, *Christianity as Psychology*, 55.

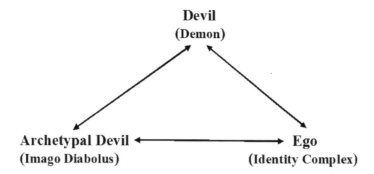

Once again, just as in the healthy developmental relationship, here too the ego's relationship to archetypal evil is both enhanced and enhances its relationship to transpersonal evil. Consequently, the more a person relates to transpersonal evil the more likely that person is to develop a personality that is governed by evil. The individual's life will be experienced as more meaningless, more self-centered, and narcissistic. And the person will experience to a greater extent a drive for power which becomes less and less fulfilling as he or she feels more and more out of control.

The unholy trinity of ego—*imago diabolus*—Devil is only one form that possession may take, although it is the most dramatic and difficult. Most times one will encounter what have been referred to as lesser demons. Here the demon takes the place of the devil proper, and relates to an inner complex which corresponds to its functioning at that time. The aspect of an unholy trinity is maintained, and the functioning is the same, it is merely the manner in which the demonic wholly other comes through the psyche that is different.

In the grand ego—*imago diabolus*—Devil, the possession is by Satan himself, and occurs at the depths of the soul. However, demons also possess in lesser ways, by addressing themselves to other complexes within. For example, for a person whose possessed behaviors are those of sexual addictions the complex may be more closely associated with a sexualized complex (rather than a power complex, Father complex, etc.) and the demon would be understood to be a demon of lust. Conversely, if during the exorcism the demon is named a demon of lust, it can be understood that it will function by addressing itself to the unconscious sexual aspects of the person. This can be seen in any combination of behaviors be they murder, violence, power, shame; the list is seemingly endless. The naming of demons is often merely recognition of their function upon the soul and the complex to which they attach within the psyche.

In such a scheme there is need not only for a psychological intervention, but also for one which is spiritual. Thus, spiritual exorcisms are performed. But the exorcism is a ritual, or a healing method, directed at the individual's spiritual, or transpersonal, relationships. The exorcism does not broach the intrapsychic relationships of the ego. So even after such a purging of the person's relationship with transpersonal evil there is still a necessity for working on the psychological level for complete healing to occur. This is where much of the current work with those who are possessed is not successful.

Many see possession only as a transpsychic, or spiritual, disease and so only provide the spiritual cure: exorcism. Others deny the reality of the transpsychic and only deliver the psychological treatment. To do either alone is not enough. Because each relationship of the ego—to the transpsychic and the intrapsychic—enhances the other relationship, both relationships must be broken so that the ego may reestablish the healthy relationships to both Self and God.

The implications for healing, therefore, are two-fold. Due to the energy and influence supplied by the wholly other spirit, exorcism of some sort is needed to sever the influence exerted upon the psychic contents. This is a cutting of the relationship between the wholly other spirit and the afflicted person's psyche. However, once done, the aspect of the psyche with which the spirit was interacting must also be dealt with. This becomes the role of psychotherapy and spiritual direction: psychotherapy to work toward the healing of any wounds or weakness that may have made the person vulnerable, and spiritual direction to assist with the development of the virtues needed to strengthen and bolster the psyche.

This work of exorcism, psychotherapy, and spiritual direction appears to function simultaneously rather than in a progressive manner. It is not that we begin with exorcism, then move to psychotherapy and spiritual direction, but rather that each is occurring simultaneously. The exorcism may be inhibited without psychotherapy as the patient may find the possessing spirit desirable in some unconscious manner. A person with a poor self-image will find a spirit of pride rather useful, even if they are not fully aware of it. As exorcism demands some level of awareness and conscious rejection of the independent spirit, psychotherapy assists to bring the motives and unconscious complexes actively into the healing work. Likewise, psychotherapy alone is not sufficient, but a form of psycho-spiritual education in the virtues will assist, this being the province of spiritual direction. And to complete the circle, neither psychotherapy nor spiritual direction may have much effect without the prayers and actions of exorcism.

There is a parallel here between possession and addictions to the point where the possession may be viewed as a form of spiritual addiction. Addiction work demands much the same coordination of work as just outlined. An addict may find that psychotherapy is not sufficient to break the compulsive behavior, but that social interventions are also necessary; interventions such as removing the patient from friends and associates who are not working toward sobriety. The addict also needs psycho-spiritual education in new ways of living, essentially in developing virtues. This method is an effective method of chemical dependency treatment: removing the patient through residential treatment or having them at Alcoholics Anonymous meetings with other sober individuals; psychotherapy sessions, and a sponsor to assist in psycho-spiritual education.

The parallel here is clear: however, the "bad friends" that draw the addict back into the detrimental behaviors in our case are spirits that want to keep the individual ensnared. This is rather a good metaphor for understanding the working of possession. It is not that a spirit *gets into* a person's soul and takes it over, but that the spirit is like the controlling, bad friend that exerts an influence upon the psyche of the patient.

With this model it is easier to conceptualize the Christian differentiation of degrees of possession. Biblically, the only term used for possession is demonization. Traditionally there have been three degrees of demonization outlined: temptation, oppression (or obsession), and possession. The degree is determined by how much control the "bad friend" has upon the person. For example, some alcoholics may be tempted to return to drinking, but have the will to say no. This is considered a temptation. Others may be so inundated by the cajoling of friends to go out to a bar, feeling they will be abandoned if they say no, that they succumb and drink. This is an oppression. Finally, another alcoholic has someone place a drink before them, tell them to drink, and it is as if they cannot stop their hand from picking up the glass. They are totally out of control of their will and so their body. This is possession. Again, in our case it is not merely a human friend exerting the influence, but a spirit.

Much of the foregoing is from a religious, and transpersonal, perspective. By adopting such a perspective we can more easily understand the transpersonal and parapsychological aspects of the cases of possession encountered in this work. Yet, as stated earlier, studies into transpersonal phenomena are not yet well accepted and the adoption of this view is still the prerogative of those who take a faith stance. To the psychologist that holds to materialism these matters remain in the dark, but this may change in the future. Psychology is still young and much of it still continues to hold to a positivistic view which is already being abandoned by the older, harder sciences of physics, chemistry, and biology. As psychological thinking continues to follow the developments of these other areas of study, it too may come to grapple with that nonphysical, metapsychological arena which some physicists have already called "the mystery." Then the spiritual and the psychological explanations will no longer be in conflict, but will be viewed as two aspects of one, unified reality.

Bibliography

Alexander, W. M. *Demonic Possession in the New Testament: Its Relations Historical, Medical, and Theological.* New York: Scribner's. 1902.

Alland, A. "Possession in a Revivalistic Negro Church." *Journal for the Scientific Study of Religion* 1.2 (1961) 204–13.

Almond, P. C. *Mystical Experience and Religious Doctrine: An Investigation of the Study of Mysticism in World Religions.* Berlin: Mouton, 1982.

Bach, Paul. "Demon Possession and Psychopathology: A Theological Relationship." *Journal of Psychology and Theology* 7 (1979) 22–26.

Bayley, R. *The Healing Ministry of the Local Church.* Oklahoma City: Presbyterian Charismatic Communion, 1983.

Barker, M. G. "Possession and the Occult: A Psychiatrist's View." *Churchman* 94.3 (1980) 246–53.

Barlow, D., et al. "Gender Identity Change in a Transsexual: An Exorcism." *Archives of Sexual Behavior* 6.5 (1975) 387–95.

Basham, D. *Deliver Us from Evil.* Lincoln, VA: Chosen, 1972.

Beck, S. T. *Outline of Biblical Psychology.* Edinburgh: T. & T. Clark, 1877.

Bennett, D. *The Holy Spirit and You.* Plainfield, NJ: Logos, 1971.

———. *Moving Right Along in the Spirit.* Old Tappan, NJ: Revell, 1983.

———. *Nine O'Clock in the Morning.* Plainfield, NJ: Logos, 1970.

Berends, W. "Biblical Criteria for Demon-possession." *Westminster Theological Journal* 37 (1975) 342–65.

Berwick, R., and R. Douglas. "Hypnosis, Exorcism and Healing: A Case Report." *American Journal of Clinical Hypnosis* 20.2 (1977) 146–48.

Bilo, Y. "The Moroccan Demon in Israel: The Case of Evil Spirit Disease." *Ethos* 8 (1980) 24–39.

Bolen, Jean. *Gods in Everyman: A New Psychology of Men's Lives and Loves.* San Francisco: Harper, 1989.

Bourguignon, E. *Possession.* San Francisco: Chandler & Sharp, 1976.

———. "World Distribution and Patterns of Possession States." In *Trance and Possession States,* edited by R. Prince, 3–34. Montreal: University of Montreal, 1968.

Bozzuto, J. "Cinematic Neurosis Following 'The Exorcist': Report of Four Cases." *Journal of Nervous and Mental Disease* 161.1 (1975) 43–48.

Bradford, B. *Releasing the Power of the Holy Spirit.* Oklahoma City: Presbyterian Charismatic Communion, 1983.

Brook, T. *Riders of the Cosmic Circuit*. Batavia, IL: Lion, 1986.

Bryan, C. P. *The Papyrus Ebers*. London: Bles, 1930.

Carty, C. M. *Padre Pio: The Stigmatist*. Rockford, IL: TAN, 1963.

Come, A. *Human Spirit and Holy Spirit*. Philadelphia: Westminster, 1959.

Courlander, H., and R. Bastien. *Religion and Politics in Haiti*. Washington, DC: Institute for Cross-Cultural Research, 1966.

Crown, S. "Exorcism: Concepts and Stratagems." *Journal of the Royal Society of Medicine (London)* 72.3 (1979) 220–21.

Davis, D. "The Psychology of Exorcism/Dismiss or Make Whole?" *Journal of the Royal Society of Medicine (London)*, 72.3 (1979) 215–18.

Del Guercio, G. "Zombie's Secret: Voodoo Myth Is Uncovered." *San Francisco Examiner*, July 10, 1985, Section E, p. 1.

Devillers, C. "Haiti's Voodoo Pilgrimages: Of Spirits and Saints." *National Geographic* 167.3 (1985) 395–408.

Dominian, J. "Psychological Evaluation of the Pentecostal Movement." *Expository Times* 87 (1976) 292–97.

Dourley, J. P. *The Psyche as Sacrament: A Comparative Study of C. G. Jung and Paul Tillich*. Toronto: Inner City, 1981.

Douyon, L., et al. *Voodoo in Haiti*. Cassette Recording, Tape #8452. Third International Conference, Nov. 11–16, Southern California Neuropsychiatric Institute, La Jolla, CA, 1984.

Dow, G. "The Case for the Existence of Demons." *Churchman*, 94.3 (1980) 199–208.

Doyle, A. C. *The History of Spiritualism*. Vols. I & II. New York: Doran, 1926.

Ehrenwald, J. "Possession and Exorcism: Delusion Shared and Compounded." *Journal of the American Academy of Psychoanalysis* 3.1 (1975) 105–19.

Eliade, M. *Shamanism: Archaic Techniques of Ecstasy*. London: Routledge & Kegan Paul, 1964.

Ellenberger, H. *The Discovery of the Unconscious: The History and Evolution of Dynamic Psychiatry*. New York: Basic, 1970.

Elliot, A. *Chinese Spirit-Medium Cults in Singapore*. Norwich, CT: Jarrold and Sons, 1955.

Fenichel, O. *The Psychoanalytic Theory of Neurosis*. New York: Norton, 1945.

Frankfort, H., et al. *The Intellectual Adventure of Ancient Man*. Chicago: University of Chicago, 1946.

Freud, S. "A Seventeenth-century Demonological Neurosis." In *Standard Edition of the Complete Works of Sigmund Freud*, edited by J. Strachey, 19:69–105. New York: Norton, 1961.

Gettis, A. "Psychotherapy as Exorcism." *Journal of Religion and Health* 15.3 (1976) 188–90.

Goethe, J. W. *Faust*. New York: Apple-Century-Crofts, 1946.

Hall, R., et al. "Demonic Possession: A Therapist's Dilemma." *Journal of Psychiatric Treatment and Evaluation* 4.6 (1982) 517–23.

Harding, E. *The Value and Meaning of Depression*. Paper presented at the meeting of the Analytical Psychology Club of New York, 1970.

Harner, M. *The Way of the Shaman: A Guide to Power and Healing*. New York: Bantam, 1980.

Henderson, J. "Exorcism, Possession, and the Dracula Cult: A Synopsis of Object-relations Psychology." *Bulletin of the Menninger Clinic* 40.6 (1976) 603–28.

————. "Exorcism and Possession in Psychotherapy Practice." *Canadian Journal of Psychiatry* 27.2 (1982) 129–34.

Hendry, G. S. *The Holy Spirit in Christian Theology.* Philadelphia: Westminster, 1956.

Hesse, H. *Demian.* London: Peter Owen & Vision Press, 1960.

Hexham, I. "Theology, Exorcism and the Amplification of Deviancy." *Evangelical Quarterly* 49 (1977) 111–16.

Hurry, J. B. *Imhotep: The Egyptian God of Medicine.* Humphrey Milford, UK: Oxford University Press, 1926.

Huxley, A. *The Devils of Loudun.* New York: Harper & Brothers, 1952.

Isaacs, T. Craig. *Revelations and Possession: Distinguishing Spiritual from Psychological Experiences.* Kearney, NE: Morris, 2009.

Jastrow, M. *The Civilization of Babylonia and Assyria.* Philadelphia: Lippincott, 1915.

Jordon, N. "What's in a Zombie?" *Psychology Today* 18.5 (1984) 6.

Jung, C. G. *The Archetypes and the Collective Unconscious. The Collected Works of C. G. Jung, vol. 9.* Princeton: Bollingen Foundation, 1959.

————. *Memories, Dreams, Reflections.* New York: Pantheon, 1963.

————. *The Practice of Psychotherapy. The Collected Works of C. G. Jung, vol. 16.* Princeton: Bollingen Foundation, 1966.

————. *Psychology and the Occult.* Princeton: Princeton University Press, 1977.

————. *Psychology and Religion: West and East. The Collected Works of C. G. Jung, vol. 11.* Princeton: Bollingen Foundation, 1969.

————. *Psychological Types: The Collected Works of C. G. Jung, vol. 6.* Princeton: Bollingen Foundation, 1971.

————. *The Spirit in Man, Art, and Literature: The Collected Works of C. G. Jung, vol. 15.* Princeton: Bollingen Foundation, 1966.

————. *The Structure and Dynamics of the Psyche: The Collected Works of C. G. Jung, vol. 8.* Princeton: Bollingen Foundation, 1960.

————. *Two Essays on Analytical Psychology: The Collected Works of C. G. Jung, vol. 7.* Princeton: Bollingen Foundation, 1966.

Kapferer, B. "Mind, Self and Other in Demonic Illness: The Negation and Reconstruction of Self." *American Ethnologist* 6.1 (1979) 110–33.

Kaplan, H., and B. Sadock. *Comprehensive Textbook of Psychiatry/IV, vol. 2.* 4th ed. Baltimore: Williams and Wilkins, 1985.

Kay, William K., and Robin Parry, eds. *Exorcism and Deliverance: Multi-Disciplinary Studies.* Milton Keynes: Paternoster, 2011.

Kelsey, M. *Christianity as Psychology.* Minneapolis: Augsburg, 1986.

————. *Discernment: A Study in Ecstasy and Evil.* New York: Paulist, 1978.

————. *Tongue Speaking: An Experiment in Spiritual Experience.* Garden City, NY: Doubleday, 1964.

Kenny, M. G. "Multiple Personality and Spirit Possession." *Psychiatry* 44.4 (1981) 337–58.

Kieckhefer, R. *European Witch Trials: Their Foundations in Popular and Learned Culture, 1300–1500.* Berkeley: University of California Press, 1976.

Kiev, A. "The Psychotherapeutic Value of Spirit-Possession in Haiti." In *Trance and Possession States,* edited by R. Prince, 143–48. Montreal: University of Montreal Press, 1968.

Kildahl, J. *The Psychology of Speaking in Tongues.* New York: Harper & Row, 1972.

Kiraly, S. J. "Folie a deux: A Case of 'Demonic Possession' Involving Mother and Daughter." *Canadian Psychiatric Association Journal (Ottawa)*, 20.3 (1975) 223–28.

Koch, K. *Christian Counseling and Occultism*. Grand Rapids: Kregal, 1972.

———. *Occult Bondage and Deliverance*. Grand Rapids: Kregal, 1971.

Kuhn, T. S. *The Structure of Scientific Revolutions*. Chicago: University of Chicago Press, 1970.

Langely, M. S. "Spirit-Possession, Exorcism and Social Context: An Anthropological Perspective with Theological Implications." *Churchman* 94.3 (1980) 226–45.

Lechler, A. "The Distinction between Disease and the Demonic." In *Occult Bondage and Deliverance*, edited by K. Koch, 153–90. Grand Rapids: Kegal, 1976.

Linn, M., and D. Linn. *Deliverance Prayer*. Ramsey, NJ: Paulist, 1981.

Ludwig, A. M. "Altered States of Consciousness." In *Trance and Possession States*, edited by R. Prince, 69–95. Montreal: University of Montreal, 1968.

Mackarness, R. "Occultism and Psychiatry." *Practitioner (London)* 212.1269 (1974) 363–66.

Maduro, R. "Hoodoo Possession in San Francisco: Notes on Therapeutic Aspects of Regression." *Ethos* 3 (1975) 425–45.

Martin, M. *Hostage to the Devil: The Possession and Exorcism of Five Living Americans*. New York: Reader's Digest, 1976.

Marty, M. E., and K. L. Vaux. *Health/Medicine and the Faith Traditions*. Philadelphia: Fortress, 1982.

Masters, A. *The Devil's Dominion*. New York: Putnam, 1978.

May, G. *Care of Mind/Care of Spirit*. San Francisco: Harper & Row. 1982.

———. *Will and Spirit: A Contemplative Psychology*. San Francisco: Harper & Row, 1982.

May, R. *Love and Will*. New York: Norton, 1969.

———. "The Problem of Evil: An Open Letter to Carl Rodgers." *Journal of Humanistic Psychology* 22.3 (1982) 10–21.

May, R. *The Cry for Myth*. New York: Norton, 1991.

McAll, R. K. "Demonosis or the Possession Syndrome: Extract from an article by R. K. McAll." *International Journal of Social Psychiatry (London)* 17.2 (1971) 150–58.

———. "Ministry of Deliverance." *Expository Times* 86 (1975) 296–98.

———. *Healing the Family Tree*. London: Sheldon, 1982.

McDonnell, K. *Charismatic Renewal and the Churches*. New York: Seabury, 1976.

Meigs, J. T. "Pastoral Care Methods and Demonology in Selected Writings." *Journal of Psychology and Theology*, 5.3 (1977) 234–46.

Metraux, A. *Voodoo in Haiti*. New York: Oxford University Press, 1959.

Moody, E. J. "Urban Witches." In *On the Margin of the Visible: Sociology, the Esoteric, and the Occult*, edited by E. A. Tiryakian, 223–36. New York: Wiley & Sons, 1974.

Moore, E.G. "Theories Underlying Exorcism: Theological and Psychic." *Journal of the Royal Society of Medicine (London)*, 72.3 (1979) 220–21.

Neher, A. "A Physiological Explanation of Unusual Behavior in Ceremonies Involving Drums." *Human Biology* 34 (1962) 151–60.

Neumann, E. *The Place of Creation*. Princeton: Princeton University Press, 1989.

Obeyesekere, G. "The Idiom of Demonic Possession." *Social Science Medicine* 4 (1970) 97–111.

————. "Psychocultural Exegesis of a Case of Spirit Possession in Sri Lanka." In *Case Studies in Spirit Possession*, edited by V. Crapanzano, 235–94. New York: Wiley, 1977.

Oesterreich, T. K. *Possession, Demoniacal and Other, among Primitive Races, in Antiquity, the Middle Ages, and Modern Times*. New York: University Books, 1966.

Office of the General Assembly. *Report to the Special Committee on the Work of the Holy Spirit to the 182nd General Assembly: The United Presbyterian Church in the United States of America*. New York: United Presbyterian Church in the USA, 1970.

Omand, D. "Exorcism: An Adjunct to Christian Counseling." *Counseling and Values* 21.2 (1977) 84–88.

O'Shield, F. B. *Dealing with the Enemy: Satan*. Cassette Recording No. S3-E'80-FBO. Oklahoma City, OK: Presbyterian Charismatic Communion, 1980.

Pao, P. *Schizophrenic Disorders: Theory and Treatment from a Psychodynamic Point of View*. Madison, CT: International University, 1979.

Parente, P. *Beyond Space*. Rockford, IL: TAN, 1961.

Parrinder, G. *Mysticism in the World's Religions*. London: Sheldon, 1976.

Pattison, E. "Psychosocial Interpretations of Exorcism." *Journal of Operational Psychiatry* 8.2 (1977) 5–21.

Pattison, E. M., and R. M. Wintrob. "Possession and Exorcism in Contemporary America." *Journal of Operational Psychiatry* 12.1 (1981) 13–20.

Pearson, P. R. "Psychiatry and Religion: Problems at the Interface." *Bulletin of the British Psychological Society (London)* 30 (1977) 47–48.

Peck, M. S. *People of the Lie: Hope for Healing Human Evil*. New York: Simon and Schuster, 1983.

Pederson, J. *Israel: Its Life and Culture*. London: Oxford University Press, 1940.

Perry, J. W. *The Far Side of Madness*. Upper Saddle River, NJ: Prentice-Hall, 1974.

Poloma, M. *The Charismatic Movement: Is There a New Pentecost?* Boston: Twayne, 1982.

Prince, R., ed. *Trance and Possession States*. Montreal: University of Montreal Press, 1968.

Pulver, M. "The Experience of the Pneuma in Philo." In *Spirit and Nature: Papers from the Eranos Yearbooks*, edited by J. Campbell, 107–21. Princeton: Princeton University Press, 1954.

Pursey, B. *The Gifts of the Holy Spirit*. Oklahoma City: Presbyterian and Reformed Renewal Ministries International, 1984.

Putnam, Frank. *Diagnosis and Treatment of Multiple Personality Disorder*. New York: Guildford, 1989.

Quebedeaux, R. *The New Charismatics II*. New York: Harper & Row, 1983.

Rahner, H. "Earth Spirit and Divine Spirit in Patristic Theology." In *Spirit and Nature: Papers from the Eranos Yearbooks*, edited by J. Campbell, 122–48. Princeton: Princeton University Press, 1954.

Raschke, C. A. *Painted Black*. New York: Harper, 1990.

Rizzuto, A. *The Birth of the Living God: A Psychological Study*. Chicago: University of Chicago Press, 1979.

Robertson, P. *Answers to 200 of Life's Most Probing Questions*. Virginia Beach, VA: Christian Broadcasting Network, 1984.

————. *Beyond Reason*. New York: Morrow, 1985.

————. *Knowing the Will of God*. Virginia Beach, VA: Christian Broadcasting Network, 1985.

Ross, M., and O. Stalstrom. "Exorcism as Psychiatric Treatment: A Homosexual Case Study." *Archives of Sexual Behavior,* 8.4 (1979) 379–83.

Russell, J. B. *The Devil*. Ithaca, NY: Cornell University Press, 1977.

————. *Lucifer*. Ithaca, NY: Cornell University Press, 1984.

————. "Medieval Witchcraft and Medieval Heresy." In *On the Margin of the Visible: Sociology, the Esoteric, and the Occult,* edited by E. A. Tiryakian, 179–90. New York: Wiley, 1974.

————. *Satan*. Ithaca, NY: Cornell University Press, 1981.

————. *Witchcraft in the Middle Ages*. Ithaca, NY: Cornell University Press, 1972.

Sakheim, D. K., and S. E. Devine. *Out of Darkness: Exploring Satanism and Ritual Abuse*. New York: Lexington, 1992.

Sall, M. J. "Demon Possession or Psychopathology: A Clinical Differentiation." *Journal of Psychology and Theology* 4 (1976), 286–90.

————. "A Response to 'Demon Possession and Psychopathology: A Theological Relationship." *Journal of Psychology and Theology,* 7.1 (1979) 27–30.

Sanville, J. "Therapists in Competition and Cooperation with Exorcists: The Spirit World Clinically Revisited." *Clinical Social Work Journal,* 3.4 (1975) 286–297.

Sargent, W. *The Mind Possessed: A Physiology of Possession, Mysticism and Faith Healing.* Philadelphia: Lippincott, 1974.

Saunders, L. W. "Variants in Zar Experience in an Egyptian Village." In *Case Studies in Spirit Possession,* edited by V. Crapanzano, 177–91. New York: Wiley, 1977.

Saxenmeyer, G. "Approaching the Ministries of Healing and Exorcism." *Journal of Pastoral Counseling,* 11 (1976–77) 32–36.

Scanlon, M., and R. Cirner. *Deliverance from Evil Spirits*. Ann Arbor, MI: Servant, 1980.

Schendel, E., and R. Kourany. "Cacodemonomania and Exorcism in Children." *Journal of Clinical Psychiatry,* 41.4 (1980) 119–23.

Schilling, H. *The New Consciousness in Science and Religion*. Philadelphia: Pilgrim, 1973.

Schwartz-Salant, N. *Narcissism and Character Transformation*. Toronto: Inner City, 1982.

Seligmann, K. *The Mirror of Magic*. New York: Pantheon, 1948.

Shape, A. D., et al. "Deprogramming: The New Exorcism." *American Behavioral Scientist* 20.6 (1977) 941–56.

Sigerist, H. E. *A History of Medicine, vol. 1*. New York: Oxford University Press, 1951.

————. *A History of Medicine, vol. 2*. New York: Oxford University Press, 1961.

Smith, M., and L. Pazder. *Michelle Remembers*. New York: Congdon & Lattes, 1980.

Sophrony, A. *A Monk of Mt. Athos*. Crestwood, NY: St. Vladimir's Seminary Press, 1973.

Spiritualist Manual. Milwaukee, WI: National Spiritualist Association of Churches, 1955.

Stinnett, C. R. "Demonic Possession in Modern Man." *Pastoral Psychology,* 6 (1955) 35–42.

Sudre, R. *Parapsychology*. New York: Citadel, 1960.

Summers, M. *The History of Witchcraft and Demonology*. New York: University Books, 1956.

Tanquerey, A. *The Spiritual Life: A Treatise on Ascetical and Mystical Theology*. Tournai, Belgium: Society of St. John the Evangelist, 1930.

Teguis, A., and C. Flynn. "Dealing with Demons: Psychosocial Dynamics of Paranormal Occurrences." *Journal of Humanistic Psychology,* 23.4 (1983) 59–75.

Truzzi, M. "Definition and Dimensions of the Occult: Towards a Sociological Perspective." In *On the Margin of the Visible: Sociology, the Esoteric, and the Occult,* edited by E. A. Tiryakian, 215–22. New York: Wiley & Sons, 1974.

———. "Witchcraft and Satanism." In *On the Margin of the Visible: Sociology, the Esoteric, and the Occult,* edited by E. A. Tiryakian, ?–?. New York: Wiley, 1974.

Underhill, E. *Mysticism.* New York: Dutton, 1961.

Valois, W. "The Integrative Aspects of Possession Trance." PhD diss., California School of Professional Psychology, Berkeley, 1983.

Van Dam, W. *Spiritual Warfare: Occultism and Demonology.* Recording No. W-I'79-WVD. Oklahoma City, OK. Presbyterian Charismatic Communion, 1979.

Vergote, A., and A. Tamayo. *The Parental Figures and the Representation of God: A Psychological and Cross-Cultural Study.* The Hague: Mouton, 1981.

Virkler, H., and M. Virkler. "Demonic Involvement in Human Life and Illness." *Journal of Psychology and Theology* 5 (1977) 95–102.

von Franz, M. L. *Projection and Re-collection in Jungian Psychology: Reflections of the Soul.* London: Open Court, 1980.

———. *The Shadow and Evil in Fairytales.* Zürich: Spring, 1974.

Walker, S. *Ceremonial Spirit Possession in Africa and Afro-America.* Leiden: Brill, 1972.

Ward, C., and M. Beaubrun. "The Psychodynamics of Demon Possession." *Journal for the Scientific Study of Religion* 19 (1980) 201–7.

Webb et al. *DSM-III Training Guide.* New York: Brunner/Mazel, 1981.

Weller, P. *The Roman Ritual.* Milwaukee: Bruce, 1964.

White, H. W. *Demonism Verified and Analyzed.* Richmond, VA: Presbyterian Committee of Publication, 1922.

Whitmont, E. C. *The Symbolic Quest: Basic Concepts in Analytical Psychology.* Princeton: Princeton University Press, 1969.

Wikstrom, O. "Possession as a Clinical Phenomenon: A Critique of the Medical Model." In *Religious Ecstasy: Based on Papers Read at the Symposium of Religious Ecstasy Held at Abo, Finland on the 26th–28th of August, 1981,* edited by N. G. Holms, 87–102. Stockholm: Almqvist & Wikshell, 1982.

Wili, W. "The History of the Spirit in Antiquity." In *Spirit and Nature: Papers from the Eranos Yearbooks,* edited by J. Campbell, 75–106. Princeton: Princeton University Press, 1954.

Wilson, M. "Exorcism: A Clinical/Pastoral Practice which Raises Serious Questions." *Expository Times* 86 (1975) 292–95.

Wink, W. *Naming the Powers: Language of Power in the New Testament.* Philadelphia: Fortress, 1984.

Wise, R. *Healing of the Past: Recovering Emotional and Mental Wholeness.* Oklahoma City, OK: Presbyterian and Reformed Renewal Ministries International, 1984.

Yap, P. M. "The Possession Syndrome: A Comparison of Hong Kong and French Findings." *Journal of Mental Science* 106 (1961) 114–37.

Yogananda, P. *Autobiography of a Yogi.* New York: Philosophical Library, 1946.

Made in the USA
Middletown, DE
11 February 2018